WITHDRAWN

PROTECT YOUR PET

PROTECT YOUR PET
More Shocking Facts

ANN N. MARTIN

NEWSAGE PRESS
TROUTDALE, OREGON

PROTECT YOUR PET:
More Shocking Facts
Copyright 2001© Ann N. Martin

NewSage Press
PO Box 607
Troutdale, OR 97060-0607
503-695-2211

website: www.newsagepress.com
email: info@newsagepress.com

Cover Design by George Foster
Book Design by Patricia Keelin
Cover Photos © Sumner Fowler

Distributed in the United States and Canada by
Publishers Group West 800-788-3123

Note to the reader: This book is an informational guide. If you have questions regarding the health of your animal companion and a possible problem related to diet, consult a professional veterinarian, preferably one who is knowledgeable in nutrition.

PUBLISHER'S CATALOGING INFORMATION

Martin, Ann N., 1944-
Protect your pet: more shocking facts /Ann N. Martin.

Includes bibliographical references, resources and index.
ISBN 0-939165-42-2
1.Pets---Feeding and feeds. 2. Pets---Health. 3. Pets---Feeding and feeds--Contamination—-United States. 4. Pets---Feeding and feeds--Contamination—-Canada. 5. Pets---Feeding and feeds— Contamination--United Kingdom. 6. Pet Food Industry—-United States. 7. Pet Food Industry--Canada. 8. Pets---Vaccinations—-United States. 9. Pets—-Vaccinations---Canada. 10. Pets---Vaccinations--United Kingdom. 11. Pets---Cancer. 12. Pets---Cruelty. 13. Pets---Mad Cow Disease. 14. Pets---Raw Meat Diet.

Printed in the United States on recycled paper with soy ink.

1 2 3 4 5 6 7 8 9 10

For Chuck, who brings me joy and love.

ACKNOWLEDGMENTS

This book would have never reached fruition without the work and dedication of many people. First and foremost my publisher and editor, Maureen R. Michelson, for her faith, understanding and patience through another book. You were tough but fair and the effort and time you have spent on this book are very much appreciated. I thank you. Thanks must also go to Tracy Smith, the copy editor. Thank you both for an excellent job in correcting mistakes, eliminating unnecessary text, and asking questions in order to make this a readable book. It was a pleasure to work with both of you.

Also, a special thanks to the designers who so beautifully crafted the layout: Patti Keelin for the interior design, and George Foster for the cover. And to the photographer, Sumner Fowler, whose animal portraits grace the cover of this book—thank you, those faces remind us of why we do this work!

Special thanks to the many veterinarians I corresponded with world-wide, your input was a tremendous help and made me realize the diversity of opinions on the various issues discussed in this book. Very special thanks to the veterinarians who took the time to read material and express opinions; Dr. Wendell Belfield, Dr. Jean Dodds, and my friend, Catherine O'Driscoll. Dr. Michael Fox, my friend, my mentor, I wish you peace and love.

Last, but definitely not least, thank you to my family and friends. Chuck, this book is dedicated to you because without your support it would not have been written.

Jamie, my son, thank heavens you are a computer genius otherwise all would have been lost, numerous times. My sister, Mary, who photographed me and Sarge for the author's photo, thanks. My friends, Joan and Linda of many years, thanks for being there. And to my extended family, Audrey, Sheila, Irene, Tina, and Darlene, it has been a real joy getting to know all of you.

No book on pet health would be complete without the mention of my four-legged family: Sarge, a beautiful German Shepherd; and my felines, Ben, Simon, and Jake.

To all my animal companions with whom I have shared my life over the many years, you are gone but will never be forgotten. I love you all.

CONTENTS

CHAPTER ONE   1
Digging for Facts

CHAPTER TWO   7
Rendering Plants and Pet Food

CHAPTER THREE   19
A Toxic Feast

CHAPTER FOUR   39
Pet Food Regulations

CHAPTER FIVE   57
The Latest on Mad Cow Disease and Pet Food

CHAPTER SIX   67
The Controversy of the Raw Meat Diet

CHAPTER SEVEN   91
Over-Vaccination and Animals

CHAPTER EIGHT   113
Cancer in Animals

CHAPTER NINE   125
Other Health Concerns

CHAPTER TEN   145
The Ultimate Health Risk: Cruelty

CHAPTER ELEVEN   157
Healthy Recipes

RESOURCES   175

ENDNOTES   183

INDEX   196

ABOUT THE AUTHOR   199

ONE

Digging for Facts

Afeter more than twelve years of persistent investigating and questioning, I have learned a good deal about the dangers of most commercial pet foods. No longer do I accept anything on face value. I demand definitive answers from those who call themselves "experts" on pet-related issues. Oftentimes, I need nothing less than a bulldog's tenacity to get a simple answer to a simple question from government agencies or any agency with a pet food connection. And even then many of my questions go unanswered. Most of these agencies are unwilling to provide any insight into the mysteries and vagaries of government regulations and the specific practices of pet food companies.

Fortunately, my love of animals is enhanced by my love of research and writing. My day begins at five in the morning and often extends well into the evening. My college degree in business and years of working in a Canadian tax office honed my skills for facts, figures, documentation, and accuracy. E-mail is one of my main avenues for communicating and I find the Internet invaluable.

One essential rule I follow in all of my research, particularly on controversial issues, is to document everything in writing. I am vigilant about this practice because I know many people will question, doubt, and attempt to discard my findings. Perhaps my findings are too disgusting to contemplate—for example, the rendering of dogs and cats to make pet food. I, too, don't want to believe this kind of information, but the evidence keeps pointing in this direction. Oftentimes, what I unearth and write about is not taken seriously because I am not a veterinarian or because I do not hold a PhD in animal nutrition. At the same time, I am a free agent and I only have to answer to the facts.

When it comes to the Federal Drug Administration (FDA) or the Canadian Veterinary Medical Association (CVMA), they are anything but helpful. For example, one FDA veterinarian I contacted was more than willing to provide information when I first wrote and he responded promptly. Unfortunately, he answered very few of my questions. Again I asked the veterinarian the same questions, plus a few more. Several weeks passed before he responded with very short answers. This mode of communication, and the lengthy wait in between answers, continued for nearly a year. Frustrated, I forwarded my questions to David Kessler, MD, then Commissioner of the FDA. Dr. Kessler redirected my letter to the veterinarians with the Food and Drug Administration, Center for Veterinary Medicine (FDA/CVM). I was then advised by the head of this department that if I should have any further questions, they were to be directed to him and not to Dr. Kessler. This process of gathering information took nearly two years when it should have taken only a matter of a few weeks. From that point on the replies were rather prompt, yet not too helpful.

While researching for this book, I posed a basic query to the FDA/CVM. I asked what the regulations are, if any, the agency imposes on pet food. My initial e-mail was to Sharon Benz, DVM, with the FDA/CVM, who referred me to their Public Information Specialist with the FDA/CVM. The Information Specialist provided a two-page scenario on how various agencies worked that were involved with pet foods. The information she provided was the same information I had already acquired from other sources regarding labeling, additives, illegal drug residues in meat, and Generally Recognized as Safe (GRAS) substances.

I also asked the Public Information Specialist to reply to a report from the United States Animal Health Association. This report, written in October 1997, states the CVM had discovered sodium pentobarbital in dry dog foods and that further testing was being undertaken. In my written letter to her, February 2000, a year and a half after this report was presented, I asked if the testing had been completed and if the results were available. I was informed that I should check the CVM website in the spring of 2000. Nothing was posted in the spring. In July, I again e-mailed the Public Information Specialist and asked if the report was available. She responded, "It is not ready for distribution at this time." When I asked for a date that this report would be available, I received no reply. Again, in September 2000, I wrote with the same request and was again advised that the report was not ready for publication. In late September I e-mailed the two doctors who head the FDA/CVM division, Drs. Graber and Benz, both veterinarians, hoping that they might tell me when this report would be available. Unfortunately, I again received a reply from the Public Information Specialist stating that the FDA was not releasing any data on this project until it was completed and that she had no idea when that would be. Not to be deterred, I e-mailed Jane Henney, MD, who is now the Commissioner of the FDA and awaited her reply. After waiting two months I again posed the same questions to Dr. Henney in January 2001 just as this book was going to press. Still no response.

Shortly after corresponding with the Information Specialist regarding the sodium pentobarbital, another question arose that fell within the jurisdiction of the FDA/CVM. This query relates to bovine spongiform encephalopathy (BSE) and what steps the department is taking to assure that it is not contaminating pet foods. Perhaps this request tested her patience. I was directed to the FDA website. She also provided me with a list of the duties assigned to the CVM Communicating Staff. Then the Information Specialist e-mailed me, "I think it is important for me to let you know that I cannot continue to respond to question after question from one individual." I thanked her for the information she had provided and the fact that I did realize her time was valuable. The Information Specialist had also answered all the questions I had at the moment and I told her that if I had any further questions in the future I would address them to the head of that department, Dr. Graber. The same day she replied, "I think you have misinterpreted my statement. Please direct any future questions to me rather than Dr. Graber." Although further questions on the sodium pentobarbital went either unanswered or a negative reply was received, it is an issue that I will not let die. Two years have passed since the testing of these pet foods—ample time for the research to be completed and the report released. Is the FDA/CVM hiding something? Do they feel I will just go away and forget about this report? That is not to be the case.

In 1996 when I was researching commercial pet foods for my first book, *Food Pets Die For*, the Pet Food Institute (PFI) located in the United States, was on the top of my list. The PFI is a trade association that represents the various U.S. pet food manufacturers. Two faxes were sent to this organization with my questions, but I never received a reply. In 1999 when I began writing *Protect Your Pet*, I again contacted the PFI. This time I received a reply from Nancy Cook, Director, Technical and Regulatory Affairs. Cook informed me that they had no record of the faxes I had sent prior to the publication of *Food Pets Die For* but stated that the Pet Food Institute would be happy to answer any questions.

The questions I had for the PFI were basically the same ones I had prior to the publication of my first book. This included asking if anyone was testing for the species of animals used in pet food. Two months later Cook replied to my inquiry. The questions I had posed with regard to the testing of raw material for species of animals were still not answered. Instead, Cook chose to point out the "errors and omissions" in my book. As for the pet foods that I had inquired about, I received the same story that I had received from the CVM—that "pet foods were one of the most highly regulated foods in the marketplace." I thanked Cook for her comments on my book and again asked if she would respond to my questions. After two more e-mails to Cook as a representative for the PFI, I realized that I would not likely get my questions answered.

In August 2000, I received an e-mail from Duane Ekedahl, Executive Director of the PFI. He, like Cook, provided an unsolicited short review of my first book and reiterated how this is a "well-regulated industry." I thanked Ekedahl for his critique, and asked again, "Who inspects the actual ingredients used in these foods?" Again, in September 2000, I addressed these queries to Ekedahl but never heard from him.

During the course of my research, many people with the United States Department of Agriculture (USDA) have been cooperative and helpful and answered all my questions. Without hesitation, Drs. Diane Sutton, Linda Detwiler, Nora Wineland, Janice Miller, and Beth Williams have been an enormous help with my research. Their time and effort have been very much appreciated. Kudos should also go to the many veterinarians across the United States whom I have bombarded with questions on the raw meat diet and toxic substances. Vets from clinics and shelter employees (especially in California) went beyond the call of duty to give me all the information I required. For the most part, veterinarians, pathologists, nutritionists, internists, and toxicologists, not only replied to my questions, but often asked if there was further information I required. They were also willing to let me use their names and quote them. All replied promptly and some even sent important texts.

Rendering Plants

In another area of my research, rendering plants, I was also provided with little, if any, information. When I contacted rendering plants across the United States, I questioned the material that they rendered and if they tested the raw material for drugs, pathogens, or heavy metals. Two of these facilities replied and those were plants that rendered specific sources of protein—chicken and pork products. The other plants referred me to the National Renderers Association (NRA). When I addressed my questions to Tom Cook from the NRA, I was asked to provide my address and he would forward the information. I received a booklet outlining the workings of the industry but nothing in this booklet addressed the questions I had asked. Since then I have e-mailed Cook at least twice with my questions. I have heard nothing and doubt if I ever will. One man who works for a rendering plant wrote to inform me that the rendering plants have all been advised not to respond to my queries and to direct the queries to the NRA.

Over the years I have been on many Internet pet lists (web discussion groups devoted to various methods of feeding pets and devoted to different dog and cat breeds) participating more as an observer than anything else. Although I try not to get involved in a discussion when it comes to pet foods, I did at one time and it became a lengthy battle. Two lists I subscribe to are Pro/Med and Vet/Med. Pro/Med provides good information on the various animal diseases worldwide and Vet/Med has a number of knowledgeable people both lay and professional.

Recently, a woman on the Vet/Med list asked for the name of the independent group that had analyzed pet food. She made it clear that it was not the *Consumers Report* and had no interest in any report from the Association of American Feed Control Officials (AAFCO), an organization she described as "a wolf guarding the chickens."

Later that day a post appeared from Chris Cowell, MS, principal nutritionist for Hill's Pet Foods. He suggested that this woman add another "not interested" to her list: the Animal Protection Institute (API) report, which is an in-depth report from this nonprofit organization that works on behalf of animal welfare. Cowell stated, "It [the API report] does not represent truth in its entirety and is full of half-truth and rumor with some actual facts tossed in to make it believable." He went on to write, "Also, AAFCO are not a wolf guarding the chickens, but rather state regulators that have no affiliation with industry." His response was surprising. I know the person who researched and wrote the original API report, Tina Perry, and I am confident that her research was sound and accurate.

If Cowell is a nutritionist with one of the largest pet food manufacturers in the United States, I figured he would have the answer to a question I have been asking for years: "Do pet food companies actually test the raw material (meat meals) to ascertain the source of the meat?" I informed him that a simple yes or no would suffice, and to skip the lengthy explanations that lead nowhere. The following day I received a number of private posts from individuals applauding what I had said in my post to the pet food nutritionist. However, I never received a response from Cowell regarding my ongoing question to pet food manufacturers. One small step for the animals! My digging for information will continue—I want answers for the sake of all our animal companions.

Two

Rendering Plants
and Pet Food

The most interesting research for this book revolved around what was happening to the carcasses of euthanized pets. I was aware that thousands of these animals were being sent to rendering plants but I wasn't sure as to how they were getting there. Were the pet carcasses coming from shelters, pounds, or veterinarian clinics? I began by contacting shelters throughout the United States, and I soon realized from the replies I received that there was no doubt that many of the shelters, pounds, and veterinary clinics were sending pets to rendering plants. Eventually I found out that although this did happen in many states, it seemed particularly prevalent in California, so at first I focused on California rendering plants.

Rendering of Pets

After acquiring a list of U.S. shelters from websites, I e-mailed them. The replies I received named two companies in California and Nevada that were picking up dead animals in these states: D&D Disposal and Koefran Services. Some veterinary clinics also mentioned these two companies, although other clinics used incineration facilities or their clients chose to bury their pets privately or at a pet cemetery. I was amazed to find that although shelters and clinics were aware that the final disposition of pets is rendering, no one seemed to question what that implied. To them it was merely a means of disposal. And they certainly didn't suspect that rendering would necessarily lead to possible inclusion in pet food product.

An employee at a humane society in California wrote that in his area, Escondido, D&D Disposal picks up approximately one hundred bodies each week. In that same area, there are three other shelters and more than one hundred veterinarians using the same disposal company.

D&D Disposal was rather hard to locate, but fortunately one shelter did have a couple of addresses for it. One location is in Vernon, California, which lies on the edge of Los Angeles in an industrial area with a population under five hundred. Through maps and a research center I found that D&D Disposal shares the same address as West Coast Rendering. In fact, West Coast Rendering owns D&D Disposal. The other address for D&D Disposal is in an upscale residential area in Westwood near the University of California, Los Angeles (UCLA). Located in West Los Angeles, this is certainly not an area where any kind of animal could be disposed of. It was clear that these animals were being sent to the West Coast Rendering plant in Vernon.

In this area of Vernon I was also able to locate another rendering plant, Baker Commodities, within a block of West Coast Rendering. Baker Commodities is also known for picking up euthanized animals. The Vernon Chamber of Commerce has a wonderful website that provides information on the various industries located in Vernon. While I was attempting to locate West Coast Rendering through the Chamber of Commerce, I learned about another industry located within blocks of both rendering plants—a large pet food company that produces several popular brands of pet food.

Koefran Incorporated, or Koefran Services, was another disposal company on my list. A company search showed it has three addresses: a post office box in San Francisco, and facilities in Reno, Nevada, and Provo, Utah. Again, I looked up companies in the area that might have knowledge of what this company was processing. One lead led to another and I found that Koefran Services also was a subsidiary of a rendering plant, Reno Rendering. In addition, Reno Rendering owns a company called Nevada Byproducts that produces meat by-products. All of these companies are at the same location. In Utah, Koefran Services also picks up animal carcasses with the approval of county commissioners.

The rendering of pets also exists in another part of the country—Florida. On January 5, 2000 an article appeared in the *Gainesville Sun* regarding a shelter in Alachua County, Florida and the method it was forced to use to dispose of euthanized animals. This shelter disposes of about eleven thousand euthanized dogs, cats, and other animals every year through rendering. The newspaper article states: "Employees who face the daily stresses associated with having to put animals to sleep bear the additional burden of taking them to be ground up into other substances animal control Director Barbara Snow told county commissioners. The employees must drive the bodies to the Griffin Industries rendering plant in Hampton, in Bradford County, lift them off the truck and heave them into a pit exposing themselves to foul odors, putrid substances underfoot and having to see the grinding going on."[1]

According to one of the employees at Griffin Industries, who will remain anonymous, the company sells rendered material to pet food companies. I contacted one of the pet food companies that purchases the rendered material from Griffin Industries, but company representatives refused to comment on its source of raw material.

Rendering Plants

In early 2000, I contacted fourteen of the larger rending plants in the United States and Canada and asked if they rendered companion animals. I also asked if they tested the rendered material for pathogens, drugs, hormones, heavy metals, and pesticides. Of the fourteen, four replied. One rendering company, American Proteins, stated that it renders only poultry by-products.[2] It also stated that it tests its products, although the company did not tell me what it tests for. Three other companies, John Kuhni and Sons, West Coast Reduction Ltd., and National By-Products Inc,[3] suggested I direct my query to the National Renderers Association (NRA).

A short time later, I contacted Tom Cook from the NRA and posed the same questions. The information he sent was a twenty-one page booklet on the National Renderers Association. Nothing in the booklet addressed the rendering of companion animals although it did provide some insight into a voluntary program called the Hazard Analysis and Critical Control Points (HACCP) to control bacteria.

The HACCP program is employed by many slaughterhouses where meat is processed for human consumption. Meat inspectors have attacked this program because it leaves much of the meat inspection up to the individual company employees. Chemicals, including pesticides, herbicides, antimicrobial agents, and other drugs in rendered material are also considered in the booklet. The prime concern seems to be the potential harmful effects these chemicals have on livestock and poultry but does not seem to address the harmful effects these elements might have on pets. As I've mentioned, this is a voluntary program and as with most voluntary programs it sadly lacks any real accountable structure. I did go back to Cook at the NRA, twice, and asked him to address my questions, but that has been to no avail.

The rendering companies that chose not to reply to my inquiries include Baker Commodities, Inc., Los Angeles, California; Anamax Corporation, Green Bay, Wisconsin; Birmingham Hide and Tallow Co., Birmingham, Alabama; Darling International Inc., Irving, Texas; Griffin Industries Inc., Cold Spring, Kentucky; Moyer Packing Co., Souderton, Pennsylvania; Sacramento Rendering, Sacramento, California; Tucson Tallow Inc., Tucson, Arizona; Valley Proteins, Inc., Winchester, Virginia; and Western Mass Rendering Co., Inc. Southwick, Massachusetts.

One rendering plant on the East Coast, Valley Protein, was in the business of rendering pets for fifty years but in March 2000 it put an end to this practice due in part to bad publicity. Valley Protein sold rendered material to pet food companies although it claimed that the material containing dog and cat carcasses was going primarily to fertilizer and live-stock feed. The Humane Society of Warren, Virginia used the services of Valley Protein. "The cost is $50 per trip and sometimes, when the shelter is extremely busy, the truck must make three trips per week," reported the *Warren Sentinel* in March 2000. "The shelter stores its animal carcasses in oil drums in a freezer, and can only store four drums without requiring disposal."[4] The only alternative now for these shelters, pounds, and veterinary clinics is either to find another rendering plant or have the animals cremated, which is far more costly then rendering.

Baker Commodities, with rendering plants in Seattle and Spokane, Washington; Rochester, New York; Phoenix, Arizona; and Hanford, Long Beach, and Los Angeles, California is another company that also picks up euthanized companion animals. Some shelters in Spokane told me that they have contracted with Baker Commodities to pick up their euthanized animals. Washington State University also sends some of its animal cadavers to Baker Commodities for rendering. According to Charlie Powell, Public Information Officer for the Veterinary College, Washington State University, "Baker Commodities is the rendering company in Spokane, and twice weekly they collect cadavers from the diagnostic laboratory cooler."[5]

Regulations for Rendering Plants

The Washington State Department of Agriculture regulates the rendering industry through two programs. The first is the Animal Health Program, which oversees rendering plants and collectors. This program licenses facilities and trucks to ensure sanitation and handling and disposal of carcasses plus animal wastes from processing and slaughter. This program only deals with meat food animals, not rendered companion animals.

The second program, the Feed and Fertilizer Program, regulates commercial animal feeds. These inspectors check rendering plants for Good Manufacturing Practices. This program focuses on prohibited mammalian proteins and their segregation during the manufacture of feeds. Kathy Connell, Assistant State Veterinarian, Washington State Department of Agriculture Food Safety and Animal Health Division, explained in a letter from the Department of Agriculture, "Rendering plants can and do accept companion animals for rendering. The use of this material would be prohibited from use as ruminant feed."[6] I did question why euthanized companion animals were prohibited from use in ruminant feed but unfortunately Dr. Connell could not answer this question.

In 1996 the FDA/CVM acknowledged that it is aware of the rendering of pets and the use of this material in pet foods, "However, that is not to say that the practice of using this material is condoned by the CVM."[7] Pets are a cheap source of protein and their use in pet foods is a viable alternative to cremation or burial. Hard to believe, but it is happening, and it is legal.

Legal Ingredients for Use in Pet Food

As my research into commercial pet food began to unfold, I was shocked at what legally can be used in pet foods. Most pet food companies would have us believe that they use only quality ingredients. We have all seen the advertising that shows prime cuts of meat, whole chickens, stocks of whole grains. In most cases, this is false advertising. In all my years of research into this industry I have found little, if any, ingredients that are used in most commercial pet foods that would be considered to be anything but garbage. Pet foods are a viable alternative for meat packers, grain operations, and even brewers to dispose of material that otherwise would be dumped into the landfill.

Protein is extremely important for the health and welfare of our animals but I had never considered what the sources of protein actually are. Terms such as "meat," "meat by-products," and "meat meals" listed on those attractive cans and bags of commercial pet foods are catch-all phrases that may include a wide array of dangerous and mysterious possibilities.

The term "meat" as defined by the Association of American Feed Control Officials (AAFCO), "is the clean flesh derived from slaughtered mammals and is limited to the part of the striate muscle which is skeletal or that which is found in the tongue, in the diaphragm, in the heart, or in the esophagus; with or without the accompanying and overlying fat and the portions of the skin, sinew, nerve, and blood vessels, which normally accompany the flesh."[8] Of the three terms, "meat" would be the best of the ingredients used in pet foods.

"Meat by-products" is described by the AAFCO as "the non-rendered, clean parts, other than meat, derived from slaughtered mammals. It includes, but is not limited to, lungs, spleen, kidney, brain, livers, blood, bone, partially defatted low temperature fatty tissue, and stomachs and intestines freed of their contents."[9] This is material deemed unfit for human consumption; however, it can be used in pet food. Lungs filled with pneumonia or tuberculosis are condemned for human consumption but however can be used in pet foods. It is also legally acceptable to render livers infected with flukes (small parasites) for pet food.

Blood cleared from slaughterhouse floors, including sawdust, can be used in pet food. Basically, any animal that is diseased will be condemned for human consumption; however, the carcass can be rendered and used to feed our pets. Delmer Jones, Chairman of the National Joint Council, USDA Meat Inspectors, explained, "Animals, hogs, cattle, and poultry are condemned and used for pet food. They are condemned for disease, also spoiled for lack of refrigeration; old products and products that become contaminated during processing."[10]

"Meat meal" is another term often used on labels, and can include dead zoo animals, road kill that is too large to be buried at roadside, condemned material from slaughterhouses, 4-D animals, (dead, diseased, dying, and disabled), and euthanized dogs and cats. Yes, our pets can end up as sources of protein in pet foods. Hundreds of thousands of pets are rendered each year, and although the pet food industry denies that this is happening, there is no uniform testing done to be sure products do not contain pet remains.

The AAFCO "Ingredient Definitions" also list other dubious ingredients that can be used: hydrolyzed hair, dehydrated garbage, and even manure, swine waste, ruminant waste, poultry waste, and what is described as "undried processed animal waste products."[11] Undried processed animal waste products are excreta from any animal except humans. When I contacted the AAFCO I found out that these ingredient definitions applied to pet foods and livestock feed.

Legal Ingredients for Dry Pet Foods

Many of the dry dog foods are comprised of grains, corn, wheat, or rice. I've seen numerous advertisements by major dog food companies stating that the prime ingredient in their product is meat. Meat, meat meal, or meat by-products may be listed as the number-one ingredient, but if you read the label you will notice that yellow corn, corn gluten meal, ground corn, or other grains are listed as the second, third, and even fourth ingredient. In the pet food industry this is called "splitting." Splitting is when grains, usually corn, are added and listed in its various forms—ground corn, gluten meal, yellow corn. If corn is added as just corn then the levels would far exceed the meat in the diet and therefore would have to be the first ingredient listed on the label. By breaking the corn into its various forms it looks as if meat is indeed the main ingredient in the food when in fact corn is the prime ingredient.

Many recalls of pet foods have occurred in the last ten years due to contamination. These are usually foods that contain grains that have become contaminated with one of the many dangerous mycotoxins, which will be discussed in Chapter Three. One such recall occurred in November 1998 when Doane Products Company recalled approximately fifty brands of its pet food. The foods were implicated in the deaths and illnesses of several dogs. As with other recalls, this food was also contaminated with mycotoxins found in moldy corn. The company stated that it has an extensive corn testing program for the detection of these toxins. Apparently the testing was not sufficient to control this outbreak.

We often hear of meat that has been recalled from the human food chain but have you ever wondered what happens to the millions of pounds of meat that may be contaminated with the deadly salmonella, listeria, or E. coli? In April 1999, Thorn Apple Valley, a meat and poultry processing plant, recalled ten million pounds of hot dogs, poultry, and lunch meat that were potentially tainted with listeria. According to a news report by Elizabeth Cohen, Medical Correspondent for CNN Interactive, the president of Thorn Apple Valley, Joel Dorfman, said the product could be irradiated and sold to Russia, which permits such sales. The USDA disagreed, stating that meat unfit for human consumption could not be "reconditioned." Instead of that proposed solution, Mr. Dorfman then stated that his company "now plans on cooking the meat, which will kill the listeria and selling it as pet food. U.S. federal law permits the sale of condemned meat as pet food."[12]

Since cats are carnivores, they require meat in their diets, or at least supplements that include taurine. Taurine is an essential amino acid that cats do not produce on their own. The label on one popular cat food reads, "Poultry by-product meal, ground yellow corn, wheat, corn gluten meal, soybean meal, brewers rice...." This is a *perfect* example of splitting: grains comprising the next five ingredients after the poultry by-products. The composition of this diet is primarily grain.

Because many pets are now allergic to grains, pet food companies have decided that a viable alternative is potatoes. Potatoes that can be legally used to make pet food have been described as containing "varying amounts of inedible or rotten potatoes, french fries, chip, skins, and fats or oils from frying operations."[13] According to the AAFCO, potatoes can be "residue of potato pieces, peeling, culls, etc., obtained from the manufacture of processed potato products for human consumption."[14]

Another questionable ingredient is beet pulp. Most people reading "beet pulp" on the label assume this is coming from red beets that we eat. However, beet pulp does not refer to red beets but to sugar beets. What is going into the pet foods is the residue after the sugar is extracted from sugar beets.

Veterinarians and Pet Food

In 1998 the Animal Protection Institute (API) and the Veterinarians for Animal Rights published the results of a survey the nonprofit organization had distributed to 700 veterinarians with 150 responding. The survey included questions regarding pet food. "More than 90% of veterinarians responding to the survey said they have concerns about pet foods," according to the API report. Later in the that same report the API concluded, "If the American public knew what went into their dog's and cat's commercial food, you'd see some major changes in purchasing choices."[15] The most frequently cited concerns by veterinarians involved the poor quality of meats, fats, and grains used in the products.

These same veterinarians were asked about their knowledge of small animal nutrition: 82.1 percent answered that their knowledge on nutrition came from what they were taught at veterinary school. Further questioning revealed that of the 141 veterinarians who replied to the question, "Do you sell dog and cat food in your practice," 108 replied that they did and that the brand sold most often was Hill's Science Diet. This seemed rather contradictory given the fact that the veterinarians stated they had concerns about the ingredients used in pet food products. Is there a reason that the veterinarians sell pet foods in their practice?

This conflicting information led me to question the level of involvement major pet food companies have in veterinary schools and their subsequent influence on veterinarians—and whether this could contribute to a conflict of interest.

If you ask your veterinarian where he or she acquires his or her knowledge on small animal nutrition, in most cases you will learn that their "nutritional information" comes from the Hill's Company. In an article from the *Wall Street Journal*, reporter Tara Parker-Pope writes, "Hill's now funds a nutrition professorship in nearly half of the nation's vet schools. Hill's employees wrote a widely used textbook on small animal nutrition that is distributed for free to students. Hill's also sends practicing veterinarians to seminars on wringing more profit from clinics and offers the only formal nutrition-certification program for clinic technicians."[16] Although other pet food companies do teach pet nutrition courses, Hill's is the prime source of information in veterinary colleges.

Hill's, along with other large pet food companies, are very involved with other aspects of the veterinary profession. In 1997 Hill's pledged $1 million to the American Veterinary Medical Association (AVMA). "These funds will support the AVMA convention and a myriad of other meetings in disaster relief, animal welfare, educational symposia, and veterinary practice management," according to a press release from the AVMA.[17] Robert Wheeler, President and CEO of Hill's, went on to state in the same press release how Hill's already supports the profession, from scientific presentations at national veterinary meetings to furnishing diets to the thirty-one veterinary colleges and sixty-eight technology schools.

Not only does Hill's provide free pet food to colleges to be used in their teaching hospitals but they also sell Science Diet pet food to the veterinary students "at a heavy discount—$6.50 per unit (case or 20 lb. bag) to students, staff and faculty in the College."[18] In addition to providing discounted pet food for future veterinarians, and free pet food to colleges, Hill's goes one step further when it comes to the veterinary profession. Hill's states in its company newsletter: "Hill's demonstrates its commitment to support future veterinarians through programs that provide financial aid and education in the field of clinical nutrition."[19]

In 1998 Ralston Purina made a $10,000 endowment to the University of Minnesota College of Veterinary Medicine to establish the Purina Student Leadership Award. Sarah Abood, DVM, Purina Pet Nutrition Scientist, states, "Purina presented the donation to the veterinary school to provide a positive link between students and Ralston Purina."[20] The bulletin goes on to report that the award also recognizes the efforts of veterinary students who worked in a Purina booth set up at the Minnesota State Fair. "Fourteen veterinary students worked in the booth during the two week fair held in early September in St. Paul. To prepare students for answering consumers' pet questions and offering nutritional advice, Purina provided six hours training in basic pet nutrition and marketing tactics."[21]

In September 1999 Ralston Purina announced that it was funding the first veterinary emergency/critical care and nutrition residency in the United States at Tufts University. "Dr. L. Chan, DVM, a 1998 graduate of Cornell University College of Veterinary Medicine, has been chosen through the residency matching program to serve as the Purina emergency/critical care and nutrition resident," explains a Ralston Purina newsletter.[22]

With the pet food industry having such a presence at veterinarian colleges it leaves little room for veterinary students to investigate alternative methods of feeding pets. I don't know of any university that seriously examines the feeding of a homemade diet for pets.

When veterinarians eventually set up their own practices, pet food representatives naturally promote their prescription and nonprescription diets to sell in these veterinary practices. What happens if a veterinarian speaks out against the industry? Tom Lonsdale a veterinarian who practices in Australia is a good example. Dr. Lonsdale vociferously claims that processed canned and dried pet food is ruining cats' and dogs' health. He is now being threatened with deregistration if he does not keep quiet.

As with the veterinary associations in the United States and Canada, the pet food companies and the associations that license the veterinarians in Australia have an unholy alliance. *Nexus Magazine*, in its article, "News Snippets from Australia," reports, "Dr. Tom Lonsdale has been accused of professional misconduct by the Australian Veterinary Association (AVA) for voicing his concerns over the increasing links between the AVA and the pet food industry."[23] In a lecture before the staff and students, Faculty of Veterinary Science, New Zealand, Dr. Lonsdale expressed his feelings regarding this unholy alliance, "Veterinarians gain legitimacy and privileges as guardians of the public welfare in respect to animal health. The profession has failed badly in its duties." In this regard to the Australia veterinary profession, Dr. Lonsdale writes, "The Association [Australian Veterinary Association] was in receipt of direct and indirect sponsorship from two large multinational pet food companies. This occasioned bitter criticism of the implied conflict of interest. Rather than limit or stabilize their involvement the AVA has recently entered a sponsorship agreement with a third American multinational pet food corporation."[24]

I have to agree with Dr. Lonsdale. Pet food companies should not be involved in the veterinary profession. When you consider the detrimental effects some of these foods can have on our pets, veterinarians, the people who provide medical care for our pets, should not be involved in selling these products. In my opinion it would be the same as human doctors dispensing from their practices particular brands of foods for various ailments.

If veterinarians are going to continue selling pet foods then I feel it is incumbent on them to know the ingredients being used in these products and the effect these ingredients are having on the animals. Don't take the word of the sales representatives. Go to the company involved and ask in-depth questions. If satisfactory answers cannot be provided, don't sell the product. In my opinion, anyway you look at it, this is a conflict of interest.

THREE

A Toxic Feast

Most consumers assume that pet foods are safe, wholesome products that our pets thrive on. If you are like I was before 1988, you never stop to consider who regulates the pet food industry—or who inspects the ingredients or even the source of the ingredients used in pet foods. I once assumed that pet food ingredients caused no harm to my animal companions.

It was only after I began some persistent questioning of exactly what the contents listed on pet food labels really meant did I begin to realize how difficult it was to determine just what was in the product. Basically, labels are vague. What is legally allowed in pet food is extensive. Labels do not indicate the hidden hazards that can be contained in cans and bags of pet foods that our pets ingest daily.

After talking to state officials about precautionary testing of pet foods, I learned there is no testing undertaken nor is it required by law. Inordinate amounts of heavy metals, hormones, drugs, pesticides, pathogens, and toxins have been found in pet foods, but due to lack of testing and strict regulations, they are allowed in pet foods.

To say the least, I am angry knowing about the myriad of substances that can be used legally in pet foods, and yet consumers are told in endless ads and television commercials that their pets get a complete and nutritiously balanced meal from commercial pet foods.

If enough pets become ill from a particular commercial pet food, the news media will report recalls of a particular product. However, I wonder how often individual pets become ill from commercial pet food while their owners and veterinarians remain unaware of the cause. The pet suffers, the symptoms are treated, and most likely, the pet continues to eat the same pet food that caused the problem in the first place. Unfortunately, it is only the exceptional veterinarian who considers an animal's diet as the potential cause of the problem.

Not only are our pets eating many foods containing levels of antibiotics, hormones, and pesticides, but when our pets become ill they are also treated with a wide variety of drugs and antibiotics. Consider the case of my own dog, Sarge. Before he came into my life, Sarge's caring owner took him to the vet numerous times and he was put on a wide array of drugs for ear infections and nasal problems. The inflammation in Sarge's nose was finally diagnosed as discoid lupus. When all else failed, the veterinarian turned to steroids.

When Sarge came into my care, we switched to a holistic veterinarian who completely changed his treatment regimen. The veterinarian took Sarge off prednisone with its many side effects, and put him on natural steroids, which are derived from fruits and vegetables. These natural steroids have kept his discoid lupus under control for over a year. Sarge also gets an array of vitamins, minerals, and supplements to build up his immune system.

Traditional drugs such as prednisone may keep conditions under control in the short term, but what are the side effects in the long run? Would it not be better to attempt to alleviate the underlying cause of the problem? Perhaps one of the primary goals for healing should be to build up the animal's immune system with natural substances such as whole foods, supplements, vitamins, and minerals. It may take longer to treat the condition with natural methods but the pet is not incurring the side effects often experienced on prescription drugs.

In addition, both Sarge and my cats are fed a homemade diet that includes meat, grains, vegetables, and fruits. Diet is of primary importance for good health not only for pets but also for humans. In the years I have cooked for my pets I've always made sure that any meat is lightly cooked to the point that the juices run clear.

Although this book is devoted primarily to animal companions and their health, humans who eat meat should also be concerned. We are seeing more and more recalls of tainted meat. This meat is sold in grocery stores and in restaurants. Dangerous bacteria such as salmonella, campylobacter, and E. coli have killed thousands of people. The Consumers Union, a non-profit organization that publishes *Consumer Reports*, tested store-bought chicken and found "Campylobacter, a rod-shaped bacterium, is the leading cause of food poisoning nationwide, in 63 percent of the chickens tested, while Salmonella was found in 16 percent of the chicken."[1]

The following will give you a good idea of what is legally allowed in commercial pet foods. You decide what you want to feed your animal companion.

Euthanized Pets in Pet Food

In my first book, I wrote about the shipping of animal carcasses—including dogs and cats—to rendering plants. In the plants these remains become the raw material that is sold to many pet food companies to make their pet food products. To this day, many pet food companies deny this practice; however, there is a strong body of evidence that indicates this happens—and frequently. (See Chapter Two.) Because pet food companies don't test the raw material they can deny or claim that they have no knowledge of rendered pets in the material they purchase. However, this doesn't make the facts any less truthful. Hopefully, my first book, and now this book, will continue to raise public awareness. Pet owners ultimately will be the ones who have to demand accountability from pet food companies to stop these practices.

The product the plants render comes from various sources: garbage from grocery stores; grease and spoiled food from restaurants; road kill too large to be buried at the side of the road; sick farm animals who have died for reasons other than slaughter; food substances condemned for human consumption; and euthanized dogs and cats from shelters, pounds, and veterinary clinics. All this material is dumped into huge containers at the rendering plants, cooked at temperatures between 220°F and 270°F (104.4°C to 132.2°C) for twenty minutes to one hour. The cooked material is centrifuged to separate the grease and tallow from the raw material. This material is finely ground and the end product is meat meal.

Beyond the startling realization that dogs and cats are potentially eating dogs and cats under the guise of "pet food," there are some serious health problems related to this rendering practice. For starters, sodium pentobarbital is a barbiturate used to euthanize companion animals and, to some extent, livestock. When animals eat pet food that has gone through the rendering process, it is likely that they are ingesting a euthanizing drug.

Ashley Robinson, DVM, with a degree in Veterinary Microbiology, undertook a study with several colleagues from the University of Minnesota in 1985 on the levels of sodium pentobarbital in rendered material. They wanted to ascertain if, after rendering, the material still contained levels of this euthanizing drug. The results of the study, published in the *American*

Journal of Veterinary Research, concluded that sodium pentobarbital "survived rendering without undergoing degradation."[2]

In late 1999, I contacted Dr. Robinson to find out if any further testing had been done on rendered material by the University of Minnesota. He replied, "No further studies have been carried out, to my knowledge, on residues from sodium pentobarbital."[3]

In my opening chapter I mention that the Food and Drug Administration, Center for Veterinary Medicine (FDA/CVM) began a study on the levels of pentobarbital and that it had found some in dry dog foods. Numerous times I requested the results of these analyses in 1999, but the CVM has refused to release them stating "the report is not complete." The FDA/CVM has given no indication when it will publish this information. I question if the results of the study will ever be made known to the public.

Basically, consumers have no way of estimating the levels of euthanizing drugs in pet food, and the label does not tell us. Each batch of rendered material contains a different percentage of animal sources. Under present regulations, testing would have to be done on a can-to-can or bag-to-bag basis to determine if there are any residues from these drugs, and if so, how much.

As I mentioned earlier, the rendering industry in the United States and Canada is largely a self-regulated industry. Agencies such as the Association of American Feed Control Officials, (AAFCO), the Pet Food Institute, the Canadian Veterinary Medical Association (CVMA), the Pet Food Manufacturers Association, a Canadian agency, and other government agencies do not undertake testing pet food for euthanizing drugs. The consensus seems to be that the levels of euthanizing drugs contained in the finished material are in such small levels that it would not cause any harm. However, what they seem to fail to take into account is that pets are more than likely ingesting this product on a daily basis.

Antibiotics in Pet Food

Some 50 percent of the antibiotics manufactured in the United States are dumped into animal feed according to *Food Chemical News* an industry publication on the use of chemicals and drugs that are allowed or banned in foods. Although the FDA is attempting to cut back on the amount of antibiotics that farmers can feed to cattle, new drugs continue to be approved for use in livestock. The number of drugs withdrawn by the FDA is miniscule compared to the numbers it approves for use.

On factory farms, pigs, cows, veal calves, and poultry are continually fed antibiotics. Primarily *penicillin* and *tetracycline* are dispensed in a vain attempt to eradicate the many ills that befall these animals in a factory farm's crowded and often unhealthy living conditions. "United States drug manufacturers produce thirty-one million pounds of antibiotics annually,"[4] writes Dr. Michael Fox in his book *Eating With Conscience: The Bioethics of Food.* Farmers feed nearly half of these antibiotics to farm animals. This high-level drug use means millions of dollars for the pharmaceutical companies. For the factory farmers, antibiotic use means fewer animal deaths and larger profits while animals are quickly fattened with the assistance of hormones and drugs before slaughter. The antibiotics in the animals are in the meat we consume as well as in the environment due to the massive levels of livestock waste from factory farms that translate into agricultural runoff.

New and more powerful antibiotics are being developed to treat human illnesses. The so-called "wonder drugs" of the 1950s and 1960s, such as penicillin, tetracycline, and streptomycin, are no longer viable in treating some illnesses and diseases in humans because we have built up a resistance to them. "Widespread overuse of antibiotics is resulting in the evolution of new strains of virulent bacteria whose resistance to antibiotics poses a great threat to human health,"[5] according to the Humane Farming Association, an organization of over 140,000 members dedicated to the protection of farm animals. "Doctors are now reporting that, due to antibiotics uncontrolled use on factory farms, these formerly life saving drugs are often rendered useless in combating human disease."[6]

Humans eating meat from animals treated with antibiotics are building up a resistance to many of these drugs. The search continues for new and stronger antibiotics to treat various infections that the older drugs, penicillin and tetracycline, can no longer treat.

In 1999, The Humane Society of the United States (HSUS) sent a letter to Jane Henney, MD, Commissioner, U.S. Food and Drug Administration, advising that the U.S. Centers for Disease Control, the National Academy of Sciences, and the World Health Organization "recommend that the use of any antimicrobal for growth promotion in animals should be banned if it is (1) used in human therapeutics or (2) known to select for cross-resistance to antimicrobials used in human medicine."[7]

Often antibiotics are given to all of the animals on the farm as a preventative measure rather then to actually treat the disease. So, whether or not animals have symptoms, they are given antibiotics across the board. Because of the inhumane, overcrowded, and unhealthy environment of factory farms, animals are much more susceptible to disease, and thus, are given antibiotics, regardless.

For example, *oxytetracycline* is an antibiotic given to cattle for treating pneumonia, foot-rot, diphtheria, bacterial enteritis, and leptospirosis. In swine, oxytetracycline is used to treat bacterial enteritis and pneumonia. In chickens and turkeys, oxytetracycline is used for respiratory disease and fowl cholera. Withdrawal times for this drug prior to slaughter varies from twenty-two days for cattle and swine to five days for chicken and turkey. Farmers usually follow this procedure.

Chloramphenicol is a powerful, broad-spectrum antibiotic which, because of its detrimental side effects, is used on humans as a last resort in treating bacterial infections. The *Antimicrobial Use Guidelines*, a book issued by the University of Wisconsin Hospital, describes the side effects of this drug on humans as follows: "Chloramphenicol can cause life-threatening bone marrow depression,"[8] a form of aplastic anemia. According to the Department of Food Safety, Residues in Animal Foods, "Chloramphenicol was never approved for use in food animals. However, veterinarians found that it worked well to treat stubborn cases of diarrhea and pneumonia in calves and pigs, so they prescribed it."[9]

Although not used often, this product can be used in the treatment of dogs with bacterial infections that are resistant to treatment with other antibiotics. Dogs given low levels of chloramphenicol daily develop signs of reduced appetite and weight loss. As for cats, chloramphenicol can be very dangerous. Mark Papich, DVM, MS, BS, and Associate Professor of Clinical Pharmacology at North Carolina State University, explained, "Cats have been found to be extremely sensitive to this drug and ingestion of very small amounts can be fatal."[10] In cats, a dose of 50 mg/kg for seven days "has produced severe anorexia, depression, and bone marrow changes."

Chloramphenicol is heat stable, which means it can withstand the temperatures of rendering, degrading only 30 percent at 375°F (190.5°C). In addition, dogs treated with this drug who have died, may be rendered and processed back into livestock or cattle feed. The heat degradation of many of these antibiotics is questionable. Little is known because drug companies usually test only for shelf life of a drug at 150°F. Some drugs are tested to ascertain the residues at cooking temperatures, 250°F to 350°F. In a report in the *Journal of the Association of Official Analytical Chemists* on the effects of storage and processing on various antibiotics in meat, "The effects of cooking and cold storage on the biological activity of the residues of ampicillin, chloramphenicol, oxytetracycline, streptomycin and sulphadimidine were varied; in some instances the effects were minimal, in others nil."[11]

More Dangerous Drugs

Antibiotics are just one of the drugs that degrade little, if any, in processing. The *Ionophores* family of drugs, monensin, salinomycin, lasalocin, are used in both poultry and livestock feed. In poultry feed they are used as growth promoters. In ruminants these drugs are used to reduce bloat, acidosis, and bovine pulmonary emphysema. There is no withdrawal period for these drugs when given to cattle and to poultry.

In 1990 in Canada, a number of dogs died from eating a commercial dog food that had become contaminated with *monensin*. This family of drugs is extremely toxic to both horses and dogs. The America Board of Toxicology lists the clinical signs of monensin intoxication in dogs as "ataxia, mild muscular weakness of the hind limbs, respiratory muscle paralysis."[12] Lasalocid residue in commercial foods fed to dogs was reported by Drs. Safran, Aizenberg, and Bark, veterinarians, "Lasalocid, accidently introduced into a commercial dog food, was found to be the cause of neuromuscular toxicosis in 10 dogs."[13] With supportive therapy there was gradual improvement in all dogs despite the severity of clinical signs. Symptoms develop within six hours to two weeks after food exposure.

In 1997 veterinarians from Utrecht issued their final investigative report on cats who had ingested a cat food produced by Spillers Petfoods in the United Kingdom. This cat food contained a dangerous drug, salinomycin. "The coccidiostatic drug *salinomycin*, which was present in the vitamin premix supplied by a third party, was considered the cause of neuropathy."[14] A conclusive report on this was sent to all veterinarians in the Netherlands because of the unique nature of the outbreak. The onset of clinical signs in cats is sudden and the progression is often rapid.

Ivermectin, is a broad-spectrum antiparasitic agent used in the treatment and control of gastrointestinal nematodes and to control infections in cattle. Cattle must be taken off this drug thirty-five days prior to slaughter. The label cautions: "Do not use in other animal species because severe adverse reactions, including fatalities in dogs, may result."[15] Interestingly, this is a drug that is given to dogs as a heartworm preventative. *The Journal of the Veterinary Medical Association* (JVMA) has reported cases of dogs who have received this medication. One report states, "Within 2 hours of oral administration of ivermectin, the dog had hind limb ataxia. Neurologic signs progressed rapidly until the dog was in a semicomatose state at admission 20 hours later. The dog improved gradually under supportive care."[16]

Another report in the JVMA states, "Ivermectin toxicosis has been reported frequently in Collies: however, other breeds may have idiosyncratic reactions at low doses."[17] Great care must be taken when administering this medication for heartworm prevention. Drugs, whether used in livestock or administered to pets, can pose problems.

Many animals going to slaughter contain levels of these drugs, primarily antibiotics, in amounts higher then allowed. These animals, or parts of the animals, are tagged and marked: "Inspected and condemned." Dairy farmers are advised to avoid rump shots and instead inject drugs in the neck or in front of the shoulder. The "Dairy Initiatives Newsletter," published by the University of Minnesota, regarding injections to cattle states, "A recent packing plant survey found that nearly three-quarters of dairy carcasses showed damage from injections given in the rump."[18] Damage from the injections in the rump can still be obvious more than a year after the animals receive these shots and this area is condemned for human consumption. Part of the Meat Inspection Act relates to "stick marks" (injection sites). Although these areas can be condemned for human consumption they can however be used in pet foods.

Hormones in Pet Food

Giving livestock hormones to promote growth is a typical practice with factory farming. *Estradiol,* a naturally occurring hormone of progesterone and testosterone, is injected because the animal's body is not producing enough hormones to achieve the weight gain the farmer wants. A number of these types of hormones are injected subcutaneously, that is, under the skin of the animal's ear.

Of greater concern are the synthetic hormones: trenbolone acetate, *zeranol,* and *melengestrol acetate.* These are implanted in the animal's body usually under the skin on the back of the ear or attached as ear tags. These cattle heads, including implants, are rendered. In the publication, *Animal*

Nutrition, the authors state: "Extensive use is being made of synthetic and purified estrogens, androgens, progestogens, and growth hormones to stimulate growth and fattening animals that will be slaughtered for meat. Because of the health concerns for humans ingesting excess levels of these synthetic hormones, the FDA requires extensive toxicological testing in animals to determine a safe level in meat for these compounds. Furthermore, the FDA has required that the manufacturers demonstrate that the amount of hormone left in the meat after treatment is below the safe level."[19]

Bovine Growth Hormone (rBGH) also known as rBST or PosilacE has been banned from use in Canada and many other countries, but is used on cattle in the United States. In 1993 the FDA approved rBGH, a genetically engineered hormone produced by Monsanto that increases milk production in dairy cows. Health Canada, a department of the federal government, would not allow the use of this hormone after it was found that, "30 percent of the rats given the drug reacted with increased levels of antibodies, and some have lesions and cysts in their thyroid glands,"[20] according the *Toronto Globe and Mail* in September 1998. Many U.S. dairy farmers have reported numerous health problems in their cattle while on this drug, including early death.

Pesticides and Insecticides

In addition to antibiotics, drugs, and hormones, add pesticides and insecticides, which are sprayed on, or injected, and used in ear tags on animals raised on factory farms. (Insecticides are also used in flea and tick control products for dogs and cats, which are explained in depth in Chapter Nine.)

Insecticides and pesticides are sometimes applied to livestock for pest control, and can possess residual action that can persist for months. In his paper, "Insecticide-Impregnated Cattle Ear Tags," Lee Townsend, PhD, reports. "...to control horn and face flies, farmers and ranchers use organophosphate insecticides such as *diazinon, fenthion, pirimofos methyl*, or *diazinon* plus *chlorpyrifos* combination."[21] In particular, fenthion is used to control cattle grubs and as an aid in controlling lice on beef and dairy cattle. The withdrawal time for fenthion is forty-five days prior to slaughter.

Because of concern to the environment, the Environment Protection Agency (EPA) has withdrawn many of the chlorinated hydrocarbons from use. Farmers and ranchers now use *organophosphates*. Although less of an environmental problem, organophosphates are more toxic then the chlorinated hydrocarbons they replaced. A professor of Veterinary Pharmacology at Purdue University, Gordon Coppec, in his paper, "Pharmacology of Pesticides" writes that "there are long term (months) effects on some enzyme systems in animals not showing overt toxicity that may still cause deleterious reactions to other drugs, e.g. succinylcholine."[22] In humans, "Symptoms of mild organophosphate pesticides include frequent headaches, general fatigue, dizziness, and mild indigestion. More serious poisoning can induce vomiting, lung failure, convulsions and death."[23]

In 1999, the EPA took steps to ban two pesticides in the organophosphate family: *methyl parathion* and *azinphos methyl*. Journalist Tom Kenworthy of the *Washington Post* reports, "There was concern about the possible toxicity to humans, particularly to the developing nervous systems of infants and children."[24] Methyl parathion, one of the most toxic organophosphates, is used as a crop spray as well as a control for mosquitoes. *Azinphos methyl* is in the same family and basically used for the same purposes. A fact sheet from the United States Information Services in August 1999 states, "Methyl parathion also poses a high risk to birds and aquatic invertebrates. It is highly toxic to honey bees. Canceling the orchard uses is expected to significantly reduce risks to honey bees and birds."[25]

Although methyl parathion is primarily a spray for crops it is also used on grain crops, which cattle ingest. The FDA/CVM monitors tissue from slaughtered animals for many of these chemical compounds. What happens to the animals found to contain high levels of these substances? "Animals with illegal residues will be condemned by the Food Safety Inspection Services (FSIS),"[26] explained the CVM. Condemned animals are sent to rendering facilities to be rendered for animal feed or pet food.

One pesticide that made the news in 2000 is *chlorpyrifos*, which is sold under the trade name of Dursban and Lorsban. (The use of this pesticide in flea and tick preparations is discussed in Chapter Eight: Cancer in Animals.) Chlorpyrifos can be used to kill mosquito and fly larvae. According to two veterinarians with the University of Missouri, College of Veterinary Medicine, chlorpyrifos is also used on cattle in "ear tags with permethrins for face flies, gulf coast ticks, spinose ear ticks, stable flies, house flies and lice."[27] (*Permethrins* is a humanmade form of the naturally occurring pyrethrins, a substance derived from chrysanthemum.)

Millions of consumers have used products containing chlorpyrifos on their gardens and lawns, and as an indoor bug spray. In June 2000 the EPA took steps to phase out chlorpyrifos citing possible health risks to children. "After a lengthy review, the EPA concluded that chlorpyrifos sold by Dow AgroSciences under the trade names Dursban and Lorsban poses a risk to children because of its potential effects on the nervous system and possibly brain damage."[28] Can you imagine the effect that this substance must have had on our pets who breathed this substance on a daily basis from flea collars and from the grass they walk on?

Minerals and Metals in Pet Food

Zinc, copper, and iron are minerals listed on the labels of most pet food. The lab that tested the commercial dog food I questioned in my own court case (described extensively in my first book) also found additional minerals in the dry dog food. Minerals that were found, but not listed on the label included: silver, beryllium, cadmium, bismuth, cobalt, manganese, barium, iron, molybdenum, nickel, lead, strontium, vanadium, tungsten, phosphorus, titanium, chromium, sodium, potassium, aluminum, calcium, magnesium, and selenium. Some of these are trace elements that are found naturally in food and therefore do not have to be listed on the labels.

One of the veterinarians whom I contacted with regard to my court case, Cecil F. Brownie, DVM, PhD, Toxicologist, at North Carolina State University, provided his comments regarding the metals in the pet food I had analyzed. On the level of iron in the food, he commented, "Iron can be tolerated at very high levels depending on the form administered, the age, and animal species given iron. Dogs, being monogastric, (having one stomach) should be able to tolerate (even though not this high of a concentration), the 295 mg. per kg. of food level administered in this diet."[29] Dr. Brownie felt that the level of 295 mg. found in the pet food I had fed my dogs was a high level compared to what dogs require.

According to *The Basic Guide for Canine Nutrition* published by Gaines Pet Food Company the level of iron in a dry dog food should be 54 mg. per kg. of food. High levels of iron in the diet can also interfere with the absorption of phosphorous. Although I was feeding my dogs what I thought was a quality commercial pet food, they were getting more minerals, as indicated by the analysis of the dog food, than was listed on the label.

Levels of lead were also found in the food I had analyzed: 3.27 mg. per kg. of food. I subsequently learned that research conducted at the Connecticut Agricultural Experiment Station detected "quantities" of lead in liver and kidney organs of cattle. Organ meats are prime ingredients in many canned pet foods. The results reported by three veterinarians in their paper, "Lead Content of Pet Foods," indicates "of the canned cat food tested, a cat ingesting six ounces of pet food per day, the daily intake of lead would range from 0.15 to 1.2 mg. For the dog food tested, a dog ingesting fifteen ounces of pet food would be receiving levels of 0.43 mg. to 2.4 mg. per day. Lead in any level should not be in pet food as it is very toxic."[30]

The Connecticut Agricultural Experiment Station also tested two types of dry cat food. The results state, "Based on consumption of 120 g. per day, the cat would ingest 0.42 mg. and 0.72 mg. of lead, or 1.4 and 2.4 times the 0.3 level considered unsafe for a child. By comparison, a dog or cat is much smaller than a child."[31] Unquestionably, commercial pet foods may contain dangerous levels of heavy metals.

Assorted Toxins in Pet Food

Mycotoxins are molds that infect grain crops, especially corn, and grow in these crops when conditions are damp or wet. These molds are also found in peanuts. The family of mycotoxins are numerous and include: *aflatoxin B1, ergotism, citrinin, vomitoxin, zearaleone, and ochratoxin*, to name a few.

Grains for human consumption are tested to ascertain levels of mycotoxins. Any grains that contain over the allowable level in human foods can be used legally in livestock feed and pet foods. Usually the contaminated grains are mixed with grains that do not have a high level of these toxins, thus cutting down on the high level. Symptoms in dogs who have eaten mycotoxins include loss of appetite, refusal to eat, suppression of the immune system, reproductive failure, and in some cases death.

Aflatoxin B1 is among one of the most toxic substances known to humankind. Measured in parts per billion (ppb), minute quantities can kill animals and humans. In the case of grains grown for human consumption, testing for this toxin is mandatory. However, this is not the case within the pet food industry. In June 1988, *The Veterinary Journal* reported a number of cases of dogs who had succumbed to aflatoxin B1 in their diets. Autopsies indicated the cause of death in these animals: "Aflatoxins have been shown to cause liver cancer in laboratory animals at levels as low as 1 part per billion."[32] Peanut shells, a source of fiber used in some commercial pet foods, are one of the prime sources of aflatoxins.

In November 1998, mycotoxin-tainted dog food was linked to the death of twenty-five dogs in Texas. The Doane Products Company, a manufacturer of pet foods for a number of other companies recalled over fifty brands of food. The CEO of Doane Products, Doug Cahill, stated, "Our first concern is for the safety of family pets."[33] It might be interesting to find out how this contaminated grain actually got into the pet food. From the information I have acquired, most pet food companies advise that they test the grains to ascertain the levels of mycotoxins in the grains they purchase. If levels are high then the contaminated grain is mixed with uncontaminated grains to bring down the levels of the mycotoxins.

Deoxynivalenol (DON), the mold or fungi that causes the mycotoxin called *vomitoxin*, is rampant in both the United States and Canada. Vomitoxin is the most prevalent of the mycotoxins found in pet foods, and is usually cited as the cause of illness in pets when a pet food is found to contain contaminated grains. Often pets will refuse to eat a food that contains contaminated grains, but if they do eat a food contaminated with vomitoxin, the animal is likely to have symptoms of vomiting, weight loss, and for young animals, vomitoxin can cause severe diarrhea.

It has been shown that milling and heat treatment do not mitigate vomitoxin from grains. The Food and Nutrition Department of South Dakota State University reported in a research paper, "In extruded corn grits, extruded dry dog food, and autoclaved moist dog food, there were no significant reductions."[34]

In its 1995 "Enforcement Report," the FDA reported on the recall of dry dog and cat foods. Nature's Recipe, the company involved in the recall, assessed their losses at $20 million.

In the United States in 1995, the FDA recalled foods included 3,557,493 pounds of dry dog food and 921,035 pounds of dry cat food. "Products are adulterated with the mycotoxin, vomitoxin, which may cause dogs and cats to become ill (vomiting and/or diarrhea),"[35] states the FDA report. With this level of recall of dry commercial pet food, pet owners feeding commercial foods are taking big risks with their animal companions' health.

Illegal Drugs Used on Animals

Although all drugs used on livestock and for use in pets are approved by the FDA, the use of illegal drugs has caused health problems for people ingesting the meat from animals given these drugs. One such drug, *clenbuterol,* "a growth promoting drug in the beta-agonist class of compounds. Its illegal use in show animals is linked to its ability to induce weight gain and a great proportion of muscle to fat," according to the Food Safety and Inspection Service (FSIS).[36]

In Spain, there have been recent reports of acute poisoning of humans from their consumption of liver from clenbuterol-treated animals.[37] When Gail Eisnitz, author of *Slaughterhouse,* began an investigation into this drug she discovered that the USDA had been advised of its use in veal calf feed in 1989 and apparently chose to do nothing. "Even though clenbuterol had already been the subject of a major international crackdown in Europe, here in the United States it wasn't until five years later with the U.S. Customs Service received a similar tip, that someone decided to investigate," reports Eisnitz. "Despite the dangers posed to the American public from clenbuterol in the food supply, federal regulators tried to keep their investigation under wraps."[38]

I correspond often with Gail Eisnitz, and she is a person who cares deeply about the welfare of animals. Her investigations have lead to numerous charges being launched against companies for the misuse of drugs and the treatment of animals going to slaughter. Her book, *Slaughterhouse,* is an eye opener for anyone who wants to learn about the meat industry.

In Canada, clenbuterol is used as an injectable, and in various oral dosages it is for horses only. In May 1998, the U.S. Food and Drug Administration approved it for use in horses with chronic pulmonary diseases. Jay Richards, *Las Vegas Review Journal,* describes how the drug works on horses, "Clenbuterol dilates bronchial passages to increase a horse's oxygen intake, thereby enhancing its stamina."[39]

There have been cases of clenbuterol being smuggled from Canada into the United States. A veterinarian in Cordell, Oklahoma, Jerry Bonhomie, was sentenced to eight months in a federal prison for conspiring to buy more than $64,000 in illegal drugs. The Center for Veterinary Medicine published this case in 1999. "Dr. Bonhomie admitted that between at least 1988 and 1994 he purchased more than 1,000 bottles of clenbuterol from a Canadian veterinarian and resold it to his veterinary customers so they could use it to illegally enhance the muscle mass of their lambs and cattle entered in various livestock shows."[40]

If animals are found to contain levels of these drugs, they are condemned for human consumption. These dead animals are usually sent to plants for rendering and nothing prevents this material from being used in pet foods.

Bacteria in Pet Food

Salmonella, E. coli, campylobacter, and *listeria* are bacteria that can find their way into human food as well as into pet food. Pet food companies randomly test for salmonella in the raw material they use. However, one problem with random testing is that salmonella, even in minute amounts, can re-infect other material very quickly. Salmonella contaminates meat products but can be eradicated by cooking. Material from slaughterhouses unfit for human consumption such as lungs, livers, and intestines from cattle and swine are easily contaminated with salmonella. Unless the pet food companies—to which this rendered material is shipped—test every batch, there is a very good chance of contamination.

In his book, *How to Have a Healthier Dog*, Wendell Belfield, DVM, writes about a little girl who was hospitalized with a gastrointestinal infection. The health department investigated and found a sick dog in the house who tested positive for salmonella. Examination of the commercial dog food the animal had been eating turned up the presence of two types of salmonella. "Twenty-five samples, representing four different manufacturers and two retail store brands, were purchased," writes Dr. Belfield. "The products of two of the manufacturers were found to contain bacterial contamination. Eleven samples of the original suspect product were examined and all were found to contain salmonella. As many as eight different strains were isolated in one bag."[41]

Jeff Bender and Ashley Robinson, veterinarians at the Department of Clinical and Population Sciences at the University of Minnesota, researched salmonella in animals. From their findings, they report, "An epidemic in a Minnesota cattery several years ago was caused by Salmonella newport and S. typhimrium. There was severe mortality in kittens over a six-month period, which eventually resulted in a decision to depopulate. The most likely source of this infection was the feeding of so called '4-D' meat (meat from dead dying, diseased, and debilitated livestock), as salmonellas were isolated from this particular product."[42] Routinely, 4-D meat is used for commercial pet foods. About five years ago a deadly strain of salmonella surfaced, DT 104, which has proven to be resistant to many antibiotics. This strain can be transmitted to pets through the ingestion of the contaminated meat or poultry. Although cooking destroys this bacterium, unless the processing area is kept spotlessly clean, contamination can and does reoccur.

Escherichia coli or *E. coli 0157:H7* is another bacterium that can cause serious illness both in humans and pets. This bacterium is usually found in the intestinal track of cattle. Gastrointestinal problems in pets caused by E. coli often go undiagnosed. Donald Strombeck, DVM, writes, "Escherichia coli in food represents 'fecal contamination,' and that is more common for some ingredients in pet foods than in foods for human use. For example, meat meal found in many pet foods is prepared from dead animals contaminated with fecal types of bacteria (coliforms). It is possible that Escherichia coli is an important cause of infectious gastrointestinal disease in animals."[43] There has also been concern that E. coli can be passed from pets to humans although further research in this area is needed.

Listeria are not heard about as often as salmonella and E. coli but nonetheless a problem to be concerned about. In recent years there have been numerous recalls of hot dogs and processed meats containing listeria. In a research study on the poultry industry undertaken by the Russell Research Center, a department of the United States Food and Drug Administration, Agriculture Research Services in Athens Georgia, notes, "Listeria were rarely found in the hatchery or on the live animals, however once they did enter the processing plant many of the carcasses became contaminated before leaving the processing area."[44]

Pets are prone to listeria, which have been isolated in cultures taken from dogs. One dog displayed an acute onset of circling and depression. A clinical examination revealed conjunctivitis, abdominal pain, anemia, and various other symptoms. Despite antibiotic treatment the dog died. Drs. H. Schroeder and I.B. Reusberg, veterinarians from the Veterinary College in Pretoria, describe their findings: "On autopsy, widespread inflammatory lesions were found to be present in the lungs, liver, spleen, meninges, lymph nodes, adrenal glands and kidneys."[45]

Campylobacter is another bacterial agent affecting humans and pets, and can be found in cattle, poultry, and pigs. Contamination is caused by intestinal spillage during slaughter. The offal, liver and kidneys, used for pet foods, reportedly are more heavily contaminated with campylobacter than the carcasses. The Food Science and Technology Institute reports, "Dogs and cats can also suffer from campylobacter diarrhea and they may transmit it to humans if hygiene is poor."[46]

Chicken is the prime suspect in cases of campylobacter. "Six years ago, tests conducted by the Centers of Disease Control and Prevention (CDC) found that 30 percent to 70 percent of all chickens were infected with Campylobacter," according to a 1997 article in *The New York Times*. "Now better detection methods suggest 70 percent to 90 percent of chickens carry the bacteria."[47]

More accurate testing methods for bacteria in meats indicate a more serious situation than previously assumed. Because bacterial contamination has become rampant in meat, humans are advised to cook all meat to avoid the serious, if not fatal, consequences from ingesting undercooked meat. Now, humans are advised to cook all meat very well. However, pet foods testing is not standardized and is inconsistent. For example, meat meal, coming from rendering plants, may be tested occasionally. Pet food companies may test the raw material—occasionally. But standards are loose and lax.

Many times I have posed the same question to a veterinary nutritionist at popular commercial pet food companies: "What testing is undertaken on the raw material to ascertain the species of the protein, and the levels of pathogens, drugs, heavy metals, pesticides, and hormones?" As of January 2001, I had not received a reply.

However, even if a rendering company tested the product for contamination and it was found negative, cross-contamination can occur very easily. If the pet food company receiving the raw material does not test the entire batch, it is possible that the raw material could be contaminated.

Diseased Animals Rendered for Pet Food

Cows, pigs, sheep, chickens, and turkeys also carry diseases—a vast array of diseases. Brucellosis, leptospirosis, caseous lymphadenitis, bovine squamous cell carcinoma, clostridial diseases in cattle (blackleg, malignant edema, clostridium sordellii, enterotoxemia), osteomyelitis in turkeys, ascites in poultry, and arthropathy in hogs and cattle, avian encephalomyelitis, Marek's disease, and liver flukes, just to name a few. Animals found with these diseases at the time of slaughter are usually condemned or the parts of the animals that are affected are condemned. This material can either be sold to pet food companies or breeders, or sent off to the rendering plants.

Brucellosis is a bacterial disease that can infect cattle, sheep, goats, dogs, and humans. Cats seem to be resistant to these bacteria. Linda March, Information Specialist for the University of Illinois, College of Veterinary Medicine, provides some insight into how this disease is transmitted in dogs. "The major route of brucellosis transmission in dogs is through direct contact of an infected, aborted fetus, or uterine discharge. They may become infected by eating contaminated meat, fetal membranes, aborted fetuses of livestock or drinking contaminated, unpasteurized milk."[48] Signs of infection in dogs may include spontaneous abortion, infertility, infected reproductive organs, arthritis, disc disease, fever, hind limb weakness, lethargy and/or general lymph node swelling.

According to the University of Illinois, College of Veterinary Medicine, "Brucellosis is difficult to treat. It may take a long period of antibiotic therapy to fully rid the dog of the bacteria."[49] It is possible for humans to become infected with canine brucellosis although transmission from dogs to people is relatively uncommon.

Leptospirosis is a bacterial disease that affects cattle, swine, wild animals, domestic animals, and humans. "A significant percentage of human cases are acquired through direct contact with the urine of infected livestock or with contaminated soil or water," according to Donald Hundson, DVM, from the Veterinary College at the University of Nebraska.[50] In dogs this disease causes elevated body temperature, vomiting, muscular stiffness, weakness, and inflammation of the kidney. Antibiotics (streptomycin, chlortetracycline, or oxytetracycline) are often used successfully in cattle.

Clostridial bacteria infect cattle with unique characteristics. E.J. Richey and E.L. Bliss, DVMs from the University of Florida describe some of the characteristics of clostridial bacteria: "(1) the ability to multiply only in the absence of oxygen; (2) the ability to survive adverse conditions by transforming into highly resistant forms called spores; and (3) the release of potent toxins during the process of multiplying."[51] Malignant edema occurs as a wound infection in cattle, which then gravitates to lower portions of the body such as the belly wall or lower limbs. Death usually occurs within twenty-four hours.

Because clostridial bacteria can be present throughout the carcass of an animal that died of the disease, researchers have suggested that cattle who have died from a clostridia infection be completely burned or buried in a deep grave after covering the carcass with quicklime.

It is strongly suggested that all cattle be vaccinated for this disease. "Clostridial vaccines can cause tissue reaction and swelling and sometimes abscesses and scar tissue. No matter which clostridial vaccine you use, it should always be given subcutaneously, and preferably in the side of the neck. That way, any tissue damage that occurs can be easily trimmed out at slaughter without sacrificing good parts of the beef carcass."[52]

This is the procedure outlined by the American-International Charolais Association, a group devoted to raising and showing Charolais cattle. When the animal is slaughtered, any areas of the carcass that are bruised or contain "stick-marks" are cut out and labeled unfit for human consumption. However, these same parts can legally be sent to rendering plants and used for pet food.

Liver flukes are found primarily in cattle in Florida. Cattle become infected after eating tiny tadpoles that have attached themselves to vegetation. Once ingested and after reaching the small intestines, the fluke larvae are released from the tadpole. These larvae enter the abdominal cavity and then penetrate the liver. Finally the fluke larvae enter the bile duct where they mature and begin to produce eggs that are carried in the bile to the gut, thus completing the liver fluke cycle. Charles Courtney, DVM, PhD from the University of Florida, explains, "The best way to learn whether or not flukes are present on your ranch is to follow your cull cow to slaughter and find out whether or not their livers were condemned for flukes."[53] Diseased livers, kidneys, and lungs of cattle, swine and livestock are major components of pet foods.

A number of viral and bacterial diseases are found in poultry. *Avian encephalomyelitis* is a viral infection that affects chickens of all ages and has been observed in turkeys. From what I have read in the last few years the signs of encephalomyelitis in chickens and turkeys resemble that of what has been seen in cattle infected with bovine spongiform encephalopathy (BSE). BSE is the disease that has caused the death and slaughter of thousands of cattle in the United Kingdom. It affects the brains of cattle. Cattle begin to stagger, fall down, and eventually die. Over eighty humans in the United Kingdom have died from a disease linked to the meat from cattle with BSE, Creutzfeldt-Jakob disease (CJD). Texas A&M University describes this viral disease in poultry as, "Lack of coordination, nervousness, a jerky or irregular gait, falling over with outstretched wing, and muscular tremors especially noticeable in the head and neck."[54]

This phenomena is outlined in a paper by the Physicians Committee for Responsible Medicine written in 1996, in which it was characterized as more like Mad Chicken Disease. "While it is unlikely that encephalomalacia in chickens has any relationship to disease in other animals, the poultry industry merits close scrutiny for its contribution to cattle disease, because chickens are fed cattle remains and, in turn, chicken manure is routinely fed to cattle."[55] Dogs and cats are also fed the remains of cattle and chickens and if there is any relationship of this disease to BSE, rendering does not kill this virus.

Another virus that affects poultry is *lymphoid leukosis*. This disease is characterized by the formation of lymphoid tumors, particularly in the liver and spleen. Although the liver and spleen are commonly involved, other visceral organs may be affected.[56] Osteopetrosis is the bone form of this disease in poultry and although it was first thought to be a disease of older birds, it is now known to be quite common in young chickens and is one of the more serious causes for broilers to be labeled condemned.

Although many of these diseases can be obliterated in the rendering process, I know that I do not want my pets to eat material that has been condemned *for any reason*. All of these diseased parts of animals are going to rendering plants. When you combine diseased animals with the potential dangers of drug and hormone residues, heavy metals, mycotoxins, and bacteria, you have a toxic mix that the pet food industry describes as "complete and balanced."

– FOUR –

Pet Food Regulations

Like millions of pet owners, I was under the impression that the pet food industry was regulated to the extent that human foods are regulated. I assumed that government agencies oversaw the ingredients that go into the food we feed our companion animals. According to a document put out by Purina, "Pet foods are among the most highly regulated products on the market."[1] As much as I want to believe this statement, my research finds otherwise.

If we are to believe what we read, the pet food industry in the United States is regulated by the Food and Drug Administration (FDA); the Federal Food, Drug and Cosmetic Act; and the Fair Packaging and Labeling Act. In addition, voluntary regulations for the United States Department of Agriculture (USDA) and state regulations are established by the Association of American Feed Control Officials (AAFCO). Impressive as all of this sounds, none of these agencies actually regulate what ingredients are contained in rendering products sold to commercial pet food companies for use in pet food.

The FDA and AAFCO are supposed to be the driving forces in the regulations on pet food. According to Linda Grassie, spokesperson for the Food and Drug Administration, Center for Veterinary Medicine (FDA/CVM,) the position of the agency is to "establish standards for all animal feeds; proper identification of the product as a pet food: net quality statement (weight, volume, or count); name and place of business of the manufacturer; packer or distributor; and proper listing of all ingredients in descending order of predominance by weight and identification by their common or usual names."[2]

However, the FDA does not test nor investigate as to what are the contents of the products from rendering plants nor the *quality* of the ingredients. In brief, I found no laws that state diseased cattle and companion animals cannot be rendered and used for pet foods. In the case of companion animals, no government agencies oversee the numbers of carcasses sent to rendering plants and no records are kept. All the states that responded to my inquiries agree that there are no regulations that prohibit the rendering of any animal, including dogs and cats.

A prime example is California. Douglas Hepper, DVM, staff veterinarian for the Department of Agriculture, Meat and Poultry Inspection Branch (MPI), oversees the regulations for raw ingredients entering rendering plants. In a personal correspondence with me, he clearly defined acceptable raw ingredients to be "inedible and condemned materials from California Department of Food and Agriculture (CDFA) and USDA-inspected establishments; livestock and horses who have died on farms; and used, inedible kitchen grease from restaurants and institutions." Dr. Hepper also stated, "MPI does not test raw material entering rendering plants for levels of pathogens, drugs, hormones, heavy metals, and pesticides. MPI does not have any jurisdiction over companion animals entering rendering plants. However, it is legal in California for companion animals to be rendered."[3]

In this chapter I explain how these various agencies are involved in the regulation of pet food. As you will see, shockingly, there are very few regulations for protecting our pets from unhealthy or harmful material that can be legally rendered into products sold for manufacturing pet food.

The Food and Drug Administration, Center for Veterinary Medicine

The primary duties of the FDA/CVM are to focus on health claims made by the pet food companies, especially if they are labeled for the prevention or treatment of a disease. The FDA/CVM confirms that research supports these companies' claims. For example, the FDA/CVM investigated pet food companies that claimed their cat foods "will prevent Feline Urological Syndrome (FUS)." When it could not be proven that the cat food actually prevented FUS, the FDA required the pet food companies to remove this claim from their packaging. The FDA/CVM had given the pet food manufacturers ample time to change their labels. When some did not comply, the FDA and state officials seized hundreds of tons of cat food. One company, whose products were seized, assured the FDA that the product would no longer be labeled for the prevention of FUS and sold in the

United States. However, U.S. pet food companies can take this same pet food with the same false claim and continue to sell it in countries without legislation—Canada, for one.

The FDA/CVM's duties also include the labeling of products: proper identification of the product, net quantity statement, manufacturer's address, and proper listing of ingredients. When there are health risks from an ingredient or additive in a pet food, the FDA asks for "scientific evidence" that shows that this is the case. It can then prohibit the use of a questionable ingredient or require the manufacturers to modify an ingredient's use. Most of the input that the FDA/CVM has when it comes to dog and cat food is product labeling.

One preservative, *ethoxyquin*, came under question by this agency a number of years ago. Ethoxyquin, a preservative used in a number of pet foods, is a concern to many pet owners. Ethoxyquin can be put into the mix by a feed grain mill, a rendering plant, or by a pet food company. Developed in the 1950s by Monsanto, ethoxyquin was first used as a stabilizer and has also been effective as an insecticide and pesticide. According to literature provided by the FDA/CVM, only when a pet food company uses ethoxyquin does this preservative have to be listed on the label. The suppliers of the raw material, feed grain mills and rendering plants can add ethoxyquin but this will not be listed as an ingredient on the label because they are only the *suppliers* not the *producers* of the finished pet food product.

A few years ago, the FDA/CVM began receiving reports from dog owners attributing a myriad of adverse effects to the presence of ethoxyquin in dog food. A FDA/CVM consumer booklet states, "The reported effects include allergic reactions, skin problems, major organ failure, behavior problems and cancer. However, there is little available scientific data to support these contentions, or to show other adverse effects in dogs at levels approved for use in dog foods. As such, there is no scientific basis to warrant change in the regulatory status of ethoxyquin at this time."[4] The FDA/CVM, requires scientific data to investigate most health concerns in pets.

The United Animal Owners Association, and in particular, consumer Carol Barfield, protested the use of ethoxyquin in pet food. Because of the allegations made by breeders concerned about foods containing ethoxyquin, Monsanto commissioned an accredited, independent laboratory to conduct a three-year study on its product. In 1996, the results of this study were disclosed.

The study, a feeding trial, was conducted on Beagles (the breed of choice for testers). One group was fed food that contained 180 to 360 parts per million (ppm) of ethoxyquin. According to *Petfood Industry* magazine in the May/June 1996 edition: "Consistent with previous work, the researchers noted liver pigmentation changes and elevated liver enzymes that depended on the dosage of ethoxyquin. The minimal liver pigmentation that occurred at 180 ppm, in females, was not considered clinically significant because there were no liver enzyme changes or associated pathological changes in the liver or other organs. In addition the dogs' overall health was not affected."[5]

As a result of consumer complaints, and the results of the independent study, in 1997 the FDA requested that levels of ethoxyquin be reduced in dog food. "FDA's Center for Veterinary Medicine (CVM) requested that the maximum level for ethoxyquin in complete dog foods be voluntarily lowered to 75 parts per million (ppm). Under the current food additive regulations, ethoxyquin is allowed at levels up to 150 ppm in complete dog foods."[6]

Unfortunately, ethoxyquin was not completely eliminated from commercial pet foods, just lowered. The FDA advised that if further information became available on the safety of ethoxyquin at 75 ppm in dog food, or shows it to be an effective antioxidant at levels below 75 ppm, the CVM will consider further action.

The second case that the FDA/CVM describes in its literature concerns propylene glycol, a humectant that has been used in semi-moist pet food for about fifteen years. Propylene glycol is a second cousin to antifreeze. Propylene glycol has been proven to be a major contributor in feline cardiac disease according to research accepted by the FDA. The FDA publication, "Understanding Pet Food Labels," states: "It [propylene glycol] was known to cause overt anemia or other clinical effects. However, recent reports of scientifically sound studies show that propylene glycol reduces red blood cell survival time, renders red blood cells more susceptible to oxidative damage, and has other adverse effects in cats consuming the substance at levels found in semi-moist food."[7]

As of January 2001, the FDA/CVM prohibits the use of propylene glycol in semi-moist cat food. Propylene glycol was in semi-moist cat food for approximately fifteen years. How many cats have suffered and died from ingesting this substance? How many thousands, if not millions, of dollars have been spent on veterinary bills to treat the illnesses caused by propylene glycol?

The Federal Food, Drug and Cosmetic Act

The FDA also has jurisdiction over the Federal Food, Drug and Cosmetic Act, which applies to human as well as animal food. Section 201(a)(3) of the Act reads: "A food shall be deemed to be adulterated if it consists in whole or in part of any filthy, putrid, or decomposed substance, or if it is otherwise unfit for food." Section 201(a)(4) reads: "if it has been prepared, packed, or held under unsanitary conditions whereby it may have become contaminated with filth, or whereby it may have been rendered injurious to health."[8]

While the Act sounds good, again, the material created at a rendering plant is not tested by any independent agency to ascertain what it is composed of. We are aware of what legal ingredients are allowed in pet food products, and we know the actual sources of much of this food, including dead, diseased, disabled and dying animals, garbage from slaughterhouses, road kill, and euthanized dogs and cats. All of these can be rendered under deplorable conditions and sold as sources of protein for pet food. From my research, it is apparent that the FDA, which oversees the Food, Drug and Cosmetic Act, is aware of what is being used in pet foods yet takes no steps to enforce this Act. Repeatedly, I have queried various government agencies as to the testing of the ingredients in these foods. No government agency tests either raw or finished products from rendering plants to see exactly what this material contains.

The Association of American Feed Control Officials

The main body responsible for regulations and guidelines for the pet food industry is the Association of American Feed Control Officials (AAFCO). The AAFCO is an association comprised of state and federal agencies, primarily agriculture departments. Also included in AAFCO's roster are people from pet food companies, feed associations, drug companies, and even the National Renderers Association, all of whom have a connection to the pet food industry.

For many years the National Research Council (NRC) provided books containing information on the nutrients required by dogs and cats. However, according to David Dzanis, DVM, former veterinary nutritionist with the Center for Veterinary Medicine, "The recommendations of the National Research Council were once used as the basis for nutritional adequacy, but they are no longer considered valid for this purpose."[9]

In 1974 the pet food industry created a group called the Association of American Feed Control Officials (AAFCO). At that time, the AAFCO chose to adopt the NRC standards rather than develop its own. The Animal Protection Institute (API), in its 1996 *Investigative Report*, showed why the NRC standards were soon abandoned by the AAFCO. "The NRC standards required feeding trials for pet foods that claimed to be 'complete' and 'balanced.'"[10]

The pet food industry found feeding trials to be too restrictive, so AAFCO designed an alternative procedure for claiming the nutritional adequacy of pet food. Instead of feeding trials, the AAFCO undertook chemical analysis of the food to determine if the food met or exceeded the NRC standards. What they did not take into consideration was that chemical analysis does not address the palatability, digestibility, and biological availability of the nutrients in these foods.

Today, the AAFCO testing protocols are minimal, and in my opinion, quite inadequate. The testing protocol requires that only eight dogs, older than one year, must start a feeding test. For six months dogs must be fed the food that is being tested. The dogs finishing the test must not lose more then 15 percent of their body weight, and six of the eight dogs must finish the test. On pet food labels, the AAFCO states that the pet foods that pass the AAFCO guidelines, have passed stringent tests. In my estimation this "stringent testing" is a misstatement.

The AAFCO regulates labeling, ingredient definitions, and product names. Its canine and feline "nutrient profiles" are primarily nutrient minimums with maximums stated. Manufacturers of pet food are only required to comply with the regulations, if any, of their particular state or the states in which the product is sold. However, the AAFCO has no enforcement authority. This organization does not undertake any analytical testing on pet food nor does it determine the sources of protein, fiber, or fats used in the product. It does provide an extensive list of "feed ingredient definitions," which gives a wide margin for the pet food industry to use the cheapest ingredients available. Again, if a particular state adopts the AAFCO guidelines, it must also adhere to the ingredient definitions.

In 1995, I wrote to a number of state officials who are members of the AAFCO to solicit their particular state's position on various areas of pet food regulations and testing. Most responses were vague and none of the states that replied prohibited the use of companion animals in commercial pet foods. In February 2000, I again wrote to the various states, some replied, some did not. The questions were basically the same questions I asked in 1995 for my first book *Food Pets Die For*. From the responses I received in 2000, I must conclude that basically nothing—regulations, testing, or ingredients used—have changed since 1995 when I first questioned state officials. The pet food industry is still virtually self-regulated. Below are the questions and some of the responses I received.

1. Are the ingredients used in meat meal, tankage, and digest restricted to specific animals?

The replies to this question varied because ruminants, as of June 1997, can no longer be used in cattle feed because of mad cow disease concerns. This feed must be marked with the phrase: "Do not feed to cattle or other ruminants." Other than the material fed to ruminants there are no restrictions on species of animals that can be used in pet foods. Most state agencies responded that they use the AAFCO guidelines.

2. Would state officials undertake testing as to the quality of grains and fats used in commercial pet foods?

Some states monitor grains used in animal feeds for molds such as aflatoxin, fumonisin, and vomitoxin. Mississippi officials stated, "Probably not unless a specific problem was identified." A New Hampshire official replied, "State officials, to the extent their authorities allow, would be able to test grains and fats used as feed ingredients."[11] Any testing undertaken on fats are to determine the amount of crude fat. Basically, none of the states replied specifically to my query on the testing of fats.

3. Is the raw material used in pet foods tested to ascertain levels of pesticides, hormones, antibiotics, drugs, heavy metal, and bacteria?

Again, some states test the material that is being used for animal feed. Tony Claxton, the AAFCO representative from Missouri wrote, "The QA's [quality assurance] of the pet food companies I believe would require some level of surveillance over ingredients they receive."[12] The representative from Nebraska wrote, "These ingredients are tested by the pet food industry more than anyone else, however, I don't know how extensive they test each of the above."[13] Donna DiCesare, New York Department of Agriculture, wrote, "NYS does not test the raw materials used by the pet food industry. Only in a consumer complaint resulting from animal illness would we test finished products for adulteration and try to trace it to its source."[14]

4. Does your state prohibit the use of rendered companion animals in pet foods?

State officials' responses to this question are discussed in Chapter Two. Twenty-six states replied, among them Florida, which replied that it does not have any pet food regulations.

5. What would the role of your department be regarding commercial pet foods?

Most of the states have regulations patterned after the AAFCO pet food regulations. Indiana official Ann Brueck wrote, "Products are sampled by random by state inspectors and tested for truth in labeling and may be tested for adulteration if contamination is suspected."[15] It seems in Oregon there is not even adherence to AAFCO regulations. When asked what role its department has regarding pet foods the reply was, "None—they are exempted from our commercial feed laws."[16]

The states that do adhere to the AAFCO regulations report that any testing they might undertake was to see that the product was in compliance with the label guarantees. In other words, if the product said it contained 22 percent protein the product would be tested to see if it met that criterion. No state tests for the actual content of the pet food.

Mr. Steve Wong, California, wrote, "There has not been any change in the California Feed Law regulations regarding the ingredients for commercial feed (livestock feed). These laws and regulations do not pertain to pet foods although ingredients manufactured for commercial feed may be obtained by pet food manufacturers."[17]

The Federal Trade Commission

The Federal Trade Commission (FTC) also oversees the advertising of pet foods to prevent false and misleading statements in advertising or labeling. The FDA oversees labeling to ascertain that the ingredients meet the levels as described on the label. However, in March 1999, the FTC issued a notice to rescind the Guides for the Dog and Cat Food Industry, which empowered the FTC to guard against false advertising by pet food companies. In October 1999, the FTC announced that Section 241 had been rescinded. Among other things, Section 241 of the Act covered "misrepresenting dog or cat food in any material respect. Misrepresenting that dog and cat food is fit for human consumption. Making false statements about the conduct or about the quality of competitors' product. Using deceptive endorsements or testimonials, or deceptively claiming that any dog or cat food has received an award."[18]

The FTC felt that the FDA and the AAFCO Model Regulations adequately covered any area of misleading advertising and labeling that was contained in Section 241 of the FTC Act. The FTC determined that its Guidelines were redundant. In essence, the FTC decided to let the fox guard the chicken coop!

When I see television commercials and read magazine ads that depict fresh meat, whole grains, pure oils and fats, there is no question in my mind that many of these pet food companies are involved in false advertising. If these were ads for human foods, they would be banned and the company fined for false and misleading advertising. Unfortunately, the FTC has chosen to back off from trying to regulate the pet food industry. It seems regulating the rendering plants and the pet food industry are low priorities.

The United States Department of Agriculture

The USDA plays a small regulatory role regarding pet food ingredients. Its role revolves around meat for human consumption. According to the Meat Inspection Act, materials from slaughterhouse facilities that are unfit for human consumption are stamped and marked: "Inspected and condemned."[19] This material can be comprised of "dead animals, moribund (about to die, comatose), temperature above 105 F (106 F if swine), suspect dies in pen, animals with obvious symptoms of disease."[20] Other causes listed for condemnation are "whole carcass: tuberculosis (generalized lesions), hog cholera, pneumonia, abscesses, caseous lymphadenitis, epithelioma (involvement of parotid lymph if ocular); parts of carcass: abscesses, arthritis, bruises, contamination on the killing floor."[21]

This condemned material is sent to rendering facilities to be primarily processed into poultry feed and pet food. Because of the fear of bovine spongiform encephalopathy (BSE), ruminants are no longer fed to ruminants. However, some of the raw material can also be frozen and sold to pet food companies, zoos, and dog kennels. Greyhounds at many racetracks are fed this contaminated meat (See Chapter Ten: The Ultimate Health Risk: Cruelty).

A branch of the USDA, The Meat and Poultry Inspection Branch, also plays a minor role in pet food regulation. According to Douglas Hepper, DVM, of the Meat and Poultry Division, his department "regulates raw ingredients entering rendering plants that are inedible and condemned materials from USDA inspected establishments, livestock and horses that have died on farms and used inedible kitchen grease from restaurants and institutions. The Meat and Poultry division does not test raw material entering rendering plants for levels of pathogens, drugs, hormones, heavy metals and pesticides. MPI [Meat and Poultry Inspection Branch] does not have any jurisdiction over companion animals entering rendering plants."[22]

One of the departments under the jurisdiction of the USDA is the Food Safety and Inspection Service (FSIS). This department is in charge of inspection of meats and can issue recalls when meat is found to be diseased or adulterated. If a pet food company requests the FSIS's services, this department can also provide a special inspection service where the meat being used in pet food is inspected by the USDA. Such inspection would eliminate any dog and cat cadavers from being used in the product.

In March 1998, the FSIS and the FDA were petitioned by Farm Sanctuary, a nonprofit animal advocacy organization, which is dedicated to stopping the exploitation of animals raised for food. In its petition, Farm Sanctuary requested that all downed livestock be condemned and removed from the human food chain.

Downed animals primarily come from factory farm conditions that are inhumane, crowded, and unhealthy. Downed livestock are injured or become sick during transport to the stockyards or slaughterhouses, and are often too weak to stand or suffer broken bones from overcrowding. Still alive but "downed," the livestock are often pushed into piles by bulldozers and left, sometimes for days, until dead. Farm Sanctuary estimates that more than 90 percent of downed livestock could be avoided if more care was given to the animals throughout their lives.

From the human health standpoint, Farm Sanctuary does not want to see diseased animals or even parts of diseased animals included in food approved for human consumption. Secondly, this petition removes the financial incentive for livestock producers to put downed animals through further misery in order to get them to market for a possible profit. If livestock producers can't continue to sell downed animals as food at a premium price for human consumption, then perhaps they would be more likely to create humane conditions that eliminate the problem of downed animals.

The FSIS denied Farm Sanctuary's petition in March 1999. In a letter to the Farm Sanctuary, Daniel L. Engeljohn, DVM, wrote, "If they [downed cattle] pose no threat, the meat may be passed for human food when the disease condition does not affect the whole carcass and the diseased part can be removed to make a wholesome product."[23] The diseased portions of the downer cattle are usually disposed by rendering. The end result may be product sold to pet food companies.

In this same letter, Dr. Engeljohn states that diseases in cattle such as, "bovine leukemia, bovine immunodeficiency virus, brucellosis, rabies, and Johne's disease, are considered to be meat borne zoonotic diseases, diseases that can be spread from animals to man. Thus, it would be extremely remote that any of those diseases would be passed on by consumption of red meat animals."[24] It is my guess that our pets are not the only ones eating diseased material.

The FDA is still considering the petition filed by Farm Sanctuary. There is growing support for this petition among consumers as well as among the most reputable producers of cattle who are concerned about strengthening consumer confidence in the cattle industry.

The Pet Food Institute

The Pet Food Institute is an association representing the interests of the various pet food companies in the United States. When I first began to investigate the pet food industry in the early 1990s, I wrote to the Pet Food Institute and queried as to what its role is regarding the ingredients used in pet foods. I received no reply. Before the publication of my second book I again approached the Pet Food Institute and received a reply from Nancy Cook, Director, Technical and Regulatory Affairs. I asked the following questions:

1. Is anyone testing the species of animals being used in meat meals?

2. Are any agencies undertaking certification to assure that the material used in pet food does not contain companion animals, diseased material from slaughterhouses, 4-D animals, road kill, or zoo animals?

3. Are tests undertaken to ascertain levels of pathogens, drugs, hormones, heavy metals, pesticides, and additives, which may also be found in these products?

On April 28, 2000, I received a reply from Cook. She pointed out that the Institute "appreciated the opportunity to address with you the many errors and omissions in that book [*Food Pets Die For*] which we consider to be very serious."[25] She then wrote: "Please be advised that members of the Pet Food Institute, which represents 95% of the pet food produced in the United States, have taken steps to assure that no such ingredients (rendered cats and dogs) are used in their products."[26] Although I appreciated her response, basically, I still did not receive specific answers to my questions.

On August 23, 2000, Duane Ekedahl, Executive Director of the Pet Food Institute, e-mailed me with his response. He also gave me his personal review of my book and wanted to correct some "misunderstanding regarding the quality of ingredients used in commercial pet food."[27] He advised that by-products provide an important source of quality nutrition. Further, that federal and state regulations apply to pet food and that the pet food companies have taken steps to prevent the inclusion of ingredients derived from rendered dogs and cats in the products.

In my reply to Ekedahl at the Pet Food Institute, I basically reiterated the same questions I had asked Cook. I received another e-mail from Ekedahl on September 6, 2000. His response was similar to his previous response: "The AAFCO Official Publication defines acceptable feeding ingredients and provides a process for the formal review and acceptance of new ingredients. Federal law does the same, and the Food and Drug Administration (FDA) regulations list other ingredients that are permitted for use in animal feed, as well as those that are banned from such use."[28] He also stated that because of the quality of the pet foods available today and the time spent on research, a number of diseases that used to be common-place in veterinary medicine, such as those associated with taurine deficiency in cats, have virtually disappeared.

What Ekedahl failed to consider in his taurine example is that the diseases associated with the lack of taurine were not seen in cats prior to the widespread use of commercial pet foods. Taurine, an amino acid found only in meat, is now added as a supplement to pet foods.

In my next e-mail to Ekedahl, I asked him the same questions and advised that if he was going to tell me that federal and state agencies oversee pet foods then please provide the names of the people who undertake the inspections and analyses, and I would be pleased to contact them. I received no reply. Again I e-mailed my query to Ekedahl on September 7, 2000. As of January 2001, I was still waiting for a reply.

Canadian Regulations

Because I am a Canadian my search for information on pet food originated here. For years, the only government regulation that applied to pet food in Canada was the Labeling Act. This Act merely states that the label on pet food must contain the name and address of the pet food company, weight of the product, and if the pet food was made for a dog or a cat.

Canada now has the Fair Business Practices Branch of the Competition Bureau of Industry Canada. This organization is responsible for the administration of the Consumer Packaging and Labeling Act and the Misleading Advertising and Deceptive Marketing practices provisions of the Competition Act. This division does not regulate pet food labeling and advertising but will investigate trade and consumer complaints of misleading and deceptive marketing.

I have recently been advised by the Information Center of Industry Canada that, "Industry Canada has initiated a project which is a voluntary code for the labeling and advertising of pet foods. This document was prepared in consultation with stakeholders such as the Canadian Veterinary Medical Association, the Pet Food Association of Canada, the Canadian Health Institute of Canada, the Canadian Kennel Club, Health Canada, and the Canadian Food Inspection Agency. Albeit voluntary, this code should be completed by the spring of 2000."[29] As of January 2001, this project has not been completed.

Aside from the Labeling Act, which is under the Federal Ministry, Canada has two voluntary organizations involved with Canadian-made pet foods. These voluntary organizations are the Canadian Veterinary Medical Association (CVMA), which purports to be an impartial third-party group, and the Pet Food Manufacturers Association (PFMA). The CVMA program was established in 1996 and only oversees Canadian-made pet foods. Like the U.S.'s AAFCO, the CVMA inspects food not for content but to be sure that the pet food manufacturers conform to label requirements.

Another requirement for certification by the CVMA is that the pet must find the food palatable, therefore the company must conduct feeding trails. CVMA tests pet food for its nutritional value and levels of nutrient digestibility. Again, as with the United States, no testing is undertaken to ascertain sources of protein, carbohydrates, or fats. No testing is undertaken for levels of pathogens, drugs, pesticides, or heavy metals. If any testing is done for drug residues it is conducted by the manufacturer, not the CVMA.

Participating pet food manufacturers are asked to sign a "voluntary declaration" that states that the meat used comes from government-inspected plants.[30] This notion of "government-inspected plants" can be troublesome. Yes, the meat may be from government-inspected plants. Yes, the meat may be government inspected. But what they neglect to mention is that the meat from these slaughterhouses, destined for pet food, has been designated by the inspector as "unfit for human consumption." This can include lungs, bowels, digestive tracts, and euthanized pets, or it can be diseased and contaminated material—only the meat inspector knows.

In 1989 the cost to have a pet food certified by the CVMA ran between $8,000 and $15,000 (Canadian). This cost covered plant inspection, digestibility trials, and chemical analysis. Subsequent plant inspections and lab fees are estimated to be $5,000 to $8,000 per formula, per year. None of the large multinational companies are involved in these voluntary programs in Canada. The multinationals, primarily U.S. based, claim that they conduct their own inspection services, feeding trials and chemical analysis, and therefore, the CVMA certification is unnecessary. For the most part, the products that are certified by the CVMA are house brands and generic products. (House brands usually carry the label of the store that is selling them, generic brands can carry the name of any company.)

In 1993, a colleague questioned a source of protein used in one of the foods certified by the CVMA. She contacted its Ottawa office and expressed her concern. She requested that the CVMA investigate and contact her. Instead of dealing with the issue, the CVMA turned the information over to the pet food company involved and asked that it deal with the situation. The consumer's question regarding the sources of protein was never answered.

The Pet Food Association of Canada (PFAC) is the second voluntary organization in Canada. In the last two years I have heard nothing about this organization and have to wonder if it even exists. To date I have not seen a pet food that bears its certification logo. As with the CVMA, no testing is undertaken by PFAC to ascertain the sources of protein used in the foods that it supposedly certifies. PFAC believes that self-regulation is more acceptable than government or third-party intervention.

The PFMA leaves it to the individual pet food companies to supply any data relating to the nutritional quality of their products. As part of its consumer advertising literature in 1990, PFAC stated that it would "provide government officials with a current list of participating products for the monitoring of product and label claims."[31] The "Nutritional Assurance Program," initiated by the PFAC, claimed that it would provide both the federal and various provincial governments with documentation showing the adequacy of the foods it endorsed.

In February 2000, I contacted both the federal and Ontario provincial governments. After being shuffled from one department to the next in the federal government it was clear that no one had ever heard of the Pet Food Association of Canada and its "Nutrition Assurance Program." No documents were ever filed with the federal or any of the provincial governments. The PFAC was required to provide both provincial and federal governments with the tests on the nutritional adequacy of the foods it promotes. It did not.

The United Kingdom

The United Kingdom has the Pet Food Manufacturers Association (PFMA). This is another voluntary organization that oversees the pet food industry for the U.K. In a letter from the PFMA I was advised that "PFMA only uses materials from animal species which are generally accepted in the human food chain in the U.K. For example, this rules out the use of any materials from horses, ponies, whales and other sea mammals, kangaroos, dogs and cats."[32] The letter also stated that it uses only animals that are inspected and passed as fit for human consumption. Because of the number of cats who have died from contaminated pet food—contaminated with bovine spongiform encephalopathy (BSE) or mad cow disease—they no longer use specified bovine tissue that includes the head, spleen, thymus, tonsils, brain, spinal cord, and large and small intestines. These materials are now incinerated to prevent the spread of BSE.

Vague Pet Food Labels

The prime concern with most of these agencies is the labeling of their products, not the ingredients used. Labels are supposed to provide us with all the information we require to make an informed decision on the appropriate food for our pet. However, ingredient statements in pet food disclose only vague information and terms, such as meat meal, meat by-products, digest, and tankage. Labels do not disclose the actual species of animal these are derived from.

In 1996, *Cats* magazine published an article by the president of AAFCO, Roger Hoestenbach. In it, he states that the number-one reason why "exact ingredients" are not listed is because of label space.[33] How much more label space would it take to eliminate "meat meal" and provide the exact source of this meat meal, such as kangaroo, raccoon, diseased cattle tissue, chicken feet, dogs, or cats? In human food, if the product contains chicken, it is so stated. If the product is a meat pie you will find the kind of meat listed on the label. Not so with pet food.

The FDA/CVM and the AAFCO are supposedly interested in the accurate labeling of pet food. We are made aware of the percentage of protein, fat, carbohydrates, and moisture that are in these products but we have no indication if they provide the nutrition our pets require. David Bebiak, DVM, Director of Pet Nutrition and Care Research at Ralston Purina Co., states in *The Pet Dealer*, "The purpose of pet food labels is to provide consumers with information that helps them select the best for their pets."[34]

We rely on the pet food industry to tell us that this is the "best food for our pets." We assume that the FDA/CVM is like a responsible parent overseeing ingredients used in these foods, investigating if there is a complaint. We assume incorrectly.

Consumer Recourse

What can pet owners do if their pets become ill and the pet food is suspect? With no government-enforced regulations it becomes a difficult situation. First in the line of responsibility should be the federal or state agencies, and these are usually the departments of agriculture. Rodney Noel,

DVM, Secretary-Treasurer of the AAFCO, suggested that pet owners who suspect their pets are ill from pet food "should contact the official in their state or CVM."[35] (See Resources for state agencies and organizations to contact.)

If your state agency is reluctant to take any action or investigate your complaint, I suggest that you contact the FDA/CVM immediately. (The names and numbers of these officials are also listed in the Resources section.) Remember that some states do not have any pet food regulations at all. Contact the Department of Agriculture in your state to find out if there are pet food regulations. If not, your only alternative is to contact the FDA/CVM.

If you live in Canada and the pet food is a product of the United States, contact the FDA/CVM. Do not waste your time with the Canadian Veterinarian Medical Association because it has no input into the pet foods manufactured in the U.S. Canada does have a representative on the board of the AAFCO. (Information on this department is listed in the Resource section under the state agencies.)

To file a complaint with any of these agencies you must have some proof that it was actually the pet food that caused the illness in your pet. Consult with your veterinarian and if possible get a written opinion as to the cause of the illness. The FDA/CVM will request that you submit a sample for analysis. If you submit a sample be sure that you retain some of the product in case you should feel it necessary to have another analysis done by an independent lab.[36]

Mr. Kashani from the Department of Agriculture in Washington advised, "If you purchased the pet food in question in Washington State and your veterinarian could point the cause of your pet's illness to a specific substance in pet food that could be analyzed, Washington State Department of Agriculture would obtain an official sample of the pet food and submit it to a laboratory for analysis."[37]

When I questioned one government official regarding the ingredients used in pet foods and the lack of truthfulness in advertising, he candidly responded that the only way we could expect to see full disclosure is if humans began eating dogs and cats. This is also the only way that we shall ever see this industry regulated.

Five

The Latest on Mad Cow Disease and Pet Food

In 1985 the world began to hear about a disease that was affecting cattle in the United Kingdom—mad cow disease. Cattle that contract this disease, also known as bovine spongiform encephalopathy (BSE), become uncoordinated, irritable, and finally are unable to stand. They soon die.

Researchers have found that the condition of the brains of infected cattle resemble the brains of sheep infected with a condition known as scrapie. The symptoms of scrapie in sheep include unsteady gait, itching, behavioral changes that include nervousness, aggressiveness, and isolation from the rest of the flock. All these symptoms do not occur in every case of scrapie. However, these characteristics are similar to those of cattle suffering BSE. In both conditions, the brains are riddled with holes that resemble a sponge.

According to the Veterinary Services of the United States Department of Agriculture (USDA), the number of BSE cases in cattle in the United Kingdom has risen dramatically from the onset of this disease. "By 1990 there were at least 15,000 confirmed cases of BSE in cattle and by July 1999 the number had risen to 175,065."[1] By the end of 2000, cases of BSE were reported in other countries as well, including France, Germany, Portugal, Switzerland, Belgium, Luxembourg, and the Netherlands.

BSE Transmitted to Other Species

A pressing question at this time is how BSE is being transmitted between the species. Martin Groschup, DVM, Federal Research Center for Virus Diseases of Animals, outlined three scenarios as to why this disease was transmitted. "There was a high incidence of scrapie in British sheep" was one possibility according to Dr. Groschup. (Sheep have had scrapies for hundreds of years, however, until the 1980s, there was no evidence that scrapies had ever jumped species.) Another scenario for the possible transmission of scrapies suggested by Dr. Groschup might be due to "changes in rendering, which meant that the efficiency of BSE and scrapie agent inactivation was reduced so that these agents could survive the treatments involved." The third scenario offered by Dr. Groschup is "the increased use of animal feedstuffs for cattle in the United Kingdom."[2] In 1980 rendering temperatures had been lowered in the United Kingdom, which may have allowed the scrapie to remain viable. In turn, the rendered material that contained sheep carcasses infected with scrapie was fed to cattle in feedstuffs. Thus, cattle were infected with the bovine form of this disease, BSE. Apparently, there have never been any reported cases of humans contracting scrapie, however, humans are contracting the human form of BSE, which is called Creutzfeldt-Jakob Disease.

According to Stanley Prusiner, PhD, Professor of Neurology and biochemistry at the University of California, San Francisco and a 1997 Nobel Prize recipient in medicine, scrapie and spongiform encephalopathies in cattle are not caused by a virus or bacteria. Instead, they are caused by prions. "Prions are an infectious protein without detectable DNA or RNS," explains Dr. Prusiner. "They cannot be destroyed by cooking or freezing. Ionizing, radiation, autoclaving, sterilization, bleach, and formaldehyde have little effect on them. Prions are infectious proteins that can live in soil for years."[3]

Prion diseases in humans have been around for a number of years. The disease, Kuru, is a prion disease caused by cannibalism, and was first identified in 1957 in Papua New Guinea. (Kuru is basically extinct at this point.) Gerstmann-Straussler-Scheinker is a prion disease caused by an inherited gene manifesting symptoms of loss of coordination followed by dementia. Death occurs in two to six years from the onset of symptoms. Gerstmann-Straussler-Scheinker disease was first written about in 1937 by the three doctors for whom it was named. Both of these prion diseases are extremely rare.

The third prion disease or human form of "mad cow disease" is called Creutzfeldt-Jakob disease (CJD). This disease is classified into three forms: sporadic form, which would affect one person per million worldwide; inherited form, which some one hundred extended families worldwide have been identified; and an infectious form in which about eighty cases have been identified. Creutzfeldt-Jakob Disease was seldom, if ever, seen in anyone under fifty years of age. However, in October 1989 the first case was reported of a younger person, thirty-nine years old, who developed CJD. Since that time, there have been over eighty confirmed deaths from CJD and all have been attributed to eating contaminated beef.

Feline Form of Spongiform Encephalopathy

Contaminated material from cattle infected with BSE has been rendered and used in commercial pet foods in Europe. Most scientists determined that this practice would be safe because they believed that the disease would not jump the species barrier. They were wrong.

The first case of the feline form of spongiform encephalopathy (FSE) appeared in 1990 when Max, a five-year old Siamese belonging to a Bristol, England couple, died. As of January 2000, over one hundred cats in the United Kingdom have died, with all cases attributed to diseased meat contained in commercial pet foods manufactured in Europe. Some veterinarians surmise that the actual number of cats who have died from FSE is far greater.

In the United Kingdom, the clinical signs for cats with FSE develop gradually over the span of several weeks. In a case reported in the Veterinary Record, the progression of FSE is described as follows: "Provoked attacks on family members or other household pets or as increased timidity with cats, with a tendency to hide and avoid contact. Locomotor abnormalities developed in all cases and generally affected hind limbs before forelimbs. The cats became ataxic and often further developed a rapid, crouching, hypermetric gait."[4]

In February 2000, I contacted the Pet Food Manufacturer's Association Ltd. (PFMA) in the United Kingdom. I asked what steps had been taken to eliminate the suspect material from pet foods. In an e-mail from Alison Walker, secretary for the PFMA, I was advised that "PFMA voluntarily banned the use of specified bovine tissues in the wake of the BSE crisis in 1989."[5] Other materials banned include specific risk material, head, spleen, thymus, tonsils, brain, spinal cord, and large intestines of cattle.

According to the Ministry of Agriculture, Food and Fisheries (MAFF), although meat and bone meal cannot be used in ruminant feed, it can be used in pet foods provided it is not from BSE suspects. MAFF also makes it clear that "pet food must, however, be manufactured completely separately from livestock feed so that there is no risk of mammalian meal and bone meal cross-contaminating the farm animal feed."[6] Basically, in the United States and Canada the same stipulations apply when it comes to cross-contaminating animal feed.

In 1996, six years after the PFMA voluntarily banned the use of specified bovine tissue in pet food, Anthony Bevins, a reporter for the *Independent*, a U.K. newspaper, reported that Angela Browning, an agriculture minister, confirmed with the House of Commons "that mammalian meat and bone meal-powdered residue from culled and rendered cattle is used in pet food."[7] Martyn Jones, a microbiologist and Labour Member of Parliament (MP), upon hearing this report responded, "This is an astounding revelation. This stuff is so risky that they are not even allowed to bury it, yet they are getting rid of it by passing it on to pet food manufacturers."[8]

Jones had asked Agriculture Minister Browning earlier that week how much meat and bone meat from bovine sources were being used in pet food. The minister told him that no figures were available and that he would have to ask the manufacturers. Not only were household cats contracting this disease but also many other animals in zoos were dying of spongiform encephalopathies.

According to the Ministry of Agriculture, Food and Fisheries, in their July 2000 report, the following zoo animals had died from spongiform encephalopathies: five cheetah (not including two cheetahs at zoos in Australia and the Republic of Ireland, both litter mates born in Great Britain), two tigers, three ocelot and three puma in the cat family.[9] There were also six kudu, six eland, two oryx, one nyala, one bison, and one ankole cow who died of this disease.

In November 2000, Richard Savill from the *London Telegram* reported the death of Major, a twelve-year old lion. A post-mortem examination revealed that he died of feline spongiform encephalopathy. Michael Thomas, the zoo manager, stated, "I would expect that it would have come from Major eating part of a whole carcass because it is the brain and spinal cord which carry the disease."[10]

Dogs and Spongiform Encephalopathy

For years government officials have claimed that dogs are not susceptible to a canine form of spongiform encephalopathy because there have been no known cases. Once again are we getting the truth? According to a 1997 report from *Reuters European Business*, "The British government said on Monday its scientists had found dogs were susceptible to mad cow disease but denied it had covered up the findings, which a spokeswoman described as 'Insignificant.'"[11] The statement concerned unpublished work done in

1991 on the brains of 444 dead hounds suggesting that some of these dogs had developed the first symptoms of BSE. The abnormalities found in the brains of the 444 hounds are called fibrils and are similar to those found in sheep infected with scrapie. According to Dr. Stephen Dealler, a consultant microbiologist, "You can be absolutely sure that the presence of scrapie-associated fibrils shows these dogs had the disease."[12]

However, the study was not definitive, according to U.K. government officials. The United Kingdom's Spongiform Encephalopathy Advisory Committee decided no further action was required regarding the dead hound findings. In June 1998, Iain McGill, DVM, testified before the BSE Inquiry. Dr. McGill had been involved with the investigation into the deaths of these 444 hounds.

Dr. McGill received a letter from Dr. Robert Higgins, a Veterinary Investigation Officer, who had been working with the hound survey since 1990. Dr. Higgins wrote, "This letter details spongiform changes found in brains from hunt hounds failing to keep up with the rest of the pack along with the results of (scrapie-associated fibrils) SAF extractions from fresh brain material from these same animals. SAFs were not found in brains unless spongiform changes were also present."[13]

Another medical doctor, Tony Scott, who was head of electron microscopy work on transmissible spongiform encephalopathies (TSEs) also worked with Dr. McGill on this survey. According to a statement by Dr. McGill, Dr. Scott "had no doubt that these SAFs were genuine and that these hounds therefore must have had a scrapie-like disease."[14]

Where did this investigation lead? What were the results of the survey? Again, according to Dr. McGill in the BSE Inquiry Transcripts, "I telephoned Robert Higgins six years after he first sent the slides to Central Veterinary Laboratory (CVL) in Surrey, England. I was informed that despite his submitting a yearly report to the Central Veterinary Office (CVO), including the suggestion that the hound work be continued, no further work had been done since 1991. This was surprising, to say the very least."[15]

All this information came to light after reports that a dog in Norway might be suffering from the effects of BSE. A report from the *Associated Press* in April 1997, states, "Dog lovers in Norway are nervous over reports that a golden retriever's death looks similar to mad-cow disease. Norway's TV2 reported that an autopsy of the eleven-year old dog showed changes in the brain consistent with those seen in the brains of cows who die of the disease. If the dog contracted the brain ailment, it probably was through dog food in the late 1980s, national animal health board director Eivind Liven told the national news agency."[16]

If TSEs in dogs reflect the symptoms of the disease in other animals, such as nervousness, aggression, unsteady gait, and weight loss, all indicate a disease affecting the brain. Clinical signs of TSE would be similar to that of other diseases affecting the brain. The only way to ascertain if it is TSE is to do an autopsy of the brain. I wonder if this disease is affecting dogs but is being misdiagnosed. "I believe that there have been dogs infected but I cannot prove it," wrote Steve Dealler, PhD, a microbiologist, in a personal correspondence to me in March 2000.[17]

Could cases of BSE in dogs in the United States and Canada be misdiagnosed? I e-mailed a number of veterinarians, asking, "If a dog was brought to you displaying neurological disease, what is the standard procedure?" First ruling out rabies the next step would be to see if an identifiable toxin was the cause. Unless the specific toxin is known, it would, in most cases, be cost-prohibitive to test for every imaginable toxin. Old age in a pet plays a part in neurological disease. Because pets suffering from diseases of unknown origin are usually euthanized, I also asked veterinarians, "Do the owner's usually request an autopsy to ascertain the cause?" In a personal correspondence from author and veterinarian, Richard Pitcairn wrote, "Very very few owners would request a complete autopsy on a pet dead from neurological disease. To do this properly, the skull must be opened, and I never encountered a practitioner prepared to do this."[18] I mentioned to Dr. Pitcairn that the FDA/CVM advised that no cases of either BSE or TSE existed in the United States. Dr. Pitcairn replied, "If they do not test or evaluate [for the disease], how can they know of incidents?"

Rick LeCouteur, DVM, from the University of California, Davis, suggests, "Once the problem has been localized to the brain, diagnostic tests such as CSF analysis, skull radiographs, CT or MRI imaging should help narrow down the cause."[19] One wonders how many pet owner's would actually have these procedures conducted?

Andrew Mackin, DVM, professor at the Royal School of Veterinary Studies at the University of Edinburgh, Scotland, does not believe BSE exists in dogs. "If the condition did occur in dogs, then it is highly likely that they would also succumb...in which case, it is most surprising that no veterinary pathologist to date, anywhere, has to my knowledge, reported the disease in dogs or found it on post-mortem." He goes on to write in a personal correspondence to me, "Still...we can never say with absolute certainty. Maybe one day someone will report a dog with a BSE-like disease."[20] In my opinion, perhaps the British government has seen this in dogs and has chosen to ignore the fact that dogs indeed are susceptible to this disease.

In the United Kingdom, cats developed FSE from eating commercial food that was contaminated with BSE from diseased rendered cattle. The U.K. government denies that it could happen in the United States and Canada. How it makes that determination is a mystery to me. Is the scenario any different in these countries then it was at the onset of BSE in the United Kingdom? Livestock, cattle, sheep, pigs, and goats are still rendered in the United States. So are 4-D animals and animal parts condemned for human consumption from slaughterhouse facilities. However, all of this condemned material is the basis for pet foods.

As of 1999, the brains of more than 8,400 cattle have been examined at the Animal and Plant Health Inspection Services, National Veterinary Services Laboratories, and at other state laboratories, according to the USDA, Veterinary Services. It claims the results show that "not a single tissue sample has revealed evidence of BSE in cattle."[21] There were 8,400 cattle examined in the seven years that the National Veterinary Laboratories conducted their surveillance program. Each year in the United States there are an estimated 300,000 downed cattle, which would be prime suspects for being infected with BSE. This means that only about .04 percent of the suspicious cattle are being inspected. This is a very small fraction of the downed cattle that is being tested for BSE.

Prior to the U.S. ban on feeding ruminants to ruminants in June 1997 the FDA sponsored a forum in February 1997 in St. Louis, Missouri and invited pet food company representatives, representatives from companies that provide the raw materials to the pet food companies, and representatives from the rendering industry. The FDA wanted to discuss the proposed ban on feeding ruminants to ruminants and what effect this would have on the labeling of pet foods. The FDA had suggested that warnings be put on commercial pet food labels indicating that this food should not be fed to ruminants. The FDA reasoned that pet food contained rendered material and therefore might be considered suspect. The suggestion from the FDA was that pet foods should contain a statement on the labels which read, "Contains (or may contain) protein derived from ruminant and mink tissues.

Do not feed to ruminant animals, and do not use to manufacture feed intended for ruminant animals."[22]

This spurred considerable discussion from members of the pet food industry. Duane Ekedahl, Executive Director of the Pet Food Institute, requested that the statement not be included on the pet food labels. Ekedahl explained at the public forum, "We went out during the past three weeks and did a consumer study. We had 350 mall-intercept interviews in five different cities, and here are the results of that study. 70 percent of the respondents indicated that with that label on pet foods they would buy something else. 68 percent of the respondents said if they saw that label on pet food in the grocery store and other retail outlets they would be very concerned about the safety of the ingredients of that product for their pets. Finally, and quite startling, 40 percent of the respondents indicated that they would be very concerned about humans eating beef and lamb products with that type of label at retail on their pet food."[23]

The FDA abandoned the proposed labeling of pet food because it reasoned, according to Kevin Custer of American Protein, that a company that supplies the pet food industry with sources of protein and flavor enhancers, "Consumers are not going to feed cat food and dog food to cows."[24] The FDA determined that the present labeling was adequate and that consumers are given all the information about ingredients used in pet foods!

Lamb and Rice Pet Foods

In my opinion the lamb and rice foods that many veterinarians recommend for a pet with an allergy are suspect. The USDA estimates that 4,500 pounds of sheep per day are rendered. This would produce five tons of the lamb-and-rice dog foods. Because dogs have not displayed any symptoms of BSE, or so the FDA/CVM tells us, the use of rendered sheep in dog food is acceptable.

Because this disease has been diagnosed in cats in European countries, Jim Corbin, DVM, PhD, research nutritionist and Professor Emeritus in Animal Science at the University of Illinois, suggests that "lamb meal be obtained from countries that have no scrapie infection in sheep."[25] This is an interesting statement considering millions of pounds of sheep are being rendered in the United States. And if sheep remnants cannot be fed to cattle, sheep, or mink because of the ban of feeding ruminants to ruminants, then a vast percentage of these rendered sheep are going into dog food. No wonder we are seeing a vast array of dog foods made from lamb. It's a cheap dumping site for this material.

After researching the pet food industry and other related topics for well over ten years, I am convinced of the following:

✦ Dogs indeed can be infected with a canine form of mad cow disease.

✦ BSE does exist in the United States and Canada, in large part because we have the same scenario as they had in the United Kingdom prior to the mad cow disease outbreak. Scrapie in sheep, rendering of sheep offal, outbreaks of mink encephalophy, and minimal screening of downer cattle, are all a part of the same scenario that was seen in the United Kingdom at the time of the outbreak.

Unfortunately, I think this is only the beginning of our woes with spongiform encephalopathy in all its forms, including canine and feline.

SIX

The Controversy of the Raw Meat Diet

In recent years, as a response to the problems with commercial pet foods, a growing number of pet owners now feed their cats and dogs raw meat diets. BARF, the acronym coined by proponents of the raw diet, stands for "Biologically Appropriate Raw Foods." Or it may refer to "Bones and Raw Food" diet created by an Australian veterinarian, Ian Billinghurst.

Proponents of the raw meat diet are trying to simulate the diet of wolves and wild dogs. They believe that this is a far healthier diet for their domesticated dogs. For cats the object is to feed a diet based on feline prey, primarily mice and birds, purportedly a natural diet for cats.

The basic BARF diet is comprised of raw meat and raw meaty bones, including chicken, beef, lamb, pork, rabbit, deer, and various other meats. Animal organs such as liver, kidney, brains, hearts, and tongue are also added. However, chicken seems to be the primary meat used, especially for cats, and pet owners feed their cats and dogs both the meat and the bones from the necks, backs, wings, and drumsticks. People who feed this diet also include other bones, raw meaty bones from lamb, beef, and venison. The animals on this diet are fed on a daily basis. Proponents state that the bones provide teeth cleaning and gum massage.

In addition to the meat and bones, proponents of BARF add raw vegetables and fruits, including carrots, green beans, peas, sweet potatoes, celery, and apples, among other foods. They usually run vegetables through a food processor to replicate what might be found in the stomach and digestive track of the prey in the wild. Wolves and wild dogs usually ingest the stomach contents of their prey first before they eat the actual meat.

Some pet owners add cooked grains, such as rice, millet, buckwheat, and rye. However, there seems to be a controversy among the proponents of the BARF diet as to the use of grains. Some BARF proponents state that the stomachs of prey in the wild contain a minimum of grain, and because of this, they do not encourage the use of grains. In addition, they believe grains can cause allergies in dogs. However, others think that some grain should be added because grains are found in the stomachs and digestive tracks of prey and grains provide carbohydrates. Basically, the jury is out on this aspect of the BARF diet.

The BARF diet also includes seeds and nuts, such as sunflower and pumpkin seeds, pecans, and almonds. Either flax seed or fish oil can be added because they are high in Omega 3s. Omega 3 is an unsaturated fatty acid that animals need in order to stay healthy, especially older animals. Omega 3s are naturally found in fish, wheat germ oil, and cod liver oil, or it can be added to food as a supplement.

Proponents of the BARF diet also feed their companion animals eggs including the shells for calcium. Most BARF advocates add vitamin and mineral supplements, and probiotics (found in natural yogut), digestive enzymes, kelp, garlic, and brewer's yeast. Some pet owners add herbs, including milk thistle, which is used in the treatment of liver disease; chamomile, which calms mental stress; and aloe vera for easing constipation or abetting diarrhea.

When I first heard about the BARF diet in 1995, I was amazed that people actually feed raw meat and bones to their pets. There have always been stories of farmers and ranchers feeding their dogs the discarded meat from their slaughtered animals. But beyond that, I had never heard of raw meat being fed to household cats and dogs.

While completing the research for my first book, *Food Pets Die For*, I continued to follow the growing interest in the BARF diet and gathered information from veterinarians and pet owners alike. In 1993 Ian Billinghurst, one of the primary veterinarians promoting the raw meat diet wrote *Give Your Dog a Bone*. In this book, Dr. Billinghurst cites his positive experiences and those of his clients who feed their pets a BARF diet.

Aside from these personal experiences, there are no scientific studies or more substantial findings to support the BARF diet. Other than anecdotal information, Dr. Billinghurst does not mention any specific studies to support his enthusiastic belief in the raw meat diet. The only study that I found related to raw meat diets for animal companions is the Pottenger study conducted sixty years ago, which focused on cats. When I queried Dr. Billinghurst about the Pottenger study and its efficacy, he responded, "Pottenger's study is certainly not a 'study' I rely on to justify feeding raw."[1]

Because of these concerns, I wanted more substantive answers to determine the efficacy of the BARF diet. The following are my findings, which address the questions in the order that I felt were of the greatest concern. I also carefully looked at what proponents of the raw meat diet consider its advantages.

Raw Meat Versus Cooked Meat

The most important question I have regarding the BARF diet is the safety issue concerning raw meat. Generally, it is accepted that humans should cook any meat until it is well done in order to kill bacteria such as salmonella, E. coli, and campylobacter, all of which can be life threatening. In particular, the mad cow disease outbreak in England and the increased dangers of food-borne illnesses related to contaminated meats in the United States and Canada provide strong incentives to avoid any uncooked meat. For a growing number of people, these serious concerns are reason enough to give up meat completely.

There are some highly informative and persuasive books on this topic, such as *Slaughterhouse* by Gail A. Eisnitz, which is an alarming exposé on the dangers of the meat industry in the United States. *Eating With Conscience: The Bioethics of Food* by Michael Fox, a veterinarian who has worked in animal welfare at The Humane Society of the United States since 1976, addresses factory farming and its devastating effects on animal welfare, health, and the environment. So, if uncooked meat for humans is life threatening, why isn't it for cats and dogs as well? The answers I found are explained further in this chapter.

Wendell Belfield, DVM, is a veterinarian I have communicated with since my first forays into the investigation of commercial pet food more than ten years ago. When my dogs became ill after eating commercial food, Dr. Belfield was the first veterinarian I contacted. Over the years I have come to trust Dr. Belfield's opinion and I highly respect his books, *How to Have a Healthier Dog* and *The Very Healthy Cat Book*. In an article Dr. Belfield addresses the question of feeding a raw meat diet, "As a veterinary practitioner for thirty-seven years and a veterinary meat inspector for seven years, I, in all good conscience, cannot recommend raw meat diets to my clients. My advice to my clients is cook the meat until the redness is gone. When this is done there is no vomiting, the cholesterol level is normal, and the risk of infection by microorganisms and parasites diminishes."[2]

Dr. Belfield advocates feeding table scraps. "What's wrong with carrots and peas and salads and even fruit and cooked cereal?" he asks in *How to Have a Healthier Dog*. "Nothing that I know of. I know a retired veterinarian in his eighties who has been feeding generations of dogs from table scraps. Meat, vegetables, grains, fruit. His dogs were rarely ill."[3]

In his book, *The Nature of Animal Healing*, Martin Goldstein, DVM, talks about the enjoyment his pets derive from eating leftovers, "Pasta in a pesto sauce with broccoli rabe is their new fixation. Tonight, as I was working on this chapter, I gave my dog Clayton my leftover sauteed garlic veggies over chopped lettuce salad and watched him lick the bowl clean."[4] Provided the pet owner is eating a basically healthy diet with whole foods rather than processed foods, it makes sense that the dogs too will be eating well.

In the fall of 1999 I sent a brief questionnaire regarding the raw meat diet to more than seventy veterinarians, nutritionists, pathologists, toxicologists, diagnosticians, internists, microbiologists, and immunologists in the United States, Canada, the United Kingdom, and Australia. In addition, I contacted the National Animal Poison Control Center (NAPCC) and the Center for Disease Control (CDC). The questions I asked were based on whether they had knowledge of the raw meat diet. Approximately 90 percent of the veterinarians knew about or had at least heard of this diet. Veterinarians in the United Kingdom and Australia were more aware of the ingredients used in the BARF diet then were veterinarians in the United States and Canada. If they were familiar with the raw meat diet, I then asked them to answer the following four questions:

1. *What is your opinion on feeding the raw diet to pets?*

2. *In your opinion is this diet comparable to what wolves eat?*

3. *Have you seen cases where pets have become ill or died from eating the raw diet?*

4. *Are pets susceptible to E. coli, salmonella, or campylobacter?*

5. *Would you recommend this diet to your clients?*

Some veterinarians who feed the raw diet or recommend it to their clients believe that pets are not susceptible to the many bacteria in raw meat.

Their reasoning is that dogs and cats ingest some pretty disgusting things and do not seem to get sick. In part, they note that the digestive track in dogs and cats is shorter and faster, and therefore there is less likelihood that dangerous bacteria can thrive.

However, my research shows a much different perspective. At least a dozen articles in veterinary journals describe how pets suffer the effects of salmonella, E. coli, campylobacter, and listeria from various sources. In addition, Sharon Gwaltney Brant, DVM, PhD, from the National Animal Poison Control Center noted in a personal correspondence to me, "Pathogens such as Salmonella, E. coli, Clostridium, Campylobacter, etc. have evolved 'coats' that protect them in their transit through the stomach (of cats and dogs) and allow them to take hold in the intestines."[5]

Although the digestive systems for a cat and a dog are different from that of a human, written findings by veterinarians support the belief that pets are, indeed, susceptible to these various bacteria. L. Beutin, DVM, notes in an article for the *Journal of Veterinary Medical Science*, "Certain strains of Escherichia coli behave as pathogens in dogs and cats causing gastro-intestinal and extra-intestinal disease."[6] In another article in the same journal, Y. Sato, and R. Kuwamoto, DVMs, report, "A 7 year old male dog kept indoors manifested severe watery diarrhea with generalized weakness. Salmonella Infantis was isolated from a fecal sample and the dog recovered soon after medication with ampicillin, to which the isolate was highly sensitive."[7] These are just two cases but the various vet journals list others. Granted, these cases do not relate directly to the feeding of raw meat but they do make it clear that pets are susceptible to bacteria.

In the written responses I received from veterinarians, there were some strong replies regarding pets and exposure to harmful bacteria in meat. Carla Haddix, a holistic veterinarian from Boca Raton, Florida, wrote that she does not personally recommend feeding the raw meat diet to pets although she does know of people who have fed this diet without problems. However, one case she cites is a client "who put her highly allergic dog on raw meat on the advice of another vet, and although within a few days the dog's allergies were improved, he unfortunately also got severe diarrhea requiring several days hospitalization. Who knows what bacteria were involved, if any (we did not culture) but we did isolate Hammondia spp. Coccidia, which is a parasite not common to dogs and cats but comes from raw beef."[8]

Joe Bartges, DVM, from the University of Tennessee, Department of Small Animal Clinical Science, responded to my questions, "Dogs certainly do get bacterial gastrointestinal diseases, including infections that may be transmissible to humans such as Salmonella and Campylobacter."[9] Dr. Bartges strongly stated, "I believe the so-called BARF diet does not only provide little benefit, but it incurs unnecessary risk for the animal."[10]

I also asked that because raw meat—prey—is the natural diet of wild dogs and wolves are they not susceptible to bacteria in the animals they kill? Dan Hendrix, DVM, from Houston, Texas, provided the answer to perhaps why wild dogs and wolves are not as susceptible as our companion animals whose raw meat source in these diets comes primarily from the supermarket. "While wild dogs can become accustomed to the variety of bacteria found in raw meat, one must remember that they are eating meat that is freshly killed and the bacterial contaminants which might be found therein do not have the time to multiply in large numbers as they do in processed meat. Remember, Salmonella and the other types of harmful bacteria that cause food-borne illnesses are not circulating freely in living organisms. They are contaminants introduced at slaughter."[11]

Being owned by cats for over thirty years I know that they are a little more discriminating in what they eat but they also can contract various diseases from eating raw meat. "Cats who hunt small mammals and who are fed raw meat can acquire toxoplasmosis, and can show signs such as fever, pain in the joints and muscles (they can transmit the toxo organism through their feces to humans),"[12] responded Elizabeth Poole, spokesperson for the Center for Disease Control. Toxoplasmosis is a disease caused by a parasite and can be transmitted through cat feces and by handling raw meat or eating raw or undercooked meats. When the eggs of these parasites are swallowed by animals or humans, they hatch and multiply within the muscle tissue.

Dennis Blodgett, DVM, from Virginia Tech whose field of expertise is toxicology, believes that there may be other areas of the raw meat diet that should be considered: "I would be concerned about gram negative bacteria that might grow and proliferate in the uncooked diet and die for whatever reason, leaving their cell walls containing endotoxin to be absorbed."[13] Endotoxins, even in small amounts, can cause liver damage and even death in pets. Veterinarian Donald Strombeck addresses endotoxins in his book, *Home Prepared Dog and Cat Diets*: "Endotoxin is formed from part of the cellular structure of gram negative bacteria such as Escherichia coli, normally found in the colon. "Endotoxin is released from dead bacteria. Little endotoxin is absorbed in the colon. Endotoxin produced and released in the small intestine can be absorbed and enter the body. Small amounts of endotoxin cause shock that can lead to death."[14] The mode of action for endotoxins is not entirely clear due to the fact that few studies have been done in this area.

Some pet owners have chosen to feed various meats besides the raw chicken. These meats include, beef, pork, lamb, rabbit, deer, and other wildlife. There have been reports of people going to slaughterhouses and buying necks and feet to feed to their pets. One woman actually went through vats of slaughterhouse waste to pick out rib bones and various internal organs for her dogs. Gerry Henningsen, DVM, warned, "Some beef have measles (tapeworm) and sheep often carry tapeworm in their livers; pork may still have some trichinella, and bear meat usually has lot of it; wild rabbits may carry and transmit tularemia and tapeworm."[15] The feeding of raw meat from wild animals is very risky.

When Dr. Billinghurst was questioned about the dangers of parasites in raw meat, he replied, "We must feed our modern dogs sources of meat that do not contain harmful parasites! There are plenty of ways to do that! And if in doubt worm your dog!"[16] In his book, *Give Your Dog a Bone*, Dr. Billinghurst mentions a number of meats that can be fed, including pork, buffalo meat, horse meat, kangaroo meat, rabbit, sheep—plus various organs, liver, kidney, brains, hearts, tongues. He does advise pet owners to purchase organ meats from a butcher or use organ meats derived from poultry. "The offal of many animals that dogs are likely to eat has the potential to contain cysts of the pathogenic (to man) Hydatid tapeworm," Dr. Billinghurst writes. "It is this human health aspect of feeding dogs that has been the major reason for dogs being fed cooked meat and meat products."[17]

Dr. Billinghurst also discusses feeding pets kangaroo meat. This is not one of the meats at the top of his list for feeding pets, according to Dr. Billinghurst. "Kangaroo is very lean and sometimes requires added fat."[18] But I questioned how safe is kangaroo meat? According to Dr. David Obendore, Wildlife Veterinary Pathologist in Tasmania, kangaroo meat is not a safe meat. "Kangaroos and wallabies can harbor a wide range of parasitic bacterial, fungal and viral diseases and most of the infections are inapparent (i.e. the animal looks normal). Even meat inspection procedures are unlikely to detect some infections unless gross lesions are apparent or samples are taken during testing."[19] Fortunately, kangaroo is seldom available in the United States and Canada.

Perhaps in Australia, it is easy to obtain meats from sources that can guarantee the meat is free of parasites. However, in the United States and in Canada, this is not the case. In her book *Slaughterhouse*, Gail Eisnitz makes a strong case against meat production in the United States and the extremely unhealthy situation in factory farms where more than 90 percent of the meat comes from. For instance, chicken is the primary meat used by proponents of the BARF diet, and most people buy the chicken from the local supermarket. Campylobacter, a potentially life-threatening bacteria, occurs twice as frequently as salmonella. These bacteria can cause severe diarrhea and sometimes bloody stools that might last from two to ten days, and in extreme cases cause death.

Carol Pickett, MD, from the College of Medicine, University of Kentucky, presented a paper at the American Society for Microbiology, in Atlanta, Georgia. Dr. Pickett states, "Campylobacter species associated with human diarrhea disease were successfully isolated from 100% (91 out of 91) of fresh chicken carcasses purchased at local supermarkets."[20] Dr. Pickett explains further, "All Campylobacter found on chickens should be considered potentially pathogenic: there is no good Campylobacter in a chicken."[21] What does this mean for the public? It means that fresh chicken very likely is contaminated with campylobacter and cooking is the only way in which it can be destroyed.

Parasites and Bacteria in Raw Meat

Proponents of the BARF diet state that dogs and cats do not succumb to the various bacterial contaminates in raw meat. In his book Dr. Billinghurst addresses germs in raw meat and the only references made to bacteria deal with dogs burying cooked bones and the fact that these bones could be attacked by bacteria. "Perhaps the worst of these would be the toxin released by the bacteria which causes Botulism, a deadly paralysis," notes Dr. Billinghurst.[22] He also addresses the issue of salmonella. "Raw chicken does of course carry bacteria, Salmonella. Also Campylobacter. These are of absolutely no consequence to a healthy dog."[23] My research leads me to a much different conclusion.

After reading posts from individuals whose pets became ill after feeding the raw diet, I wondered why there are no journal texts of illnesses in pets caused by the contaminates in raw meat. In my research I found a few cases, mentioned above, of companion animals suffering from listeria, salmonella, E. coli, and parasitic infections, but nothing of any substance that clearly points to the raw meat diet as the culprit.

Wendy Powell, DVM, from the University of Guelph, provided an answer to my question over the lack of journal texts on illnesses caused by contaminates in raw meat: "One of the reasons that you may not have read any documented cases of food-borne illness in animals is that it would have to be identified and then deemed important enough to publish in a journal. Journals tend to publish new research or interesting case studies. Most food-borne illness would present as diarrhea and would not be deemed important enough to put in a journal."[24]

Granted, I am aware that proponents of the raw meat diet would respond that the real reason there are no journal texts on illnesses caused by contaminates in raw meat is because there are none to speak of. This is difficult for me to accept, given my understanding of raw meat and the dangers of parasites and bacteria in raw meat, which are very problematic for both humans and pets.

Some pet owners who use the raw meat diet have serious concerns about bacteria and parasites in the meat. They suggest soaking the meat in a solution of grapefruit seed extract (GSE) to kill any bacteria or parasites that have contaminated the meat. Grapefruit seed extract is derived from the seeds, pulp, and white membrane of grapefruit. According to Allan Sachs, DC, CCN, "In hundreds of laboratory tests, GSE has demonstrated its ability to kill or inhibit the growth of a wide array of potentially harmful bacteria, fungi, viruses and protozoan parasites."[25] However Diane Gerken, DVM, PhD disagrees with Dr. Sachs's opinion of GSE. Dr. Gerken, who is with the Department of Veterinary Biosciences, Ohio State University, wrote, "I do not know of any antimicrobial agents in grapefruit seed extract. Even if there were, I would be concerned about any spores. It may prevent further growth, however that would not eliminate the risk of Salmonellosis in pets."[26]

Grapefruit extract is a substance that has been available for human use for approximately twenty-five years to kill bacteria but also to treat many human diseases. Louis Parish, MD, investigator for the Department of Health and Human Services, Public Health Service of the Food and Drug Administration, found that grapefruit seed extract is "as effective as any other amoebocide now available, perhaps more effective because it does not cause side effects."[27] According to NutriTeam, a distributor for GSE, this substance can be used for a number of health-related problems in pets including "skin fungi, parasites, or bacterial disease of the skin." It can also be used "as a general antiseptic for cages, stalls or any other contact area."[28]

Care should be taken if soaking meat in this substance as it is a bitter and acidic liquid. Pat McKay, author of *Reigning Cats and Dogs* suggests adding four drops of grapefruit seed extract to six ounces of purified water and pour over one pound of ground poultry. "Mix well. Then pour the appropriate amount of meat you are preparing."[29] People have mentioned to me that their pets, cats especially, have refused to eat meat that has been soaked in this substance perhaps because of the bitter, acidic taste. If you are soaking chunks of meat in this solution, wash it before feeding it to your animals, and perhaps this might eradicate some of the bitter taste and to make it more palatable.

There is also the theory that freezing the meat will kill bacteria. Not so. Laboratories preserve bacteria and viruses by freezing them. Cooking meat will eliminate the potential for any illnesses from the bacteria or parasites found in raw meats. Freezing meat does not kill parasites or bacteria.

The Dangers of Feeding Bones

In addition to the concerns about contaminated meat, I was also alarmed with the idea of feeding bones, either raw or cooked, to my animal companions. Veterinarians had always advised me to never feed bones to my dogs and cats.

Over the years, on occasion, I have provided my dogs with either knuckle or marrow bones—those bones filled with marrow composed mainly of fat to chew on. But allowing them to eat and swallow these bones was out of the question. I always made sure I was close by while they chewed them, just in case.

On one occasion I gave my Newfoundland, Charlie, a knuckle bone. While gnawing away on the bone, Charlie suddenly started pawing at his mouth. I looked closely inside his mouth, but I couldn't see anything. He continued to paw as if irritated, so off to the vet we went. After the veterinarian gave Charlie something to calm him down, he examined Charlie's mouth and found a small piece of bone embedded between two of his teeth. The piece of bone was small but large enough to cause great distress. That was the end of bone eating for Charlie. So, between the advice of veterinarians and my own experience with my dogs and bones, I seriously question the wisdom of feeding bones. Further inquiries and research into this topic confirm my beliefs about the dangers of raw or cooked bones.

In his book, *Give Your Dog a Bone*, Dr. Billinghurst asserts, "As dogs chew on bones, rip the flesh off bones, crush bones, that very action cleans the teeth, and massages the gums, stopping tartar, gum infections, tooth root decay, dental abscesses, and a whole body poisoned by a grossly infected mouth."[30]

Many veterinarians to whom I questioned about this topic gave me very different responses from Dr. Billinghurst's. In addition, many pet owners have written to me about a pet who died after ingesting raw bones. These people had fed their pets a raw meat and bone diet. One woman wrote, "I got the pathology report yesterday afternoon from the vet. Kenai died as a result of puncture wounds. The pyloric valve (between the stomach and intestines) was basically ripped apart, like a 'foreign body' had been stuck there."

I elicited the opinion of twelve veterinarians, all members of the Academy of Veterinary Dentistry, about feeding animals bones. Nine of these veterinarians were from the United States, two from Canada, and one from New South Wales. The questions I posed were the same for each veterinarian: "Would chewing on bones or ingesting raw bones be cause for concern? Have you, in your practice, encountered problems or seen cases where dogs have experienced problems with raw bones?"

Judy Rochette, DVM, from Burnaby, British Columbia, replied that she had seen a family of chihuahuas with white teeth and no gum disease from chewing on bones. "I think the smaller dogs get the benefit of keeping tarter off without being able to generate enough bite force to break their teeth. I have, however, seen several larger dogs who have broken their teeth from chewing bones."[31]

White, clean teeth seem to give people the impression that their pet's teeth are healthy. Wrong, says Fraser Hale, DVM, from the University of Guelph. "What I see is dogs with sparkling clean teeth with crown fractures and endocontic (pulp) disease."[32] Although the teeth may look clean, underlying problems may be occurring. Gregg DuPont, DVM, of Seattle, expressed basically the same opinion, "I do not recommend feeding bones due to the very common occurrence of fractured upper 4th premolar teeth requiring root canal treatment or extraction." Dr. DuPont noted, "Smaller bones, such as chicken bones can cause problems if pieces injure the periodontium or embed in a gingival sulcus causing a periodontal infection."[33]

Perhaps David Clarke, DVM, from New South Wales, summed it up best with his response: "I see fractured teeth every day from chewing on bones, in fact over the last 8 years bones have accounted for 65.5% of broken teeth with the canine and carnassial most represented at 83.6% which just so happens to be the teeth that dogs chew with."[34]

All the veterinarians I contacted advised against the practice of feeding bones of any kind. If you want your pet to have clean teeth, brushing seems to be the best method to follow. Some of the vets recommend giving soft nylon bones but advised against giving such items as cow hooves, raw hide bones (because pieces can be swallowed and cause the pet to choke), hard rubber and plastic bones, and pigs' ears.

As for proponents of the BARF diet imitating the "natural" diet of wolves and wild dogs, veterinarian Fraser Hale had an interesting comment with regard to the condition of wolves teeth: "A colleague in the north (way north) was doing work for a wild-life biologist and they were examining the skulls of wolves found lying on the tundra. A high percentile of these animals that had died of natural causes had fractured teeth and evidence of chronic dental abscesses. Whether or not these abscesses contributed to the demise of these animals, they would certainly have been painful."[35]

In the *Journal of Veterinary Dentistry*, veterinarians G. Steenkamp and C. Gorrel reported some interesting findings after examining the skulls of twenty-nine adult African wild dogs originating from a museum collection. They detected a wide variety of conditions similar to those seen in domestic dogs. "Although other reports suggest that captive African wild dogs suffer more extensively from dental disease than those in the wild, we concluded that these wild carnivores suffer from the same oral diseases as their domestic relatives, suggesting that a natural diet does not protect against these diseases."[36]

I believe that many veterinarians in private practice see the ills that befall dogs every day from ingesting raw bones. Linda Dugger, DVM, a veterinarian in private practice, wrote to me about a problem she had seen with animals that have ingested raw bones. "I have seen numerous intestinal perforations, broken infected teeth, esophageal irritation and colitis from these things. I performed 42 enemas on one dog who had eaten a raw knuckle bone from the supermarket. It was like ground glass going down his colon. The feces was impacted, full of bone, and dry due to his vomiting, which resulted in dehydration. The feces sliced my latex gloves when I tried to manually relieve the blockage."[37] If something like this does not discourage an owner from feeding a pet bones, I don't know what will.

Not only are the pets on the raw diet given bones to chew but bones also comprise part of their actual diet. Chicken bones purportedly supply the necessary minerals and calcium. "Unfortunately, chicken bones are not the best source of minerals to feed dogs, because they can become very sharp when they break," wrote Douglas Macintire, DVM, when I asked him about feeding raw chicken bones. "I have seen severe gastroenteritis, bloody diarrhea, and even perforated intestine as a result of chicken bones. Dogs die from eating chicken bones, and we do not recommend it."[38]

The theory is that this is a safe practice because the stomach acid dissolves the bones. Richard Hill, DVM, MA, PhD, who is an assistant professor of clinical nutrition at the University of Florida believes that "most dogs can cope with some bones but raw bones have the same risk of infection as raw meat. The acidity in the dog's stomach is similar to that in your own stomach. Some of the bone will be digested but most passes through."[39]

And what happens to the bones or bone fragments that don't pass through? What happens to the bones on the way from the mouth to the stomach? William Duke, DVM, who operates the Martin-Clark Animal Hospital in Dothan, Alabama, responded to my e-mail inquiry regarding animal companions eating raw bones. "I have personally had to euthanize two dogs that have gotten esophageal or bowel perforations from eating bones of various species," responded Dr. Duke. "I have seen several emergencies for a blockage of some sort caused by feeding dogs chicken or steak (round or T bones) calf hooves, or rawhide."[40] Mark Jackson, DVM, has also seen the problems encountered with feeding bones. "I have removed two esophageal foreign bodies [bones] from dogs on this diet."[41] These are not isolated incidents. I have spoken to many veterinarians who have encountered the same problem. These are not cooked chicken bones, but raw chicken bones that have been the source of the problems.

Yes, some veterinarians I corresponded with recommend commercial foods instead of a raw meat diet, but many recommend a diet with raw fruits, vegetables, and grains, and any meat lightly cooked. All the veterinarians stated that feeding bones, raw or cooked, is downright dangerous.

Is a Raw Meat Diet a Natural Diet?

How "natural" is the BARF diet? "Natural" is defined in the *Funk & Wagnall Dictionary* as "produced by or existing in nature: not artificial." Because I have always cooked the meat for my pets, many feel that I am depriving them of the natural diet that dogs and cats thrive on. To this statement I have to ask, how natural is a diet that is comprised of chicken purchased at the supermarket, butcher shop, or even from a farmer? Unless it is classified "organic" the poultry is full of antibiotics as well as a variety of drugs and pathogens. Is this natural?

Many proponents of the raw meat diet also add a variety of vitamins, minerals, enzymes, amino acids, and supplements. Is this natural? Despite the claims that this is a natural diet, my research and resources say, no, this is not natural.

Geoff Stein, DVM, wrote, "The problem with all these new 'natural' diets is the misguided assumption that 'natural' is better, just because it's natural. It is actually 'natural' for wolves to die of Salmonella once in awhile, too, in the wild. It is natural for mammals to die of bacterial infections, too...but we prefer to treat some with antibiotics to avoid that result... though that is *not* natural. Sometimes doing things 'unnaturally' has its advantage. Wolves would be just as healthy if they ate cooked meat (probably healthier) but that just isn't an option for them."[42]

Some pet owners feed their animal companions organic meat. However, people with multiple pets may find buying organic meat cost prohibitive. Organic is the safest way to feed not only your pets but yourself given the levels of contamination in meat. Organic also implies that the farm animals live on smaller sustainable farms, and are treated humanely until slaughter. For people who love their pets, it follows that they are compassionate for other animals. Dr. Michael Fox describes in *Eating With Conscience* the commercial factory farm poultry sheds where from seventy thousand to one hundred thousand chickens are housed. "Broiler flocks have sometimes gone crazy, and in wave upon wave, bash themselves to death in mass hysteria inside a poultry shed."[43] Not just poultry, but all livestock raised in commercial operations are subject to inhumane conditions. Agribusiness is more concerned about the almighty dollar than the health and welfare of the animals it raises.

Reports of contaminated meat and poultry from factory farms that make their way into the human food chain are rampant. In 1996,

Cox Newspaper analyzed an Agriculture Department computerized database of meat and poultry inspections. The newspaper reported that it "found 138,593 instances in which inspectors said food being prepared in packing plants was 'certain' to sicken consumers."[44] The situation is not improving. "Reports by federal food inspectors stationed at packing plants across the country offer graphic evidence of meat and poultry products containing feces and other contaminates,"[45] writes George Anthan of the *Register Washington Bureau.* The advice given by the USDA to "cook all meat until the juices run clear" is the only way to destroy bacteria contamination. Feeding raw meat is like playing Russian roulette, it's not worth the risk.

Fortunately, there are many pet owners who have not encountered problems feeding their pets the raw meat diet. You may get away with feeding raw meat for awhile but sooner or later there's a strong possibility that your pets are going to experience vomiting, diarrhea, pancreatitis from the fat in this diet, bone shards that perforate the throat, stomach or intestines, and even death at an early age. Is it worth it? I may be wrong in feeding my pets a diet that contains cooked meats but in the nearly twelve years I have fed this diet, not one of my pets has experienced health problems—no diarrhea, no vomiting, and no internal problems from ingesting raw bones. As for keeping their teeth clean, I attribute that to brushing.

The Pottenger Study

The Pottenger study was conducted by Francis Pottenger, MD, between 1932 and 1942. As a medical doctor, Pottenger used cats in various medical experiments in his research laboratory. During this time, he also examined the values of a raw versus cooked diet for cats. His feeding experiments eventually involved some nine hundred cats over a ten-year period.

The study began when Dr. Pottenger observed that the cats were poor operative risks. He was experiencing high rates of mortality among the cats "undergoing adrenalectomies for use in standardizing the hormone content of the adrenal extract he was making."[46] Neighbors in his community of Monrovia, California had donated cooked meat scraps for his laboratory cats and Dr. Pottenger supplemented the cooked meat, which included liver, tripe, brains, heart, and muscle with raw milk and cod liver oil. Portions were generally one-third raw milk, some cod liver oil (amount unspecified by Pottenger), and two-thirds cooked meat. While on this diet the cats showed a decrease in their reproductive capacity and kittens were often born with deformities and organ malfunctions.

As the cat population in his laboratory increased and he found the meat supplied by the neighbors was not enough, he placed an order with a local meat packing plant for meat scraps, which included viscera, muscle meat, and bone. He fed the meat to a segregated group of cats experimenting with different proportions of raw meat, cod liver oil, and types of milk. Some of the diets he tried included:

A. 2/3 raw meat, cod liver oil and 1/3 raw milk.
    (This was the diet that Pottenger found to be the best.)

B. 1/3 raw meat, cod liver oil, and 2/3 pasteurized milk.

C. 1/3 raw meat, cod liver oil, and 2/3 evaporated milk.

D. 1/3 raw meat, cod liver oil, and 2/3 condensed milk

E. Milk only from cows on dry feed. From cows on green feed.[47]

Pottenger found all the above diets inadequate, and with "Diet E" the cats developed rickets and early death in male kittens. Then Pottenger fed one group of cats a diet that included two-thirds raw meat from the packing house, plus one-third raw milk, and some cod liver oil. Within a few months this group of cats appeared to be in better health than the other cats still being fed Dr. Pottenger's original diet, which included the cooked meat scraps, raw milk, and cod liver oil. "The kittens appeared more vigorous, and most interestingly, their operative mortality decreased markedly," reported Dr. Pottenger in his study.[48]

Cooking and Vitamins, Minerals, and Amino Acids

After reading the Pottenger study, my question was what components, if any, of the raw meat versus cooked meat produce healthier cats? Most proponents of the raw meat diet ascertain that because the meat fed to the first group of cats was cooked, it was devoid of nutrients, vitamins, minerals and in particular amino acids with taurine being the prime one.

There is concern about the accessibility of taurine, especially for cats, because they are the only animal that cannot produce taurine independently. The assertion from proponents of the BARF diet that cooking meat destroys taurine, then led me to question if cooking absolutely destroys necessary nutrients.

To what extent, if any, are vitamins, minerals, and amino acids destroyed in the cooking of meat? Do raw meats actually contain higher levels of nutrients then cooked meats, as proponents of the BARF diet assert?

The USDA Nutrient Data Laboratory supplies information on the nutrient levels in various foods on their website (See Resources), including meat. According to the USDA's data on raw meat versus cooked meat, the vitamins and minerals in meat degrade very little when the meat is stewed or lightly cooked. (Specifically, stewed or cooked means that the meat is cooked at temperatures at the boiling point or until the meat juices run clear.) In fact, the data show that the amino acid levels were usually higher in stewed chicken as opposed to raw chicken.

For example, tryptophan, an essential amino acid that is important in the nutrition of animals, registers at 0.250 per gram in raw chicken, and 0.319 per gram in stewed chicken. Another basic amino acid, lysine, which is important for both humans and animals, registers in raw chicken at 1.818 per gram, yet, in stewed chicken, lysine registers at 2.318 per gram. Other essential amino acids such as valine, threonine, and isoleucine all show higher levels in stewed chicken than in raw chicken. These levels are also shown higher in cooked beef versus raw beef.

There is no doubt that amino acids can degrade at the very high temperatures used in pressure cooking as opposed to stewed or lightly cooked meat. Because the commercial pet food industry cooks all of its food at very high temperatures, it adds many vitamins, minerals, and amino acids to the processed and overcooked foods.

Taurine in Meat

Taurine was the one amino acid that was not listed in the USDA Nutrient Data Laboratory. Nutritionists, veterinarians, and informed pet owners have always asserted that taurine is destroyed to some extent when cooking meat. In turn, proponents of the raw meat diet insist that raw meat is the best way for cats to obtain taurine.

Cats require approximately 50 milligrams to 80 milligrams of taurine per day in their diet, although some pet owners add up to 500 milligrams as a supplement. Lack of taurine in commercial cat foods processed at very high temperatures, had caused problems with cats a number of years ago and the pet food industry began adding taurine as a supplement to all cat foods.

I still questioned if cooked meats had been the cause for the problems in the Pottenger study. I contacted John Coupland, PhD, Food Chemistry, Assistant Professor of Food Science at Pennsylvania State University, a doctor whose field of expertise is the chemical structure of various food substances. When I asked his opinion on how heat affects taurine, Dr. Coupland wrote, "Chemically, taurine (H2N-CH2-CH2-SO3H), isn't really an amino acid. It is formed biosynthetically (artificially produced) from the amino acid cysteine."[49] Although Dr. Coupland was not sure how heat would affect taurine, he wrote, "I would doubt it would be affected much."[50] Cysteine is shown in the USDA Nutrient Data Laboratory with levels of 0.349 in stewed chicken and 0.274 in raw chicken. As with the other amino acids, taurine does not degrade in cooking.

I also contacted ten doctors, medical and veterinarian, in various fields of food sciences and technology as well as professors of biochemistry and nutrition regarding the question of taurine. Two doctors, both in the field of food science and technology, responded to my query by quoting from the *MERCK Index*, 11th edition, which states that "taurine decomposes at 300°C (572°F)." This was the chemical form of taurine. When I questioned the decomposition of the chemical form versus the natural form found in meat, Hosni Hassan, PhD, Microbiology, Head of the Department of Microbiology at North Carolina State University, explained, "The decomposition temperature should be the same for a natural or a synthetic pure compound. However, in the natural food stuff (meat for example) the compound will be more stable because other components in the meat (proteins and fats) will provide a shielding (protective) effect to taurine."[51]

Robert Backus, DVM, PhD, from the Department of Biosciences at the University of California, Davis, substantiated Dr. Hassan's statement when he wrote, "Cooking should not destroy taurine. In the laboratory, we can heat taurine in hydrochloric acid to 110°C (262°F) for 24 hours without substantial destruction."[52] A number of doctors replied with very technical terms but the end results were the same: Taurine is not destroyed at cooking temperatures.

Perhaps the best answer to the taurine dilemma came from Nick Costa, PhD in Nutrition and Biochemistry, Associate Professor of Biochemistry and Nutrition at the School of Veterinary Biology and Biomedical Science,

Murdoch University in Australia. "Taurine is a very heat-stable amino acid with a decomposition point of 250°C (482°F)."[53] However, Dr. Costa did clarify that pressure cooking does destroy some taurine but that it is compensated for by manufacturers adding sufficient amounts in the mixture ingredients. "Although home cooking can degrade some of the taurine in meat, there is sufficient present to easily supply the taurine needed by cats," stated Dr. Costa.

Dr. Costa also included information on the degradation of various vitamins. "Thiamin (vitamin B1), folic acid, and vitamin C (made by dogs and cats but not by humans) show the heaviest (and most variable losses) on cooking. Minerals are not affected by cooking but can leach out into the water used for boiling, so save this." Dr. Costa added, "Shallow frying liver will reduce its vitamin A content but boiling does not affect the vitamin A content. Vitamin D and E are relatively heat stable."[54]

After receiving these numerous responses, I was convinced that cooking meat, even at relatively high temperatures, does not degrade levels of amino acids to the point that there would be a detrimental affect on the animals ingesting cooked meat. In addition, most vitamins and minerals are not degraded. And for those still concerned that cooking meat depletes the levels of taurine in the diet, they can add taurine supplements, available at most health and natural foods stores.

Enzymes

Proponents of raw meat diets also emphasize the importance of preserving the enzymes in meat, which may be destroyed with cooking. This topic has been a bone of contention for some time and there are varying opinions on this. According to Christopher Cowell, who has an MS in Animal Nutrition, "Enzymes are complex protein molecules that have very specific structures, kinetics, and uses that are sensitive to pH and temperatures. Therefore consumed enzymes are treated like any other protein, they are hydrolyzed into amino acid groups, absorbed, utilized and excreted. They do not retain functionally as enzymes."[55]

David Klurfled, MD, Chairman and Professor of the Department of Nutrition and Food Science at Wayne State University, explains in his article, *Live Enzymes from Your Food*, "This is a myth that refuses to die. Some people advocate the consumption of raw plants that contain 'live' enzymes to aid in digestion. Well, if these enzymes were really important in digesting food, wouldn't the plant ingest itself? The enzymes our stomach and pancreas make to digest most of our food are not found in plants. In fact, our own digestive process actually digests the enzymes in the food we eat. Enzymes in food are not active in our body."[56]

Enzymes are proteins and so they are treated as such by the body after being ingested. Upon entering the stomach all proteins are broken down by the stomach's acids and digestive chemicals into amino acids, which are then absorbed and utilized by the body to make new proteins, provide energy, and repair damaged tissues. Basically, the body's genetic materials contain all the information needed to make as many enzymes as needed for digestion and absorption.

William Burkholder, DVM and PhD, from Texas A&M University, explained how this information relates to dogs in a written correspondence: "We know that the dog's own pancreas secretes enzymes into the small intestines for about 90 percent of the digestion. The remaining 10 percent of digestive function comes from enzymes secreted by the stomach, the small intestine itself, and some of the resident bacteria in the lower intestine and colon. If the dog's pancreas fails to produce its digestive enzymes, no amount of raw food will compensate for the lost digestive capacity, so the amount of digestion contributed by the food is small compared to the dog's own enzymatic digestion."[57] The digestive systems of dogs and cats operate in virtually the same way—their stomach and pancreas produce the enzymes they require for the digestion of food.

Granted, there is no doubt that cooking at temperatures over 118°C for a period of half an hour or more destroys enzymes. Yet, it has also been established that enzymes, alive or dead, make little difference for dogs, cats, and humans when they are ingested. Columbia University, Health Education Program, found, "Any enzymes present in foods you eat will *not* aid the body in the digestive process."[58]

After corresponding with several veterinarians and nutritionists on the importance of enzymes in meat consumed and whether or not they are destroyed in cooking, no one seems to be sure on exactly how important food enzymes are for the metabolism and digestion, and how this relates to cats and dogs. It is too simplistic to assume that because meats are cooked, enzymes are lost. Much more research is needed to understand this process before we can make the assumption between lost enzymes and cooked meat.

The Efficacy of the Pottenger Study

After considerable research, and seeking the opinions of many veterinarians, nutritionists, and researchers, and learning much of what was discussed above, it became apparent that there were other reasons the cats did not thrive. According to modern scientific findings, unless the meat Dr. Pottenger fed the cats was pressure cooked, the vitamins, minerals, and amino acids would not have deteriorated to the point where they would cause such severe reactions in these cats.

I found other aspects of the Pottenger study that need to be questioned, including the environment in which the cats were kept as well as their overall general health. Many of the cats in the study were donated to Dr. Pottenger, and I question if there was any kind of screening done by him in terms of the health history of these cats. In addition, Pottenger's diets for this ten-year study were not nutritionally analyzed for the key dietary constituents known today but unknown then.

At that time, it was standard practice to feed pets leftover table scraps because commercial pet food was just in its infancy, and the idea of buying pet food was still a novelty. Cat owners felt that cats did well on the leftovers plus a bowl of milk, and in fact, most cats did thrive on this diet. Advocates of raw milk claim that the Pottenger study showed that it was the pasteurized milk that caused the detrimental effects on the cats. Thomas Cowan, MD, an advocate of the raw milk lobby, wrote about the Pottenger study and how this study basically showed it was the raw milk that caused the improvement in cats. Dr. Cowan concludes, "Dr. Pottenger fed similar groups of animals (usually cats) a diet of exclusively milk. Half ate cooked milk (i.e. pasteurized), the other ate uncooked (i.e. raw milk). The results were conclusive and astounding. Those that ate raw milk did well, lived long, happy active lives free of any signs of degenerative disease. Those that ate pasteurized milk suffered from acute illnesses (vomiting, diarrhea) and succumbed to every degenerative disease now flourishing in our population."[59]

Basically, there is no conclusive evidence as to why one group of cats did well while the other did not. Was it the raw meat? Was it the raw milk? Or was it some other aspect of the diet? No one can be sure.

No doubt other issues in this diet can be questioned. The amount of cod liver oil that was added to the diet is one. This amount was never specified. Perhaps when this study was undertaken, more than sixty years ago, it might have been considered a good study. However, I seriously question how Dr. Pottenger's study can be considered a viable study given today's standards for conducting scientific research. Until this study is replicated with today's standards for a controlled study, I don't think any one can state that it was simply the cooked meat that caused health problems, and the raw meat that kept cats healthy.

Dogs and Wolves and Diet

The BARF diet is based primarily on the assumption that because domesticated dogs evolved from wolves that dogs are similar to the wolf in many ways. Therefore, it is reasoned, the diet of the dog should closely follow the diet of the wolf.

Robert Wayne, PhD, an evolutionary biologist at the University of California, Los Angeles, led an international study on the evolution of dogs. In his most recent research he determined that "the origin of dogs is very old, perhaps 100,000 years ago or more."[60] Dr. Wayne's theory differs from other evolutionary biologists who study canines. He came to his conclusions by using genetic fingerprinting. "In the past the revolutionary relationship of canids have been studied by morphological approaches, but parallel changes in several evolutionary lineages can make inferences uncertain,"[61] explains Dr. Wayne on his website (See Resources). "The use of molecular and biochemical techniques to examine genetic differences among species provides an alternative way to investigate phylogenetic relationships."[62]

Although the research did show that dogs evolved from wolves, Dr. Wayne's studies indicate that this happened long before what has been originally thought. The research looked at the DNA sequence in cellular metabolism, specifically, a controlled region of mitochondrial genome that has a high mutation rate. Based on how quickly those mutations could accumulate, the research concluded that dogs could have originated as long as 135,000 years ago or as recently as 60,000 years ago.

An article in the *Seattle Times* in 1997 referred to the study undertaken by Dr. Wayne and his team of researchers. "However skeptical some biologists are of the date itself, they were impressed by the scope of the canine study, which is believed to be the largest of its kind."[63]

It is apparent from this research that although dogs may be the ancient cousins of wolves, dogs have been domesticated for many thousands of years. As a result, today's physical traits of wolves and dogs differ. For example, "dog's brain capacity, muzzle length, and strength of jaw are less than that of their progenitors," notes Norma Bennett Woolf in an article on dogs and wolves. [64]

All wolves in the wild ingest the entire animal, including the fur, feathers, and hide. Depending on where wolves live, they will eat a variety of berries and plants. In contrast, pet owners who feed their cats and dogs the raw meat diet feed them chicken from supermarket shelves, in particular necks, legs, backs, and wings. Is raw chicken from supermarkets, without feathers, a diet that wolves would ingest? According to the Northern Prairie Wildlife Research Center, "Most wolves do not kill livestock even when that food is available. In Northwestern Minnesota, wolf packs lived very near farms without killing livestock." [65] Personally, I have heard of raids on chicken coups by wolves but this usually happens in the dead of winter when no other food is available to them.

On a wolf-dog hybrid website called Lioncrushers' Domain (See Resources) that addresses the difference between wolves and domesticated dogs, I found the following most interesting: "The most important genetic difference is a gene that codes for specific hormones that trigger adult behavior (territoriality, social bonds, dominance behaviors). Consider this: humans and chimpanzees share 98.4% of their genetic structure, yet there is no question of the difference in behavior and appearance. Though that may be a very small amount that differs, that small amount is what makes humans different than chimpanzees. Likewise, that small portion of DNA in wolves is what makes them, behaviorally and physically, different than dogs." [66] We see that although wolves and dogs share many similarities, they have significant differences, similar to humans and chimpanzees.

Rosalind Dalefield from the Royal Veterinary College, whose field of study is Veterinary Toxicology holds a BVSc (Bachelor of Veterinary Science and a PhD). When asked about wolves, dogs, and diet, she wrote, "When someone convinces me that wolves live longer, healthier lives than domestic dogs, I'll start paying attention to the question of how they do it." [67] Dr. Dalefield then added, "The assumption that 'natural is good' is a value-based judgement with no scientific validity. The most toxic substance we know is botulinum toxin, and that is 100% natural." [68]

Conclusion

The Well Pet list on the Internet promotes the raw meat diet. I joined this Internet group for awhile to learn what individual pet owners experienced with the raw meat diet. Most people on the Well Pet list were pleased with how well their pets did on the raw meat and bones diet, writing about their pet's clean teeth, increased energy, and shining coats. However, some pet owners complained, stating that their pets experienced severe diarrhea, vomiting, and bone fragments stuck in the colon as a result of the raw meat diet. The proponents of this diet assured the owners that the reason their pets were experiencing diarrhea is because they were "detoxing."

Suggestions for solving the problems pets encountered with bones is to crush the bones or feed their animals strictly chicken necks, which are easier to chew and digest. I found these responses frightening and responded that if my pets were experiencing such symptoms with bones, I would be investigating further the validity of such a diet. In turn, I found quite a bit of resistance from BARF proponents when I expressed these concerns.

After researching for years the different aspects of the raw meat diet, I have concluded that I am not willing to risk my animal's health for a diet that looks highly questionable. The problems with the raw meat diet far outweigh the advantages. I respect the work Dr. Billinghurst has done. We agree on the disadvantages of feeding commercial pet foods, but I am afraid our paths part regarding alternative methods of feeding. I understand that those who feed the raw meat diet to their pets believe they are making the best possible choices they can for their pets. However, the above information from a variety of experts in various veterinary fields convinces me not to use the raw meat diet to feed my pets.

SEVEN

Over-Vaccination
and Animals

Currently, most veterinarians advise annual vaccinations for millions of animal companions for a variety of diseases. Traditionally, veterinarians advised that yearly vaccinations are the only preventative method for life-threatening diseases. However, some veterinarians now question the need for annual vaccinations.

For dogs, vaccinations include the yearly rabies vaccination although there is a three-year rabies vaccination. Depending on what U.S. state you live in and if there is a risk of exposure of pets to wild animals such as foxes, bats, and raccoons who may have rabies, then a mandatory rabies vaccine is necessary. This also applies across Canada. In the United States and Canada rabies are found in raccoons, foxes, bats, coyotes, skunks, squirrels, chipmunks, rabbits, mice, and rats. According to a pamphlet put out by the Rabies Prevention in Washington State, "A Guide to Practitioners," "While dog rabies is a major problem in much of the world, in the United States, animal control and vaccination programs assure that rabies remains rare in dogs, cats, and other domestic animals. In this country, over 90% of animal rabies cases occur in wildlife."[1]

In both the United States and Canada, it is generally required that a dog living in a high risk area must have a rabies vaccination in order to get a dog license. Other vaccinations for dogs are optional although veterinarians usually recommend annual vaccinations for parvovirus, (a viral disease causing gastrointestinal distress, which can lead to death), distemper, parainfluenza, adenovirus (which causes canine hepatitis), and leptospirosis, a potentially fatal bacterial disease that damages the liver and kidneys. Other vaccinations include Bordetella, which is the bacterial cause of kennel cough; coronavirus, which is an intestinal infection that causes vomiting, diarrhea, and depression and can cause death in puppies; and a vaccination for Lyme disease, which is spread by ticks. Lyme disease causes fever, joint pain and possibly death and can also be contracted by humans.

The yearly vaccination protocol for cats includes panleukopenia, (FP), also known as feline distemper, infectious enteritis (the equivalent to parvovirus in dogs), cat fever, and cat typhoid. All of these are highly contagious viral diseases for felines. Other cat vaccinations include rhinotrachetis and calicivirus, both upper respiratory diseases and FeLV (feline leukemia), plus the annual rabies vaccination, all of which are given annually. As with dogs, if wild animals in the area are infected with rabies, it is compulsory to have your cat vaccinated against rabies if a cat license is required. However, most states do not require cat licenses.

Unquestionably, the effects of some of these diseases can be deadly and animal companions should be vaccinated. However, what is questionable is how often cats and dogs need to be vaccinated against certain diseases. Also, the question needs to be asked, are these annual vaccinations truly effective or are they harming animal companions more than helping them?

The Pet Vaccination Education website (see Resources) describes at length the various diseases that vaccinations guard against. For example, dogs with distemper "may suffer coughing, vomiting, seizures, diarrhea, and other painful signs followed by death."[2] However, canine cases of distemper are rare in the United States and Canada, which makes questionable the methodology of administering an annual vaccine for distemper. However, parvovirus, a viral disease present throughout the United States and Canada, is still a serious threat. It causes "severe dehydration, vomiting, diarrhea and death, especially in puppies."[3] Parvovirus outbreaks are still common and serious.

The Risks of Over-Vaccination

Some major veterinary colleges such as Colorado State University, along with a growing number of veterinarians in private practice, now question if the risks of yearly vaccinations might outweigh the risks of animals contracting some of these diseases. Titer testing, described below, gives a pet owner a good indication how often an animal companion should be vaccinated. Even the American Animal Hospital Association (AAHA) cautions against excessive vaccinations. In August 1999, the AAHA released its opinion paper regarding vaccinations. The AAHA President, Michael Paul, DVM, wrote, "The intent of the opinion paper is to encourage veterinarians to consider vaccination procedures as medical decisions and not automatic actions prompted by a calendar."[4]

Although some veterinary colleges and veterinarians are stating publicly that pets are immune to these diseases for one, two, three years, and even longer after the initial vaccinations, it is still common practice in the United States and Canada for veterinarians to recommend yearly vaccinations. The necessity of frequent vaccinations is now being called into question.

Jean Dodds, DVM, a veterinarian in private practice in Santa Monica, California and one of the foremost experts in pet vaccinations, believes that vaccinations with single or combination modified live virus are increasingly recognized contributors to immune-mediated blood diseases, bone marrow failure, and organ dysfunction. Dr. Dodds also lists leukemia, thyroid disease, Addison's disease, diabetes and lymphoma as diseases that can be triggered by vaccines. "Combining viral antigens, especially those of modified live virus (MLV) type, which multiply in the host, elicits a stronger antigenic challenge to the animal," explains Dr. Dodds in an article on the immune system. "This is often viewed as desirable because a more potent immunogen presumably mounts a more effective and sustained immune response. However, it can also overwhelm the immuno compromised or even a healthy host that is continually bombarded with other environmental stimuli and has a genetic predisposition that promotes adverse response to viral challenge."[5]

In October 2000, the *Journal of the American Veterinary Medical Association* published a study that was undertaken by Dodds and Lisa Twark, DVM. The purpose of the study was to assess whether serum canine parvovirus (CPV) and canine distemper virus (CDV) antibody titers, (titer tests are discussed later in this chapter) could determine revaccination protocols in healthy dogs. For this study, 1,441 dogs were used ranging in age from six weeks to seventeen years.

The interval between the last vaccination and the antibody measurement using a titer test was from one to two years for the majority of dogs, 60 percent, and two to seven years for 30.3 percent, and one year for 9.6 percent of the dogs used in the study. The conclusion arrived at by Drs. Twark and Dodds: "The high prevalence of adequate antibody responses (CPV 95.1%; CDV 97.6%) in this large population of dogs suggests that annual revaccination against CPV and CDV may not be necessary."[6]

All packages of vaccinations carry warnings that they should be injected only in healthy animals. In the case of cats, vaccine manufacturers advise against vaccinating pregnant or nursing cats. However, many pets are not healthy when vaccinated although they might not have outward signs of health problems. Charles Loops, DVM, a holistic veterinarian from Pittsboro, North Carolina, notes that "chemically killed viruses or bacteria are injected directly into the blood stream, which is an unnatural route of infection."[7] This causes the animal's antibodies to attempt to fight off the offending virus molecules and render them harmless. If the animal's immune system is too weakened, he or she cannot fight off these viruses and can develop a reaction to the vaccine. Even small amounts of a virus that is introduced through a vaccination may be too much for sick animals to fight off. They then may fall ill from the very disease to which they have been vaccinated.

If you have concerns about vaccinating your pet, Michael Lemmon, DVM, suggests the following: "First, don't vaccinate your dog or cat when he is showing any signs of illness. If your pet is already ill, his immune system may not be able to produce antibodies the vaccination is supposed to stimulate; and he stands a chance of being overwhelmed by the small amount of virus in the vaccine, and succumbing to the illness he's being vaccinated against."[8]

Some veterinarians believe that vaccines are outright damaging to our pets. Dr. Loops writes in an article, "Veterinarians and animal guardians have to come to realize that they are not protecting animals from disease by annual vaccinations, but in fact, are destroying the health and immune system of these same animals they love and care for."[9] In the same article, Christina Chambreau, DVM, Founder and Chairperson of the Academy of Veterinary Homeopathy, expresses similar views: "Routine vaccinations are probably the worst thing that we do for our animals. They cause all types of illnesses but not directly to where we would relate them definitely to be caused by the vaccine."[10]

Cats and Vaccinations

In the early 1990s the vaccination of cats was beginning to draw concern from cat owners as well as from veterinarians who noted that cats were developing tumors within weeks and months of being vaccinated. *DVM Magazine* ran an interesting article on the possible connection between vaccinations and feline sarcomas. "In 1998, Mattie J. Hendrick, DVM, a pathologist with the University of Pennsylvania School of Veterinary

Medicine, began to notice something odd," writes Lynn Brakeman, senior editor of *DVM Magazine*, "out of the thousands of biopsies she was analyzing each week, a surprising number of cats (and cats only) were showing the same kind of inflammatory lesion at vaccine sites. By 1990, she and her colleagues had diagnosed a surprising number of fibrosarcomas in the dorsal portion of the neck and interscapular regions of cats."[11] But the question still remained as to what was causing the sarcomas to develop in cats receiving these vaccinations and how many cats were actually succumbing to fibrosarcomas?

In November 1996 a ten-member task force assembled to address the issue of sarcoma formation at injection sites of the commonly used feline vaccines. The task force included members of the American Association of Feline Practitioners (AAFP), American Animal Hospital Association (AAHA), American Veterinary Medical Association (AVMA), and Veterinary Cancer Society (VCS). The AVMA states: "The objectives of the task force were to define the true scope and incidence of the problem, determine the casual and prognostic factors of the syndrome, and develop an interim plan to educate and inform veterinarians and the public."[12] Veterinarians were to be updated on research findings and on new vaccines that were licensed.

In 1998 the task force made its initial vaccine site recommendations. "In short, the task force recommends that vaccines containing rabies antigens be given as distally as possible in the right rear limb, vaccines containing feline leukemia virus antigen (unless containing rabies antigen as well) be given as distally as possible in the left rear limb, and vaccines containing any other antigens except rabies or feline leukemia virus be given on the right shoulder."[13]

Cats often develop small lumps at vaccination sites but these bumps usually disappear within one or two weeks. Theresa A. Fuess, PhD, an Information Specialist at the University of Illinois, College of Veterinary Medicine, wrote a paper on the cancer risks in cats published by the University of Illinois. "The shortest time for cancer to develop is three months, but it can take as long as three and a half years," explained Dr. Fuess. "If your cat develops a lump that persists more than a month and a half it should be evaluated by a specialists right away. Removal of a lump at six weeks is minor surgery; at three months it is major surgery."[14]

A friend of mine who has owned Siamese cats for many years and who has had them vaccinated annually, was horrified to find that one of her cats had developed a lump at the site of the injection for FeLV within a few weeks of the vaccination. She did not delay in getting her cat to the vet where the lump was removed before it had a chance to spread. If your cat does develop a lump at the site of the injection, don't delay in seeing your vet. Surgical removal with wide margins is crucial since this type of tumor can spread quickly.

In a presentation to the American Veterinary Medical Association in 1998. Guillermo Couto, DVM and Dennis W. Macy, DVM, MS presented data to the American Veterinary Medical Association on the number of cats who may be affected with the vaccine-related sarcomas. In their paper, "Vaccine Associated Feline Sarcoma Task Force," the veterinarians state, "The prevalence of soft tissue sarcomas after vaccination varies between 1 and 1,000 and 1 in 10,000 cats. If this prevalence is to be applied to the 1991 cat population of the United States, a total of 22,000 vaccine-induced tumors developed in 1991."[15]

Another theory that has developed in the last few years is the use of vaccines containing aluminum-based adjuvants. An adjuvant is a substance that is used to facilitate immune stimulation with a killed virus. This material holds the virus in the area of the vaccination for a couple of weeks so it can be released slowly, allowing immune stimulation to take place over a period of time.

According to Wendy C. Brooks, DVM, DABVP (Diplomate, American Board of Veterinary Practitioners), "Recently, fibrosarcomas have been removed from areas of the body typically used for vaccination and, to the surprise of the veterinary profession, particules of aluminum-based vaccine ingredients (called 'adjuvants') were discovered within the tumor."[16] Aluminum-based adjuvants have been known to induce vaccine-site inflammation but the role they might play in causing fibrosarcomas is still unknown.

Feline Leukemia Virus in Cats

It was first thought that these fibrosarcomas were related to the rabies vaccination, which became mandatory for cats in 1987. However, Katherine James, DVM, reports, "In 1993 researchers from the University of California Davis showed that feline leukemia vaccines were more likely to cause sarcomas than were rabies vaccines."[17]

This is frightening news for many cat owners who religiously have their cats vaccinated every year for feline leukemia. In his book, *The Nature of*

Animal Healing, Martin Goldstein, DVM, describes cats in his veterinary practice who have been vaccinated. "I began seeing cats with immuno-suppression diseases whose medical histories bore a depressing similarity: many had been given the leukemia vaccine in the recent past."[18] Dr. Goldstein also observed increasing numbers of young cats with stomach and kidney cancers. Before veterinarians began using FeLV, he rarely saw any cases like this.

Dr. Goldstein is also suspicious of the sharply higher incidents of feline peritonitis in cats three or four weeks after they had been given an FeLV vaccination, something he had not seen prior to the spring of 1985 when this vaccine became available. In *The Nature of Animal Healing*, Dr. Goldstein refers to recent cases that Dr. Jean Dodds studied that suggest the FeLV vaccine occasionally provokes another feline disease, infectious peritonitis "by compromising a cat's immune system and thus rendering her more susceptible to it."[19] Infectious peritonitis causes fluid to accumulate in the abdomen and/or chest. Other symptoms of infectious peritonitis include signs of kidney and liver failure, anemia, weight loss, and vomiting and diarrhea, which can make it difficult for the veterinarian to diagnose feline peritonitis. Infectious peritonitis has a high fatality rate.

Feline leukemia virus can be latent in carrier cats without any signs or symptoms for many years. Susan Little, DVM, ABVP, is part owner of two feline specialty practices in Ottawa, Canada. She also works with a group of volunteers on a trap/test/vaccinate/ release program for feral cats in the Ottawa area. In 1998, Dr. Little posted a number of articles relating to cats on her website (See Resources) including the article "Feline Leukemia Virus." In this article, Dr. Little explains "The prevalence of FeLV in single cat households is about 3 percent and can be as high as 11 percent in stray cat populations. In large, multi-cat households where cats roam freely out-doors, the prevalence can reach as high as 70 percent. Cats roaming in urban areas are more likely to be exposed to FeLV (40%) than cats roaming in rural areas (6%)."[20]

Dr. Little describes the possible outcomes for cats exposed to the FeLV virus: "In about 30% of cats, an effective immune response is produced and the infection is resisted. In about 40% of cats, the virus is successful and the cat eventually becomes persistently infected and excreting virus in its saliva. Another 30% of cats do not produce immunity but also do not become persistently infected immediately. In these cats, the virus hides in the bone marrow for up to 30 months."[21] Dr. Little points out that cats whose feline virus hides in sites such as the bone marrow rarely become contagious and they are unlikely to develop the disease.

When you take your cat in for the FeLV vaccination, the vet will first take a blood test to ascertain if the cat is harboring this infection. A blood test is the only way to determine if in fact your cat is suffering from FeLV infection. If your cat tests positive for the virus, it is not necessary to vaccinate for feline leukemia because your cat already has the virus. In addition, if your cat tests positive, and there are other cats in the household, it is advised that you have all your cats tested, even though they may have been vaccinated (there is no 100 percent guarantee with any vaccine), to be sure that they are free of the disease. Regarding the FeLV vaccine, Dr. Jean Dodds stated in a personal correspondence, "This vaccine [FeLV] has relatively poor clinical efficacy. It is about 40 percent although manufacturers cite up to an 80 percent efficacy."

There is no cure acknowledged by mainstream veterinary medicine for feline leukemia. There are however some alternative health practitioners who claim anecdotal success with feline leukemia. Remember that some blood tests will show a "false negative," which means a cat may have feline leukemia even though the test shows that he doesn't. A false negative can occur if a cat is in the early stages of the disease; if the virus is sequestered in the marrow or organs, such as the liver and spleen; or if a cat is terminal because of the disease. This is not very common but it does occur, especially in young kittens.

If a cat or kitten has recently been exposed to the feline virus, the antibodies may not have had enough time for a response to appear on the test thus producing a false negative. If it is known that a kitten has been exposed to this virus a second test two weeks after the first is usually recommended. I asked Susan Little, DVM, why this test would show a false negative in a cat who was in the terminal stages of this illness. Dr. Little replied, "Because the virus can segregate itself in body organs (especially bone marrow) where it is not easily detected by a routine blood test, it is possible to have feline leukemia virus infection and test negative on a blood test."[22]

Cats who have access to the outdoors should be vaccinated for FeLV since their chances of contracting the virus increase substantially. Dr. Little advises yearly vaccinations for outdoor cats. An alternative to yearly vaccinations for FeLV are nosodes, a homeopathic oral alternative to vaccination for various diseases. Although there have been no scientific studies undertaken, it has been shown that nosodes may prevent animals and people from falling ill with the problem in question. In the case of FeLV, cats who have been given nosodes have not shown any signs of the disease. (Nosodes are discussed at greater length later in this chapter.)

Dogs and Vaccinations

In Great Britain, Catherine O'Driscoll, an author and the publisher of Abbeywood Publishing, challenges the wisdom of annual vaccinations for pets, and in particular dogs. After several years of ongoing research, and first-hand experience with her dogs' fatal reactions to vaccinations, O'Driscoll is an outspoken opponent to traditional vaccinations. She believes that the use of nosodes is a much safer alternative to vaccinations.

O'Driscoll and her husband, John Watt, have been owned by Golden Retrievers for many years. In the mid-1990s, two of their young Golden Retrievers got sick shortly after they had been vaccinated, and eventually died. Oliver, who was four years old, had been vaccinated in the hip and died less than three months later from sudden rear-end paralysis, an unexplained medical problem.

A year later his sister, Prudence, died of leukemia. Prudence had also been vaccinated but discovery of the leukemia was outside of the three-month time frame of the vaccination. O'Driscoll believes the leukemia had been developing for a long time prior to diagnosis. "After Oliver died, I spent two years asking every vet I met...why? No one could answer me," explained O'Driscoll in an interview. "Veterinarians just kept hemming and hawing. Then we took another one of our dogs to see Christopher Day, one of the U.K.'s top homeopathic veterinarians. Once again I explained what had happened with Oliver and asked Dr. Day what he thought might have caused it. He explained that he often sees animals becoming sick or dying within three months of their vaccine shot, and rear-end paralysis was a common post-vaccination problem." Dr. Day also noted that when the start date of an illness is known, 80 percent of the dogs he sees in his veterinarian practice first become ill within three months of a vaccine.[23]

After Oliver's death, O'Driscoll spent two years writing a book on Golden Retrievers, focusing primarily on their personalities and temperament. She interviewed owners of Golden Retrievers worldwide. In the course of her research, an individual sent Catherine an article written by Jean Dodds, DVM, who addresses the problem of immune-blood mediated diseases, including leukemia being on the rise in dogs since the introduction of live virus vaccines. O'Driscoll and her husband, John Watt, were alarmed by this connection. Watt, who has a masters degree in systems analysis and operational research as well as considerable statistical and research experience, thought it would be beneficial to do some independent research related to illnesses in dogs and vaccinations. So began the Canine Health Census in October 1996.

The Canine Health Census included a team of veterinarians, Dr. Jean Dodds from the United States, Dr. Christopher Day from the United Kingdom, and Australian veterinarians Tom Lonsdale and Ian Billinghurst, along with Viera Scheibner, an Australian research scientist with a PhD in natural sciences. The goal of the Canine Health Census was to understand a number of health-related issues for dogs and to gather information directly from dog owners.

Drs. Jean Dodds and Christopher Day helped draft a survey to be distributed to as many dog owners as the Canine Health Census could reach in the United Kingdom. The Canine Health Census took out paid ads in dog magazines requesting participation in the survey, and individuals distributed the questionnaires to dog owners, sometimes walking door-to-door through neighborhoods. The survey was also posted on the Canine Health Census website and mailed to pet owners worldwide. The survey was twenty-six pages long, and it was divided into several areas of concern, such as diet, vaccinations, environment, pollution, chemicals, and drugs. Pet owners could fill out the entire survey or only certain areas of the survey if they desired.[24]

The vaccine portion of the questionnaire had more than twenty general questions about an individual dog's situation and health, such as the age of the dog, when the dog was adopted, number of dogs in the household, and the dog's diet. Questions also covered topics such as when the dog was first vaccinated, and after that, was the dog vaccinated annually. Some of the questions related to the type of vaccine used: killed, live, or mixture. In addition to general questions, there was a "Time Frame" segment in the survey that asked an additional thirty questions that related to various ailments such as allergies, cancer, distemper, leukemia, liver damage, and when the dog may have developed these ailments in relation to the vaccinations.

The response to the Canine Health Census Survey was substantial. Over the first four-month period they received information on 2,700 dogs. The data gathered from this "Interim Report" showed a strong correlation between vaccinations and the onset of disease. According to O'Driscoll, "The survey showed that 68.2% of dogs in the survey with parvovirus contracted parvovirus within three months of being vaccinated. Similarly 55.6% of dogs with distemper contracted it within three months of vaccination; 63.6% contracted hepatitis within three months of vaccination; 50% contracted parainfluenza within three months of vaccination and every single dog with leptospirosis contracted it within that three-month time frame."[25]

As of December 2000, two sets of results have been collected. According to O'Driscoll, "The second survey confirms the results of the first but the picture of vaccine damage looks even bleaker." The Canine Health Census survey is ongoing and can be accessed through the website or you can request that a copy of the survey be mailed. (See Resources.)

As a result of the findings by the Canine Health Census, and inspired by the loss of her own animal companions due to over-vaccination, O'Driscoll wrote a fascinating book on her findings, *Who Killed the Darling Buds of May: Vaccines.* In her book O'Driscoll reports the results of the first survey. In August 1998, a new edition of the book was published to include the results of the second survey. In her recent book, *What Vets Don't Tell You About Vaccines,* O'Driscoll covers many aspects of vaccinations for animal companions as well as information on human vaccinations. For animals, the topics include vaccines that are mixed with deadly poisons; vaccines that shed into the environment thereby spreading disease; vaccines that can cause the diseases they are designed to prevent; and vaccines that disarm and impair the immune system.

What Vets Don't Tell You About Vaccines was the topic of a television documentary in the United Kingdom in 1998. Granada Television "World In Action" aired the documentary, "Fatal Affection," which featured O'Driscoll's book and the findings of the Canine Health Census. As a result of this documentary and public exposure to the problems with vaccinations, the Veterinary Medicine's Directorate in Great Britain requested copies of the Canine Health Census research data. Whether or not this will change the present practice of annual vaccinations for cats and dogs in the United Kingdom is still uncertain as of January 2001. But at least many pet owners in Great Britain are aware of the potential problems with vaccinations.

Since the deaths of her much-loved pets, Oliver and Prudence, O'Driscoll no longer has her pets vaccinated. Instead, she has yearly titer tests performed to determine a dog's level of immunity. She is also a strong proponent of using nosodes instead of vaccinations. (Titer tests and nosodes are explained later in this chapter.)

I have witnessed first-hand the results of over-vaccination in one of my dogs. Sarge, a beautiful six-year-old German Shepherd, came into my life when I met his human companion, Chuck Phair, who is caring and conscientious. Chuck made sure that Sarge had all his yearly vaccinations. Unfortunately in 1999 Sarge was diagnosed with discoid lupus, an auto-immune disease. Fortunately, the holistic veterinarian who treats Sarge has been able to keep the disease under control with a number of vitamins, minerals, supplements, and natural cortisone. There is no cure for lupus. I believe that over-vaccination played a major role in Sarge's contracting this disease. It is difficult to realize that you may have unintentionally harmed your animal companions by giving them annual vaccinations, which are intended to protect them.

The Cost of Annual Vaccinations

In addition to the health factors for yearly vaccinations, some pet owners have questioned the motives of veterinarians who insist that yearly vaccinations are necessary. Research indicates that the cost of vaccinations by a veterinarian average from $16 to $20 (U.S.) for a rabies vaccine. In addition, veterinarians usually charge about $30 per office visit. The total cost of the veterinary visit, plus the rabies vaccination, typically ranges from $46 to $50.

Undoubtedly, there is a substantial markup on vaccines. The website for the Omaha Vaccine Company lists the "Fort Dodge/Solvay RabVac 1" for $28.95, which includes fifty single doses.[26] This breaks down to about 79 cents per dose for the veterinarian. This does not include the cost of the needle or syringe. There are some rabies clinics sponsored by local shelters that will vaccinate a pet at a cost between $3 and $5 (U.S.). This is substantially less than a private visit to a veterinarian. These clinics are usually held in the spring and dates are posted in local newspapers.

Some veterinary clinics now offer three-year rabies vaccinations. The three-year rabies vaccine from Fort Dodge for dogs as well as for cats sells a package of fifty single doses for $44.95 per package, which is about 85 cents per dose. Veterinarians often charge $30 for the three-year rabies plus the basic office visit. Omaha Vaccine Company lists the combination vaccine, which includes Progard 5 DA2P+PV, Canine distemper, adenovirus type 2, parainfluenza, and the parvo modified live at a cost of $1.97 per dose for veterinarians. The combination vaccine, Eclipse 4 + FeLVs, vaccine for cats, which includes feline panleukopenia, feline rhinotracheitis, calicivirus, chlamydia psittaci, and feline leukemia, costs the veterinarian $5.34 per dose. When this cost is extended to the consumer, it can easily amount to $60 for the vaccination and the office visit.

O'Driscoll, who addresses the financial motivation for annual vaccinations among veterinarians, asserts in her book, "Vaccines are big business. Some estimate that 30 percent of a vet's income comes from annual vaccination boosters."[27] Current U.S. figures put it at between 8 percent and 10 percent. Five years ago, vaccinations made up about 15 percent of a veterinarian's income. However, it must be noted that there is one positive aspect of annual visits to the veterinarian's office—the opportunity to have the vet examine your animal companion for any health problems.

New Vaccination Protocol

In early 1998 Colorado State University released its "Small Animal Vaccination Protocol," which basically discouraged yearly vaccinations. In a statement issued by the Veterinary School at Colorado State University, veterinarians write, "Our adoption of this routine vaccination program is based on the lack of scientific evidence to support the current practice of annual vaccination and the increasing documentation that over-vaccinating has been associated with autoimmune hemolytic anemia with vaccination in dogs and vaccine-associated sarcomas in cats both of which are often fatal."[28]

The new program adopted by Colorado State University is dubbed "Program 1701." This program is based on a survey done by Pfizer, one of the largest vaccine manufacturers in the United States. The survey's purpose was to find out how many vaccines and vaccination protocols are being used by veterinarians in the United States. The survey findings show that are were 1,700 different vaccination recommendations in existence. Colorado State University's veterinary teaching hospital offers its clients one more vaccination protocol, "Program 1701," stating, "We are making this change after years of concern about the lack of scientific evidence to support the current practice of annual vaccination and the increasing documentation that over-vaccination has been associated with harmful side effects."[29]

Program 1701 recommends the standard three-shot series for puppies, which includes parvovirus, adenovirus 2, parainfluenza, and distemper. For kittens the program recommends panleukopenia, rhinotrachetitis, and calicivirus. Rabies should be administered after twelve weeks of age for cats, and sixteen weeks of age for dogs. Following the initial puppy and kitten immunization series, Program 1701 recommends that cats and dogs be given booster shots one year later for all the above shots, and after that, every three years thereafter for all the above diseases.

Veterinarians from Colorado State University School of Veterinary Medicine further recommend: "Other available small animal vaccines, which may need more frequent administration, i.e., intranasal parainfluenza, Bordetella, feline leukemia, Lyme, etc., may be recommended for CSU client animals on an 'at risk' basis but are not a part of the routine Colorado State University protocol for small animals."[30] As of the fall of 2000, Program 1701 has been adopted by the University of Wisconsin, Texas A&M and the American Association of Feline Practitioners. As of January 2001 these are the only colleges involved.

In speaking with numerous pet owners and veterinarians during the course of my research, I found that about 50 percent of the veterinarians in private practice in the United States are following the protocol of Program 1701. However, far fewer Canadian veterinarians use this new protocol. In the province where I live, Ontario, you cannot board a pet without a certificate of yearly vaccination or a letter from your veterinarian that specifically states why your pet cannot be vaccinated. Most kennels also require that you sign a release that relieves them from any responsibility should your pet contract a disease while boarding at their facilities.

Stephen Kruth, DVM from the Veterinary College in Guelph, advises veterinarians in Canada to follow the current recommendations of the Ontario Veterinary Association and the Canadian Veterinary Medical Association. These organizations recommend yearly vaccinations. When I questioned Dr. Kruth about this, he responded, "There is conflicting data regarding duration of immunity, and new vaccine technologies are currently being released. The Canadian veterinary community has not yet jumped on the three-year bandwagon yet, however, I suspect that we will probably move in that direction as real data becomes available."[31]

The consensus among Canadian veterinarians, including my animals' vet, is to continue vaccinating on a yearly basis. My cats, ages eight years to twenty-four years, received their initial kitten shots and have not been vaccinated since. They are strictly house cats and do not have contact with other cats outside of the house. As for our dog, Sarge, who was vaccinated annually for six years, he will never be vaccinated again due to his medical complications. If Sarge were healthy, I would opt for Program 1701 only after performing titers tests.

Vaccine Protocols for Animals with Immune Dysfunction

The following vaccination protocol was formulated by Dr. Dodds in April 2000. This is for breeds or families of dogs susceptible to or affected with immune dysfunction, immune-mediated disease, immune reactions associated with vaccinations, or autoimmune endocrine disease (such as thyroiditis, Addisons or Cushings disease, and diabetes, among others). Dr. Dodds recommends only three doses of the Modified Live Vaccine (MLV) for Distemper/Parvovirus only (e.g. Intervet Progard Puppy) given at several week intervals.

+ The first vaccination given at 9 weeks
+ The second vaccination given at 12 weeks
+ The third vaccination given at 16 to 20 weeks

When a puppy is twenty-four weeks or older, then vaccinate for rabies using a killed rabies vaccine. It is my understanding that only killed rabies vaccines are used in both the United States and Canada.

At one year, give a booster vaccine for MLV Distempter/Parvovirus. Three or four weeks later, give a booster vaccine for rabies, using the killed three-year rabies vaccine. Thereafter, do annual vaccine titer tests, which are dicussed in the following section.

Checking the Immune Response

Titer testing is one way to determine if your pet has had an immune response to the vaccine's antigen and if there are sufficient antibodies. Titer is the name for a serological test (a simple blood test) that measures a specific concentration of a given immunoglobulin. This serum antibody test indicates the levels of immunity that a pet has for a particular disease. If you have show dogs or cats, this test should be undertaken annually to make sure they are maintaining sufficient immunity.

If there is an immune response to this testing, it means you don't need to vaccinate at this point in time. However, the results of titer testing may not be adequate to satisfy the vaccination requirements when boarding your pets or when traveling internationally with your pets, although these requirements are slowly changing.

Titer tests may be a little more expensive than vaccinations. The cost for titer testing varies but should fall within the price range of $20 to $50 (U.S.). Susan and Robert Goldstein, both DVMs, suggest in their online newsletter, "Love of Animals," that you "just test for one or two of the most prevalent diseases in your type of animal. For example, we recommend that for cats, you test for distemper and upper respiratory viruses. For dogs, canine distemper and parvovirus."[32]

Dr. Dodd's protocol recommends that after one year, annually measure serum antibodies with a titer test against specific canine infectious agents such as distemper and parvovirus. This is especially recommended for animals previously experiencing adverse vaccine reactions or breeds at higher risk for such reactions such as Weimaraner, Akita, American Eskimo, and Great Dane.

Dr. Dodds states that she only uses killed (dead) three-year rabies vaccines for adult dogs and waits another three or four weeks before giving any additional vaccines. Dr. Dodds does not use Bordetella, corona virus, leptospirosis or Lyme vaccines unless these diseases are endemic in the local area or specific kennel.

Another concern to consider regarding pets and vaccinations is a possible allergic reaction, which may include hives, facial swelling, or even nausea. The worst allergic reaction can be shock or sudden death (anaphylaxis). In 1998 the University of Kansas State University's College of Veterinary Medicine, recommended that puppies not be vaccinated against lepto-spirosis, a potentially fatal bacteria disease that can damage the kidneys and liver. According to Bill Fortney, DVM, assistant professor of clinical sciences at the Kansas State College of Veterinary Medicine, "It is not uncommon for dogs to have a reaction to vaccines, causing other difficulties including death. One of the problems with the leptospirosis vaccine is that it causes more reactions than the others."[33] This same report advises against vaccines for leptospirosis, coronavirus, or Lyme disease. The risks outweigh the benefits.

Most important, remember, that no matter what vaccines are being used they are approved for use only on healthy animals. *If your pet has any health problems do not vaccinate.* If you or your veterinarian feel that your pet is healthy enough to be vaccinated, avoid the combination vaccines and request that your pet be vaccinated over a period of months. Donna Starita Mehan, DVM, a highly respected holistic veterinarian based in Oregon, advises: "Vaccinate for one disease at a time, that is, avoid multivalent [combination] vaccines. For cats, vaccinate for feline panleukopenia alone. The vaccines for the two upper respiratory viruses [calicivirus and rhino-tracheitis] can be given together. I strongly recommend against vaccination for feline leukemia or feline infections pertitonitis virus. Both vaccines are ineffective, and in my opinion, extremely hazardous."[34]

For dogs, Dr. Mehan recommends, "Give parvo separately from distempter. Do not vaccinate for leptospirosis, hepatitis, or parainfluenza. Never give the rabies vaccine at the same time as any other vaccine."[35] In addition, avoid modified live vaccines and request that killed vaccines be used although the canine distemper/hepatitis vaccine is not available in a killed virus form.

Alternatives to Vaccines

Some breeders and pet owners are turning to nosodes, which are an oral homeopathic alternative to vaccination. Homeopathic remedies are made from diluted amounts of natural substances such as herbs, seeds, barks, berries, minerals, and animal matter such as secretion or discharge.

Nosodes are taken orally and are believed to immunize the body against a specific disease. Nosodes do not have to be swallowed. They are dissolved on the mucus membranes in the mouth and then absorbed into the system.

Dee Blanco, a holistic veterinarian from Santa Fe, New Mexico, describes the composition of nosodes as "homeopathic remedies made from diseased products of whatever disease you are wanting to protect against. For distemper, nasal discharge is used. For parvo, fecal material is used. These are subsequently filtered, and sterilized, diluted and succussed as any homeopathic remedy and are administered orally."[36] Dr. Blanco explains, "Nosodes provide protection by stimulating a non-specific immunological response. They fill the susceptibility the animal has to the disease without actually producing antibodies."[37] The primary nosodes that Dr. Blanco uses are for life-threatening diseases such as parvo, distemper, and panleukopenia. She also uses nosodes for Bordatella, a bacterial disease of the lungs, for animals in kennel situations.

A German physician who earned his Doctor of Medicine degree in 1779, Samual Hahnemann, was instrumental in introducing homeopathy. Dr. Hahnemann used camphor to prevent and treat cholera and basically is credited as being the discoverer of homeopathy and the use of nosodes in Europe. It has only been in recent times, particularly the last fifty years, that nosodes have been used in the treatment of pets in North America.

Probably the best-known study on the use of homeopathy for animals was undertaken in 1986 by Christopher Day, MRCVS (Member of the Royal College of Veterinary Surgeons) in England. Dr. Day's study involved forty dogs with kennel cough at a boarding kennel. "Of the 40 dogs, 18 had been vaccinated for kennel cough before—all 18 (100%) showed typical symptoms," writes Dr. Day. "Twenty-two of the 40 dogs had not been vaccinated previously—19 (86%) of these developed the disease. The vaccine used were Parainfluenza injectable (16 dogs) and Bordetella intranasal (2 dogs)." Dr. Day further explains, "A nosode was given to all dogs who entered this infected boarding premises thereafter—a dose on entry and twice daily for 3 days. In the ensuing summer months 214 dogs were accepted for board. Of these 214 dogs, 64 were previously vaccinated and 3 of these (4.7%) developed kennel cough. The remaining 150 dogs were not vaccinated and 1 of these dogs (.67%) developed illness."[38]

The results of Dr. Day's use of nosodes shows that they were effective as an alternative to vaccinations. Since then nosodes have been developed and used successfully by holistic vets for almost all animal diseases. Dr. Day has also undertaken studies on the use of nosodes in bovine mastitis and the use of homeopathy in the control of stillborn pigs.

According to Dr. Mehan, "The biggest advantage of nosodes over vaccines is the fact that they are completely safe. There are no risks or side effects whatever. And they can be safely given to puppies and kittens much earlier than vaccines can."[39] Some holistic veterinarians discourage the use of combination nosodes because they believe this confuses the body's immune system. Instead, these vets recommend giving dogs parvo nosodes and distemper nosodes at different times, and giving cats the distemper nosodes separately.

One major stumbling block that exists with using nosodes as a form of immunization is that mainstream veterinarians consider nosodes an unconventional treatment that has not been scientifically proven to be efficacious. One controlled parvovirus nosode study did not adequately protect puppies under challenged conditions. In *Alternative Veterinary Medicine*, Susan Wynn, DVM, writes, "Unfortunately there is no convincing evidence that nosodes do prevent disease. A few studies published in homeopathic journals suggest that nosodes may decrease the severity of active disease and possibly prevent the spread of epidemics, but these studies are not well controlled."[40] Dr. Wynn suggests, "Until well designed studies are completed and thousands of pet owners make a concerted effort to help with potential retrospective studies, nosodes remain an unknown quantity, and I do not recommend using them as a sole strategy for disease prevention."[41]

If you don't want to risk vaccinating your pets, Dr. Wynn suggests titer testing, although titers are not perfect indicators of immunity. Most immunologists agree that we should not place total reliance on titers. They are, however, the best test at the present to indicate a pet's immunity to various diseases.

Debra Tibbitts, DVM, from East Wenatchee, Washington, related an experience that transformed her way thinking on vaccinations and nosodes. At the time she was working for a Saint Bernard breeder whose kennel dogs had parvovirus, at the time unbeknownst to the kennel owner. "The first litter of puppies was affected at 7 weeks of age," explained Dr. Tibbitts. "We consulted the manufacturer of the vaccine we used at the time and a custom-tailored vaccine program was initiated due to each successive litter getting parvo at an earlier age in spite of vaccinating and taking every precaution possible." The mother and her litter got sick with the parvovirus shortly after they had all been vaccinated, and one pup subsequently died. "So it was decided to try using the parvo nosodes on pups beginning at three weeks of age," explained Dr. Tibbitts. "After this was instituted, no cases of parvo occurred in successive litters and no negative side effects were seen."[42]

If you decide to use nosodes for your companion animals, keep in mind that on a purely practical level, most kennels and clinics will not accept nosodes as a form of vaccination. Also, nosodes are not recognized as valid vaccines by international customs officials.

Who Do You Believe?

Ronald D. Schultz, DVM, PhD, and T.R. Phillips, DVM, have spent many years researching the effect that annual vaccinations have on pets. "A practice that was started many years ago that lacks scientific validity or verification is annual revaccination," states Dr. Schultz. "Almost without exception there is no immunologic requirement for annual revaccination. Immunity to viruses persists for years or for the life of the animal."[43]

Don Hamilton, DVM, who practices veterinary homeopathy in New Mexico, agrees with Dr. Schultz. In an article written in 1999 Dr. Hamilton states, "Yearly 'boosters' are unnecessary, and provide no benefit if given [will not increase immunity]. Thus boosters [rabies] are either a legal issue or a manipulation issue inducing clients to come in for examination rather than directly suggesting an examination."[44]

John Fudens, DVM, is a holistic veterinarian practicing in Clearwater, Florida as well as a paralegal who has studied the law behind the rationale for yearly rabies vaccinations. Dr. Fudens claims that nationwide, rabies is nowhere near the problem the veterinarians, media, politicians, and bureaucrats would have us believe.

In an article "The Big-Scam-Rabies Vaccination," published originally in *Tiger Tribe*, Dr. Fudens discusses why annual rabies vaccinations are recommended by law. First, he explains there are two basic forms of law in the United States—constitutional law and common law. He notes that the United States was founded on constitutional law, and that common law is passed by "Administrative agencies/bureaucrats who have been given so-called authority to pass laws." Dr. Fudens explains, "So any and all mandatory rabies vaccination programs are colorable law, in that they have been passed and mandated upon the pet-owning public by certain vested interest groups. Who are these groups? First and foremost are veterinarians, in general, and veterinarian medical organizations. Second, are the local animal control personnel, bureaucrats and politicians. What are their reasons? Greed, power, and control. Both these large powerful interest groups stand to benefit greatly by having rabies mandated by colorable law."[45]

Dr. Fudens also emphasizes that veterinarians receive a large percentage of both their income from vaccines. "Therefore, if veterinarians lobby to have a colorable law passed to give rabies vaccine every year, that enhances their financial picture."[46]

⌣

Before you vaccinate your pet, read all the information you can acquire and obtain the opinions of two or three veterinarians, including holistic veterinarians. Then make your best-educated decision, based on your circumstances and the overall health of your animal companion. No longer can we assume that our veterinarians have all the answers and are up on the latest information. It is the same with our own medical doctors. Now, we must think and act similarly for our animal companions' health as we now do for ourselves.

If you decide to skip the annual vaccination protocol, I still encourage you to consider taking your animal companions for an annual vet visit. Some veterinarians believe that the yearly vaccinations are unnecessary but they still encourage yearly check-ups.

As O'Driscoll so aptly states in *What Vets Don't Tell You About Vaccines*, "No one is chasing you or me to inject us with vaccines every year so why are they chasing our pets?"[47]

EIGHT

Cancer in Animals

Veterinarians have been seeing many more animal companions with cancer than ever before, yet they are not exactly sure why this increase is happening. At present, cancers account for about half the deaths in pets over the age of ten. Some forty years ago, cancer in pets was rarely seen, but today it is common to find someone who has had an animal companion with cancer or at least know someone who has an animal companion suffering from cancer. "It's astounding how many animals under 3 years of age I see with cancer," notes Marty Goldstein, DVM, in his book, *The Nature of Animal Healing*. "It used to be a disease of old animals."[1]

Dr. Goldstein attributes many of the illnesses in pets today to their diet and to over-vaccination. He points to a 1998 survey of disease-related deaths among pets funded by the nonprofit Morris Animal Foundation that found: "Of 720 canine deaths reported, 479 were cancer-caused. The next highest category was heart-related problems (12 percent), followed by kidney (7 percent) and epilepsy (4 percent). Among 469 felines deaths, cancer also ranked highest (32 percent), followed by kidney and urinary disease (23 percent) and heart problems (9 percent)."[2]

I contacted twenty veterinarians throughout the United States to find out if individual veterinarians are finding an increase in cancer within their practices. I asked them if they had noted a rise in cancer rates over the last twenty to thirty years. If so, were certain types of cancers higher in the pet population then others?

Ihor Basko, DVM, operates the All Creatures Great & Small Clinic in Kauai, Hawaii. He has been in practice for more than twenty-five years on this beautiful Hawaiian island. Even he has found a significant rise in cancer rates among the animals brought to his clinics. "The increase is alarming,"[3] replied Dr. Basko when I asked him about increases in cancer, yet he could not give specific causes for this rise in cancer rates. Instead, as a holistic veterinarian, he believes that cancer in animals is a process related to lifestyle, a polluted world, contaminated food and water, and veterinarians vaccinating sick animals.

Lori Tapp, DVM, who has a practice in Ashville, North Carolina responded that she has noticed a rise in cancers since she graduated from veterinary college in the 1980s. Dr. Tapp responded, "I've been out of vet school for about 15 years and it seems to me that cancer has become very much more common in companion animals." Dr. Tapp also indicated that other related diseases are also on the rise. "Autoimmune disease (i.e. Lupus et al), immune-mediated diseases (allergies, FUS, asthma, etc.) and immune-related cancers (lymphoma, mast cell tumors, et al) all seem to be on the rise and they are occurring in younger and younger animals."[4] Dr. Tapp also noted that fibrosarcoma has been definitively linked to vaccines in cats.

Determining the numbers of animal companions with various forms of cancer is difficult. According to Ralph Henderson, DVM, Professor of Surgery and Oncology at Auburn University, College of Veterinary Medicine, "To know the incidence of a disease, both the affected population and the reference population must be qualified. Only a few individuals have tried to establish such programs. These are called 'Cancer Registries.'"[5] Dr. Henderson noted in his communication with me that the only successful Cancer Registry was in Contra Costa County in California in the late 1960s and 1970s.

Cancer in Dogs and Cats

According to the American Veterinary Medical Association (AVMA) some of the common types of cancer in dogs and cats are skin, breast, head and neck, lymphoma, feline leukemia complex, testicles, abdominal tumors, and bone cancers. Most of the cancers that affect humans also affect pets.

With any changes in your dog's or cat's health or personality, your veterinarian should be consulted. Some of the signs to look for are: "Abnormal swellings that persist or continue to grow. Sores that do not heal. Weight loss. Loss of appetite. Bleeding or discharge from any body opening. Offensive odor. Difficulty eating or swallowing. Hesitation to exercise or loss of stamina. Persistent lameness or stiffness. Difficulty breathing, urinating, or defecating."[6]

According to Michael Goldschmidt, DVM, Professor of Pathology at the University of Pennsylvania, various canine breeds are susceptible to particular forms of cancer. Based on an extensive computerized database of canine cases, Dr. Goldschmidt learned that benign mammary tumors were often found in small breeds of dogs such as the Miniature Poodle, Yorkshire Terrier, Chihuahua, and Maltese. "Trichoepithelioma is a benign neoplasm arising from keratinocytes of the hair follicle root sheath, hair matrix, or both."[7] The Basset Hound is the breed prone to this benign form of cancer.

The University of Illinois, College of Veterinary Medicine, also provides some insight into a breed's susceptibility to various forms of cancer. "Breeds with dark pigment in the mouth, such as German shepherds, black cocker spaniels, Scotties, and chows are prone to melanoma in the mouth."[8]

Mast cell tumors (in the connective tissue) are seen most often in short-nose breeds of dogs such as Boxers, Bull Dogs, and Boston Terriers. Large breed dogs such as Newfoundlands, Saints, Irish Wolfhounds, and German Shepherds are predisposed to bone cancers at the ends of long bones. Cocker Spaniels who develop chronic ear infections sometimes develop carcinoma in the cerumin, the wax-producing gland.

Both cats and dogs are prone to skin cancers especially in areas exposed to sunlight, i.e., in cats the pink tip of the nose and eyelid areas and in dogs with a fair complexion, exposure to the underbelly or inside of the back legs. Breeds of dogs that may be affected by skin cancers include Pointers, Bull Terriers, Pit Bulls, and Dalmations. The University of Illinois finds that Siamese cats are more prone to some cancers such as "salivary carcinomas and intestinal carcinomas, at a younger age than other breeds."[9]

If cancer is suspected, the usual procedure is for the veterinarian to do a complete physical work up on the animal. If there is a specific growth, the veterinarian does a needle biopsy. This entails inserting a needle into the growth and taking a few cells to be examined under a microscope. Tumors are assigned into three categories: high, intermediate, and low grades based on the microscopic evaluation. "High-grade tumors tend to be very aggressive, they spread early, and are difficult to treat," explained Kim Cronin, DVM, from the University of Pennsylvania. "Low-grade tumors are exactly the opposite."[10]

Traditional Cancer Treatments

Treatment for cancer in cats and dogs has come a long way since I lost my first Newfoundland to this disease twenty years ago. Diagnosis is easier with 3-D imaging and CT scans that were not then available. Many of the cancer therapies used for humans today can also be used in cancer treatment for animals. The University of California Los Angeles Medical Center (UCLA) opened a $1.5 million cancer treatment center for dogs and cats. No longer will veterinarians from the Los Angeles area have to sneak dogs and cats into hospitals for surreptitious cancer treatments on radiation machines intended for humans.

"There's a huge demand for this type of cancer treatment [radiation] for pets," noted Rodney Withers, a UCLA clinical research professor and head of the medical center's radiation oncology department. We've had a number of patients and staff ask if we could treat animals with our equipment."[11] This is a welcome breakthrough in the treatment of animal companions with cancer.

Chemotherapy is often used in the treatment of animals with cancers. Fortunately, it seldom has the same effect on cats and dogs as it does on humans. For instance, animals usually do not experience hair loss and nausea when undergoing chemotherapy. Dr. Karin Sorenmo, assistant professor of oncology at the University of Pennsylvania Veterinary College, explained, "Chemotherapy is often combined with surgery or radiation therapy to treat high-grade tumors that are likely to metastasize."[12] These drugs are given orally, intravenously, or subcutaneously and are the same drugs used to treat cancer in humans. Dr. Sorenmo pointed out that with some cancers chemotherapy extends the average lymphosarcoma survival time from just two months (untreated) to a year. And 10 percent to 15 percent of these cases never relapse.

New Medical Procedure

Veterinarians at Kansas State University's College of Veterinary Medicine are using a relatively new procedure in feline and canine cancer treatment. Radioactive beads are used when surgery is not an option or if surgery fails to remove a significant portion of the tumor.

According to Ruthanne Chun, DVM, "brachytherapy, the implanting of radioactive beads, is for dogs or cats that have certain tumors that aren't likely to metastasize."[13] Veterinarians implant these beads after surgery. The beads are sutured into the tumor bed. This therapy, according to Dr. Chun, is "much nicer" than conventional forms of therapy due to the fact that animals do not have to go under anesthesia multiple times. The duration of the therapy is vastly truncated as compared to the more conventional or external beam radiation therapy.

In November 2000, *DVM* magazine published an article on a new form of cancer treatment. Although the treatment is not available as yet it is hoped that additional studies will obtain regulatory approval for its use in treating canine soft tissue sarcomas. This treatment involves "a new gene medicine for treatment in cancer in canines." Research findings showed "shrinkage or elimination of several tumors." According to the article, "The therapy is designed to reduce the growth of the primary tumor and inhibit growth of other tumor cells by stimulating a dog's immune response to cancer."[14] It is hoped that this new "gene medicine" can be used as a primary treatment for tumor regression, thereby eliminating surgery.

Nutrition and Cancer

I cannot emphasize enough the importance of nutrition, not only to keep your animal companions healthy and cancer free, but to help them recover from illnesses, and in particular dealing with cancer. The more I research and learn about commercial pet foods versus natural whole foods, I am convinced that there is a very strong connection between inferior diets and poor health of cats and dogs. We cannot expect our animal companions to stay healthy if they live off the dregs and condemned foods of human society. In particular, nutrition plays a major role in caring for animal companions suffering from cancer. Most animals with cancer have a reduced appetite, especially if they have received treatments such as surgery, radiation, or chemotherapy. The oncology department at the University of Pennsylvania advises against pushing food on a patient or coaxing an animal to eat when he or she is feeling or showing overt signs of nausea or discomfort. In addition, veterinarians at the University of Pennsylvania advise, "Pets that gulp or drool at the sight or smell of food, turn their heads away, spit out food when placed in the mouth or bury the food under their bedding should be left alone."[15]

Tube feeding may be an alternative for some animals who have no appetite. Or you might try some creative alternatives to entice your animal companions to eat. Often a dog or cat will accept human food directly from a beloved human who is eating—the food just might look more interesting. Also, make mealtime as comfortable and as stress-free as possible. It helps to divide food into small meals. "The food ingredients that increase palatability for most dogs and cats are moisture, fat, and protein," according to staff at the Oncology Department at the University of Pennsylvania. Adding water to a dry pet food or switching to canned food may improve food acceptance. A pet's tolerance of certain nutrients must be considered when trying new foods. Animals with kidney or liver dysfunction may not tolerate high protein intake. Animals with some types of gastrointestinal disease cannot tolerate large amounts of dietary fat.[16]

With cats especially, I have found that an all-meat baby food will be well tolerated. This is not a diet to offer on a continual basis; however, it does get the cats interested in food. Do not feed your pet baby food any longer then a couple of weeks as it does not provide all the nutrition an animal requires. You might also slightly heat the food because the aroma is likely to entice a cat to eat. Another solution is to pour a little chicken broth or fat over the food.

Alternative Cancer Therapies

Dr. Basko in Hawaii is successful treating many types of disease in pets, including cancer. A holistic veterinarian, Dr. Basko believes, "With chronic diseases, especially degenerative disease, drugs do not make a difference in longevity. Most of vet medicine is intervention medicine...not much on prevention. Most of what vets hold as 'prevention' is vaccinating animals to death."[17]

How does Dr. Basko treat animals with cancer? "My approach to treating cancer includes the use of medicinal mushrooms (shiitake, maitake, reishi, tremella) plus immune system enhancers along with antioxidants, dietary changes, and enjoyable events that the animals like to participate in to boost the immune system."[18] Sometimes he will use chemotherapy or surgery along with the above-listed treatments. Like other holistic veterinarians, Dr. Basko finds that most pet owners go the conventional veterinary route first and lose precious time before they contact a holistic veterinarian.

A growing number of pet owners are turning to alternative cancer therapies to supplement traditional cancer treatments. In some cases, pet owners are foregoing the traditional chemotherapy and radiation, believing these treatments are too harsh and painful for an animal companion with no guarantees. And quite honestly, cancer treatments cost a great deal of money and medical insurance for animal companions is still an anomaly. If you are considering alternative treatments in place of traditional treatment, you will want to contact a holistic veterinarian. If you do not know how to find one, contact the American Holistic Veterinary Medical Association. (See Resources.) Herbs, supplements, and specially designed natural diets for pets with cancer are some of the main alternatives holistic veterinarians use.

In addition, some veterinarians encourage alternative therapies that help alleviate pain and discomfort for an animal with cancer. Some of these are briefly discussed below.

The TTeam and Therapeutic Touch

The Tellington Touch Every Animal Method (TTEAM) was inspired by the original findings of Moshe Feldenkrais, an Israeli engineer and nuclear physicist, who was also very active in sports, soccer, and the martial arts. He used his own body to develop a treatment he called the Feldenkrais Method. He found that simple, nonthreatening, and nonhabitual exercises reprogrammed neural pathways between injured body parts and the brain in humans. The method used by Feldenkrais and his students involved easy movements that gradually evolve into movements of greater range and complexity, such as reaching, standing, lying, and sitting. The method basically works with your agility to regulate and coordinate movement.

Linda Tellington-Jones, a horse trainer and competitive rider, adapted some of the methods Feldenkrais developed for humans and applied them for use with animals. Known for her natural/holistic approach to working with animals, Tellington-Jones first began using this method of treatment on her horses and later applied it to a myriad of other animal species, including cats and dogs. She found that by touching the animal and moving the skin in a single circle that she was able to make an animal more aware of his or her body.

"The TTEAM motion is a circle inscribed on the dog's (or other animal's body)," explains Tellington-Jones. "It is done by placing the fingertips on the body and tracing a clock-face circle from six o'clock around the dial past the starting point to eight o'clock. Practitioners adapt pressure, speed, and size of circle to the particular animal."[19] This awareness leads to an animal's greater self-confidence and enjoyment of physical contact with humans.

With TTEAM Tellington-Jones enfolds touch, movement, body language, and instructional techniques into a form that permits the animal to learn and heal in a painless and anxiety-free environment. Tellington-

Jones asserts that with TTEAM both the human and animal develop a more trusting relationship. Tellington-Jones has written several books on TTEAM and her successes in using this method with animals.

I was very skeptical when I first heard about TTEAM; however, a positive experience using this treatment method melted away my skepticism even though it still seems mysterious. In a problem unrelated to cancer, my Newfoundland, Katie, developed an odd posture. She walked with her head down and back arched. Spinal x-rays and a wide array of tests could not detect the cause. This continued for over two weeks until a friend of mine, Barbara Janelle, an expert on the use of both TTEAM and another alternative therapy, Therapeutic Touch (TT), asked if she could try TTEAM on Katie. (Janelle has also taught Therapeutic Touch for use in humans at the University of Western Ontario, and she has applied her expertise to animals.)

She worked with Katie for just over one hour and I could see no improvement. But to my amazement the next morning Katie was back to her normal gait and posture. Other then the one TTEAM session, Katie received no other treatment, and the condition never reappeared. Janelle, who is a leading North American expert on the use of Therapeutic Touch with both humans and animals, explained in an interview with me, "Therapeutic Touch supports the flow of energy through the field and results in a very fast relaxation response. In addition, it reduces pain, helps wounds heal very quickly, supports the immune system and reduces stress."[20] The difference between the kind of touch used in TTOUCH, and simply petting your dog and cat is that the brain focuses consciously on certain kinds of touching.[21]

According to the Nurse Healers-Profession Associates International, the official organization of Therapeutic Touch, this method was developed by Dolores Krieger, PhD, RN, then a professor at New York University, and Dora Van Gelder Kunz, a natural healer. In the summer of 1972, Krieger and Kunz began teaching their technique to a group of Krieger's graduate student nurses.[22] "I have worked with many animals with cancer and find that Therapeutic Touch can keep them more comfortable, as it does for humans too. TT is very effective in relieving side effects from chemo."[23]

According to Janelle, it is a mistake to look at cancer solely as a physical illness and treat only the physical symptoms. "One of the things that TT does is to support the emotional and spiritual aspects of the receiver, whether animal or human." Janelle used Therapeutic Touch to treat a dog she worked on who was undergoing chemotherapy treatments for lymphoma. She believes that the dog lived about a year longer than predicted and with a good quality of life in part due to the benefits of Therapeutic Touch.

Acupuncture

Acupuncture is another alternative treatment used by some veterinarians. It is used primarily for pain management, not to treat the cancer itself. Robin Downing, DVM, author of an informative book, *Pets Living With Cancer*, writes, "In addition to managing pain, acupuncture may help an animal cancer patient feel better in general and may boost the immune system to better battle the disease. Acupuncture can also help to increase appetite and calorie intake benefits the pet in its fight against cancer."[24]

Gary Tran, DVM, a holistic veterinarian from Louisville, Kentucky, agrees with Dr. Downing and the use of acupuncture in the treatment of cancer. "I have no luck in using acupuncture to treat cancers even though I am one of the first veterinarians certified by the International Veterinary Association way back in the early seventies," stated Dr. Tran.[25] However, Dr. Tran does find acupuncture useful in treating the pain associated with terminal cancer.

Jordan Kocen, DVM, from the South Paws Veterinary Referral Center in Springfield, Virginia states that although acupuncture cannot modify the immune system enough to control the condition, "It can, however, improve the feeling of well being and improve the way the animal feels. Also, if the patient is concurrently arthritic or in a generally weakened state, acupuncture will help."[26]

Herbs

Herbs may complement the drug and radiation treatments your animal companion is undergoing for cancer. However, if you are going to use herbal preparations, be sure to check with your veterinarian because some herbs may interfere with chemotherapy treatments. Some herbs can also be quite toxic if not used under the supervision of an holistic veterinarian trained in herbal remedies. Herbs purported to be anti-cancer substances include: green tea, garlic, ginseng, echinacea, mistletoe, cat's claw, pau d'arco, and essiac.

When Charlie, my Newfoundland, was diagnosed with inoperable cancer of the bladder he was given a short time to live. A friend suggested that I give him essiac tea as it was supposed to have cancer-fighting properties. Essiac comes from herbs such as burdock root, sheep sorrel, and slippery elm bark. I gave Charlie this substance twice a day in his drinking water and although it did not cure the cancer I am sure that it helped prolong his life another five months.

R.M. Clemmons, DVM, PhD, outlines some of the herbs that may be used in the treatment of cancer. Cat's claw comes from the Peruvian rainforest and is used by the indigenous people in Peru to treat cancer and arthritis. "Recent studies indicate that it [cat's claw] contains immune-enhancing substances, including several antioxidant compounds," notes Dr. Clemmons. "These compounds may account for the anti-tumor properties reported for cat's claw. Treatments have been reported to lead to remission of brain and other tumors."[27] Dr. Clemmons also mentions reishi and maitake mushrooms, which stimulate the patient's immune system. Pau d'arco has been reported to induce strong biological activity to cancer. Pau d'arco comes from the bark of trees that grow in Brazil, Argentina, and other tropical regions.

Other dietary supplements mentioned include milk thistle, which helps protect the liver from toxic damage and shark cartilage that is reported to have anti-angiogenic properties. In Chapter Eleven: Healthy Recipes, I have included a homemade diet recipe by Dr. Clemmons that supplies all the nutrients required for dogs with cancer.

Chiropractic

In her book, *Why Is Cancer Killing Our Pets?* Deborah Straw suggests that chiropractic therapy may also be a method of providing pain relief for pets suffering from cancer. "Chiropractic care is performed on dogs, cats, and horses, generally to provide pain relief. This treatment can offer a drug free addition to an animal's total health care regimen."[28] In her comprehensive book, Straw outlines the many different aspects of cancer from how this disease affects dogs and cats as well as their owners, to accepting the loss of your pet. Shaw also provides a list of counseling services for those who will lose or have lost a pet due to cancer.

Treating cancer in animal companions can be a costly venture, whether choosing a traditional medical route or using holistic approaches. An article in the *Washington Post* describes a cat owner whose eight-year old cat had developed a tumor as a result of vaccinations. The woman who owned the cat took a night-time job to pay the pet's veterinary bills. Another woman, owned by a Dachshund, "finished the last of her radiation treatments for a nasal tumor this month, at a cost of $5,000."[29]

With new technology many of the cancers that are killing our animal companions can now be put into remission. Tumors can be removed completely, adding years to the life of our companion animals. There is no doubt that diet and over-vaccination can play a major role in the susceptibility of cats and dogs to cancer. Also, genetics and environment can be contributing factors. In many ways, our animal companions are in the same boat as us humans when dealing with cancer—there are many unknowns and it is not always clear what method is the best. What makes it especially difficult with our animal companions is that they can't just state in a plain human language how they are feeling and what they'd like us to do!

Ultimately, you have to consider what the quality of life will be for your dog or cat, whether it is undergoing surgery, chemotherapy, or radiation. Some cancer drugs can have side effects such as vomiting, lack of appetite, and diarrhea, to name a few, and there are no guarantees of a cure. You also have to be honest with yourself and admit what you can and can't do— whether financially or emotionally—for an animal companion with cancer. Each situation is different. Given the difficult choices and emotional stress, perhaps the most important thing to remember is to go easy on yourself no matter what you decide. I believe your animal companion will continue to love you and in his or her own "animal way" will understand your choices.

NINE

Other Health Concerns

In the course of my research on commercial pet food, I have found several other pet-related concerns that are important to mention. These are topics that have jumped out like red flags, begging for more attention. Perhaps with added information, pet owners will be more willing to consider alternatives that do not carry heavy risks or side effects.

There has been a considerable increase in the use of drugs to treat animal companions for a variety of ailments. It is almost as if human beings have passed on to their animal companions their penchant for quick fixes with a pill or the latest drug. Even Prozac is prescribed for dogs who may have a "nervous disorder" or "appear to be depressed." I question if many of our ailments, both human and animal, aren't primarily related to our diets and our lifestyles.

Rimadyl

One drug that is increasingly used for dogs, and in my opinion, controversial, is Rimadyl. Ads on television and in magazines extol the virtues of Rimadyl, the trade name for carprofen. This is a drug designed to ease the pains of arthritis in older animals. However, since the introduction of Rimadyl in 1996 this drug has invoked much debate. Some veterinarians and pet owners are thrilled with the results obtained with Rimadyl, but others have seen dogs suffer and die as a result of taking this drug.

Unquestionably, osteoarthritis is a progressive, degenerative condition affecting an estimated 20 percent of all adult dogs. Some of the signs of osteoarthritis in dogs include decreased activity, stiffness, limping, difficulty in getting up from a resting position, reluctance to walk, run, climb stairs, jump, or play. Also, dogs may display aggressive or withdrawn behavior that is not typical for that particular dog's personality, and may be caused by overall soreness, especially when touched.

Pet owners are anxious to find relief for their aging animal companions, and Rimadyl looks as if it is the answer to the painful effects of osteoarthritis. For some, this is a miracle drug that has added pain-free years to the life of their dogs. For others, this is the drug that created serious side effects, and sometimes death.

Rimadyl is a non-steroidal, anti-inflammatory drug (NSAID) in the family of Tylenol and ibuprofen, developed by Pfizer, the second-largest manufacturer of drugs for animals. Originally, Rimadyl was developed for human use; however, its success came in veterinary medicine. *Wall Street Journal* correspondent, Chris Adams, reports in an article on Rimadyl, "Approved for human use in the U.S. but not marketed that way, an arthritis medicine called Rimadyl languished for nearly 10 years in developmental limbo, then emerged in a surprising new form: Instead of a human drug, it was now a drug for arthritic dogs, and became a hit."[1] In turn, Rimadyl has become a financial success for Pfizer as well. According to Michael Meyer of *Newsweek* in 1998, "Pfizer spent $21 million advertising Rimadyl, an arthritis drug introduced in 1996 that brings in more than $100 million in yearly sales."[2]

The Center for Veterinary Medicine (CVM) approved Rimadyl for use in pets in October 1996 after CVM determined a comprehensive review had been completed testing the product's safety and efficacy. Pfizer conducted the various trials on Rimadyl. The *Wall Street Journal* reports that Pfizer tested about five hundred dogs for possible side effects from Rimadyl. "Some dogs showed unusual liver function readings and one young beagle on a high dose died, but for the most part, the FDA and Pfizer didn't find side effects alarming."[3] Before long, Rimadyl became the most recommended canine arthritis pain medication. By 1999 Pfizer declared that veterinarians had prescribed Rimadyl for more than one million arthritic dogs in more than twenty-five thousand veterinary practices across the United States.

However, in late 1999 the CVM posted a bulletin, "Update on Rimadyl," that indicated adverse effects. "In spite of the high standards for safety and effectiveness that exist for FDA approval, not everything is known about a drug when it is first marketed," the bulletin explains. "Due to the limited number of animals and controlled nature of pre-marketing clinical trials, only the most common adverse effects will be observed. Uncommon effects or problems may not be discovered until after the drug has been widely used."[4]

In the same bulletin, the CVM states that in 1998, 39 percent or 3,626 of their Adverse Drug Experience (ADE) complaints from veterinarians and pet owners involved Rimadyl. However, the CVM went on to diffuse the growing evidence that there are serious side effects directly related to Rimadyl. "For any one ADE report, there is no absolute certainty that the suspected drug caused the effects," the CVM report states. "The adverse effects in these reports are consistent with those expected for NSAIDs. They typically involve the gastrointestinal system, renal/urinary system, hematopoietic (blood) system, neurological system, and liver. Approximately 13% of the 1998 Rimadyl ADE reports for dogs involved death of dog, either on their own or by means of euthanasia."[5]

Russell Swift, DVM, a holistic veterinarian, states in his article, "Rimadyl: Wolf In Sheep's Clothing," that after numerous complaints, Pfizer had to revise the insert used in all packages of Rimadyl. According to Dr. Swift, the insert now reads, "Rimadyl, like other drugs of its class, is not free from adverse reactions. Owners should be advised of the potential for adverse reactions and be informed of the clinical signs associated with drug intolerance." The insert goes on to state, "Serious adverse reactions associated with this drug class can occur without warning and in rare situations result in death."[6] Dr. Swift notes that it is important to know "that all NSAIDs actually damage joint cartilage. The result is a worsening of joint function and increased pain, which requires more drugs to control."[7]

The Senior Dog Project, a website (see Resources) developed in 1997 to inform people of health-related problems in senior dogs, advises that before any dog is put on Rimadyl, the dog should have a complete physical, including liver and kidney function tests. Once a dog starts taking Rimadyl, he or she should be closely monitored for side effects. "Carprofen, [Rimadyl] is not recommended for animals with known bleeding disorders and should not be used if a dog has a pre-existing liver disease, inflammatory bowel disease, or a known tendency towards gastrointestinal ulceration," states a warning posted on the website.[8]

Some of the adverse side effects of Rimadyl include loss of appetite, refusal to drink, unusual pattern of urination, blood in the urine, sweet-smelling urine, an overabundance of urine, urine accidents in the house, vomiting, diarrhea, black tarry stools, flecks of blood in the vomit, lethargy, drowsiness, hyperactivity, restlessness, aggressiveness, staggering, stumbling, weakness or partial paralysis, full paralysis, seizures, dizziness, loss of balance, and jaundice (yellowing of the skin, mucus membranes and whites of eyes).[9]

In October 1999, a class-action suit was filed against Pfizer by a pet owner, Jean Townsend of South Carolina. Her Labrador Retriever, George, was put on Rimadyl in September 1997. Townsend contends that Pfizer knew of the side effects of this drug yet did little to communicate them to pet owners. Both Pfizer and the CVM were aware that there might be some side effects when this drug was first marketed but both groups felt the side effects were insignificant when compared to the pain relief Rimadyl provided. Within a week of George being put on Rimadyl, he developed health problems, including loss of appetite, vomiting, diarrhea, and bloody stools. George was suffering to the point that he had to be euthanized. The case is still pending in the courts.

The Senior Dog Project website continues to post updates on this law suit. When I spoke with Jean Townsend, she told me, "The U.S. court system takes a long, long time so we just have to be patient."[10] Because the case is still pending, Townsend cannot discuss details of the court action. She does believe it was a lot of the advertising hype done by Pfizer's ad agency, Colle & McVoy, which she saw on television that convinced her to put her animal companion, George, on this product in order to relieve his arthritis.

Jean Townsend referred me to an interesting article written by Katharine Delahaye Paine, CEO of a worldwide communication research company. Paine discusses the various methods that advertising companies use to elicit people to purchase a client's product. In the case of Rimadyl, the Colle & McVoy ad agency had uncovered some interesting research that revealed women are the most likely to take their arthritic dogs to the vet to be euthanized. "Based on this research, Colle & McVoy decided to directly target women pet owners, and used a leaping golden retriever as their brand image," alleges Paine. "That leaping dog made its way into two web sites and countless pet shows, television and print ads. Stories of rejuvenated dogs were turned into a calendar, and veterinarians were exposed to leaping dog images at industry trade shows and in trade journals. And the net impact? They sold out of the product a month after launch."[11] Based on the slick advertising, Townsend believed Rimadyl could help George. I wonder how many other pet owners based their decision about Rimadyl on the advertising?

Alternatives to Rimadyl

There are alternatives to help pet owners avoid the use of controversial drugs such as Rimadyl. Ideally, it is best to take precautionary measures before your dog is stricken with a debilitating disease such as arthritis. For starters, weight and exercise are important factors in the management of arthritis. Many senior dogs do not get enough exercise and are inclined to put on weight. Don't let your pet get to the point that he or she has to be put on a diet.

If your dog is inclined to put on weight, here are a few suggestions you might try. If you give your dog treats, try nutritious foods such as carrots or celery sticks, pieces of apple, or low-fat crackers. Definitely avoid commercial pet foods, not only are these lacking in healthy whole-food ingredients, they are usually laced with fat and grease in order to be more tantalizing to your pet. If you can, provide a homemade diet, but cut back on the carbohydrates and add more vegetables and fruits. Use low-fat yogurt and cottage cheese.

Donald R. Strombeck, DVM, and author of *Home Prepared Dog and Cat Diets*, stresses that obese animals should have a complete medical checkup before any weight control management is begun. Although pet owners attempt to control the diet of their older pets, many animals will still put on weight due to a lack of exercise or other health problems. It is advised by most veterinarians, both allopathic and holistic, that your pet have a yearly medical examination.

Joe Bodewes and Holly Frisby, veterinarians with the Pet Education website, list exercise as the next step, after diet, for helping dogs who suffer from arthritis. "What we are trying to accomplish here is to restrict the amount of exercising yet still maintain adequate movement to increase or maintain muscle strength," according to Drs. Bodewes and Frisby.[12] Swimming is an excellent form of exercise for arthritic dogs but it is advised that you avoid strenuous exercise that involves jumping, which can be extremely hard on a dog's joints. Try and maintain a daily routine of exercise rather then just exercising on weekends. Weekend exercise alone can leave your dog sore for the rest of the week and reluctant to move at all.

Drs. Bodewes and Frisby also mention that it helps to keep the joints warm and it might be a good idea to put a sweater on your dog if you live in a cold climate, or keep your home a little warmer. They also recommend: "Provide a firm, orthopedic foam bed. Place the bed in a warm spot away from drafts. Next to a heat register is best."[13]

The Senior Dog Project website describes an alternative for arthritis involving a twelve-year-old German Shepherd, Lilah, who started limping after exercise when the weather was cold. Lilah receives 750 mg/day dose of glucosamine and chondroitin, which seems to work very well. Glucosamine is derived from the shells of crustaceans. Chondroitin is obtained from the tracheal rings of slaughtered cattle, which is the only known source of this material. Glucosamine is a major component of cartilage and chrondroitin enhances the formation of cartilage and inhibits enzymes in the joint, which tend to break down cartilage.

In another case, Max, a Shepherd/Rottweiler mix was on Rimadyl for three months. During the last month he was on Rimadyl the owner also gave her dog a product called Osteo Bi-Flex, which contains glucosamine and chondroitin. Max has been on this supplement for four months now without Rimadyl. He seems to be doing as well, if not better, then when he was on Rimadyl.

Regarding the effectiveness of these two products, Wendell Belfield, DVM, states, "In recent years, since the advent of glucosamine and con-droitin, the tendency in veterinary medicine, has been to treat the existing condition. These two natural substances have eliminated, to some extent, the administration of steroids, which had multiple adverse side effects."[14] Dr. Belfield's opinion is that those patients who don't respond to this therapy it is likely the condition will persist throughout their lives.

Another alternative to Rimadyl is acupuncture for arthritis. Many holistic veterinarians claim they have seen good results for arthritic dogs. Martin Goldstein, DVM, finds that a particular form of acupuncture and supplements works better for many of the animals he treats. In his book, *The Nature of Animal Healing*, Dr. Goldstein notes, "Traditional acupuncture is almost always helpful. Because it's more effective, I prefer the procedure called aquapuncture. I inject the Smith Ridge 'cocktail' of B12 and adrenal cortex, and also homeopathic Zeel or Traumeel, at the acupuncture points relevant to the patient's condition. In minutes, a pet's pain can ease, and the effects can last several weeks."[15] Both Zeel and Traumeel are classified as homeopathic combination remedies.

If your veterinarian suggests that you put your dog on Rimadyl, be sure to ask questions. Many vets are unaware of the dangerous side effects of Rimadyl. Weigh the benefits against the risks, and take your individual animal companion's health concerns into serious consideration. If you and your veterinarian feel there are no alternatives, then tell your vet that you want the lowest dosage that can be used to obtain relief. To avoid gastric upset that occurs in some dogs, be sure that you give your animal companion Rimadyl with food. As I mentioned at the beginning of this chapter, some dogs do well on this drug but others can incur serious health problems. Use Rimadyl cautiously.

Bloat

Bloat or its scientific term, gastric dilation volvulus (GDV), basically means that an animal's stomach distends with air, twists, and cuts off blood flow to the point that the animal goes into shock and may die.

Bloat occurs primarily in large, deep-chested dogs and seldom in smaller breeds. Great Danes, Irish Setters, Newfoundlands, St. Bernards, Irish Wolfhounds, Collies, and Dobermans are some of the breeds that are prone to bloat. Incidents of bloat in dogs have increased over the years based on the number of dogs with bloat admitted to veterinary teaching hospitals in the United States. According to a report by Purdue University, the dramatic increase is about 1,500 percent, from 0.036 percent to 0.57 percent of all dogs admitted between 1964 and 1994. As for cats, bloat is far less common, but it does occur.

Bloat can be a deadly situation, and one that needs veterinarian attention immediately. The signs of bloat and treatments for this situation are well defined. Bloat happens in three stages:

PHASE 1 SYMPTOMS: Pacing, restlessness, panting and salivating. Unproductive attempts to vomit (every 10 to 20 minutes). Abdomen exhibits fullness and begins to enlarge.

ACTION: Call veterinarian to advise him or her that your dog has bloat, and you are on the way.

PHASE 2 SYMPTOMS: Very restless, whining, panting continuously, heavy salivating. Unproductive attempts to vomit (every 2 or 3 minutes). Dark red gums. High heart rate (80 to 100 BPM). Abdomen is enlarged and tight, emits hollow sound when thumped.

ACTION: Apply first aid if veterinarian care is more than 10 minutes away. First aid should consist of having bloat kit on hand and previous instruction from a veterinarian on how to use the kit. This involves passing a tube through the dog's mouth into the stomach. Normally it takes two people to undertake this procedure. This type of first aid should be learned, prior to any bloat symptoms by anyone owning a breed that is prone to bloat. A "bloat kit" contains instructions, rolls of tape, stomach tube, needles, KY Jelly and a gas absorbent product such as Digel, or Gas Ease. Some owners keep a bloat kit on hand and have become adept, under veterinary guidance, at using this procedure in an emergency

PHASE 3 SYMPTOMS: Gums are white or blue. Dog unable to stand or has a spread-legged, shaky stance. Abdomen is very enlarged. Extremely high heart rate (100 BPM or greater) and weak pulse.

ACTION: Apply first aid immediately, Death is imminent! As described above, use the instructions provided with a bloat kit. Get the dog to a veterinarian immediately, even while applying first aid, if possible.

In her article, "Bloat in Review," Jocelynn Jacobs-Knoll, DVM, describes a veterinarian's diagnosis and treatment of bloat. First, the veterinarian takes an x-ray to confirm the condition. Then, with or without sedation, the veterinarian may place a tube down the dog's esophagus to the stomach. If the stomach is not twisted so far as to cut off the opening to the stomach, the tube can be passed. However, if the torsion is significant, tubing may not be possible. If the tube is passed, the veterinarian uses suction through the tube to extract material, air, fluid, etcetera from the stomach.

Once the stomach is deflated it will return to its normal position. Dr. Jacobs-Knoll explains, "Surgery can also be performed to remove air and material from the stomach and replace it in its normal position. A tacking procedure then can be done to attach the outer wall of the stomach to the inner wall of the abdomen so torsion cannot take place again at a later date."[16]

Reasons for Bloat

Over the years, there have been many explanations as to why bloat [GDV] occurs, but none are conclusive at this time. Several veterinarians at Purdue University have undertaken an extensive study of GDV. This study has been overseen by a husband/wife team, Larry Glickman, DVM, MS, and Nita Glickman, Masters Degree in Public Health (MPH). They hope to determine what are the predisposing factors of GDV, any precipitating factors, the breeds most likely to develop GDV, and ways to prevent GDV.

There are 1,989 dogs enrolled in this study, and the owners of these dogs have completed a thorough questionnaire on each dog's health history as well as participating in ongoing current status reports. "The dogs in this study had all been recruited for a case-control study of bloat risk factors. Those who agreed to participate were contacted again every few months to find out if the dog had bloated again, and if the dog was still alive."[17] This study ended in March 1999 and it is expected to take several years for the complete results to be published. However, initial findings point to some interesting factors.

When the Purdue study began in 1994 it was thought that overeating or the type of food the dogs were eating contributed to bloat. The Purdue study found that the ingestion of dry food, or dry or moistened food, really did not increase the risk of bloat. Instead, what they found to be more problematic were dietary factors such as fast eating, fewer meals per day, and fewer snacks between meals.

To the best of my knowledge, a homemade cooked diet or the raw meat diet were not taken into consideration in the Purdue study. I've checked resources in an attempt to ascertain if there had been problems with dogs being fed a home-cooked diet but have found none. In a paper for the *Journal of the American Animal Hospital Association*, Dr. Glickman reports, "Predisposing factors that decreased the risk of GDV significantly were a happy temperament and inclusion of table foods in a usual diet consisting primarily of dry dog food."[18]

The Purdue study found that in 59.3 percent of the cases of bloat that the time of bloat onset was between 6 pm and midnight.[19] Other precipitating factors such as stressful events, feeding times, and a bigger meal then usual seemed to add to problems with bloat. However, exactly why bloat continues to plague animal companions is still unknown. Veterinary schools, veterinarians, and scientists have looked at all areas, including diet, breed, chest size, exercise, stress, temperament, heredity, and even the fact that bloat may be of an infectious nature.

As a precaution against bloat, Martin Goldstein, DVM, recommends a natural diet for dogs, free of kibble. In addition, he believes that a sedentary lifestyle for dogs can contribute to bloat. Dr. Goldstein also considers over-vaccination as a possible cause for bloat, although there are no scientific grounds for this assertion. In his book, he notes some interesting findings by a woman who breeds Standard Poodles. This breeder vaccinated "one third of her dogs with the standard regimen of combination vaccines, one third with vaccines on an individual basis, and one third with no vaccines. The incidents of gastric bloat correlated exactly as she suspected it would; the combination group suffered the highest incidents of bloat, while the non-vaccinated dogs remained bloat free."[20]

Pneumonyssoides caninum infection (nasal mites) has also been considered a causative agent in bloat. A prospective one-year necropsy study was undertaken by W.P. Bendal, DVM, of the Norwegian College of Veterinary Medicine. He found that "out of 250 dogs, 17 were GDV cases and of these, 35% had concurrent nasal mite infection compared to 5% of the control population." Dr. Bendal concludes, "Nasal mite infection was found to be the most important risk factor for GDV in this study with an odds ratio and confidence interval of 27.6 (4.8-157.5)."[21] Some researchers have also speculated that bacteria in dry dog food are the culprits for bloat, but this has not really been investigated. However, until this is determined, this is one more reason to avoid commercial pet foods.

Kathy Hutton, DVM, suggests feeding a dog two or three meals daily, especially for larger breeds prone to bloat. Also, pet owners should discourage their dogs from rapid eating by giving the dog only small amounts of food at a time instead of filling the bowl all at once. Dr. Hutton advises waiting at least two hours after a meal before a dog exercises.[22] Another suggestion for dogs prone to bloat is to limit water consumption for at least half an hour after meals. Keep in mind that any dietary changes should be made over a period of time, never suddenly.

Fortunately, in all the years I have owned dog breeds that are susceptible to bloat, I have never had a problem. When I got my first Newfoundland twenty-five years ago, our veterinarian advised us to feed her two, preferable three meals a day. Since then, I followed this simple practice with all my dogs. Although I have never had cats experience bloat they also are fed three times per day.

Fleas, Ticks, and Chemicals

Rare is the pet owner who has not had to contend with fleas infesting their animal companions and their homes. At one point in my life, I had three large dogs and eight cats infested with these tiny creatures. I chose to treat them with a flea powder purchased from a pet supply store. After two applications, a week apart, the dogs seemed to have less fleas. The cats were a different story. Five of the seven Siamese had severe reactions to the point that three weeks later my beloved cat, Whiskers, died. I had used a flea powder product made specifically for cats and it contained rotenone and dichlorvos. I later learned that dichlorvos is an organophosphate that can cause severe reactions in cats.

When I applied the flea powder for cats, I made sure to rub it into the cats' fur thoroughly. Of course the cats cleaned themselves and ingested this dangerous substance. The veterinarian suspected that because Whispers was fifteen, he had a more severe reaction then did the other cats. I have not used a flea product on any of my pets since. Perhaps because of the diet I feed my cats and dogs, and because I brush and comb them often, none have contracted fleas for more than twelve years.

Many flea products advise the person applying the product not to breathe the powder and to wash their hands after application. And for good reason. These products contain dangerous chemicals that can cause health problems. We are subjecting our pets to these same substances, oftentimes applying the powders and sprays to the neck and head area where our pets cannot help but breathe the chemicals. Cats and dogs also lick themselves and ingest these chemicals.

People working with animal companions, such as groomers, pet store employees, and veterinary assistants often suffer various illnesses after exposure to flea preparations. *The Morbidity and Mortality Weekly Report*, a publication that deals with the occupational hazards of various substances, reported on some of the problems workers experience when exposed to flea control products. For example, a pet groomer treating a dog for fleas and using a tub of water containing concentrated phosmet solution, developed "skin flushing and irritation, shortness of breath, chest pains, accelerated heart rate and respiration, abdominal cramping, and nausea."[23] Another case involved a pet store employee who accidentally sprayed her face with a pyrethrin/piperonyl butoxide solution while spraying into a flea-infested cat house. "Despite immediately flushing her eyes with water, she developed eye irritation with reddened conjunctive and a burning sensation. Mild, diffuse wheezing was noted on examination."[24]

If these flea products cause such problems with humans, what are they doing to cats and dogs? The Cancer Prevention Coalition (CPC), which informs the public about preventable exposures to carcinogens, lists many brand-name products as containing either carcinogens or neurotoxins, or both. "These products include certain flea collars by Longlife, Hartz, Pet Agree, Sergeant's, and Zodiac. In addition, several of these products may have adverse reproductive effects."[25]

In my research, I was shocked to find flea collars for sale containing Dursban. This is a powerful pesticide in the organophosphate family. Produced by Dow Chemical, Dursban has been around for more then thirty-five years. It is used to kill insects in gardens, homes, and on pets. In a preliminary review of this product in 1999, the Environmental Protection Agency (EPA) found that children were at the highest risk when exposed to Dursban. The National Resources Defense Council published a paper on Dursban and the hazards of this substance. "Toxicity studies find that even low-dose exposures to Dursban during pregnancy or just after birth may decrease the manufacture of DNA and reduce the number of cells in certain parts of the brain. Combined with rodent studies of other organophosphates, the data suggest that low-level exposures to Dursban early in life may adversely affect the function of the nervous system later in live, with possible links to changes in normal learning and behavior."[26]

In June 2000 the EPA planned to limit the use of Dursban for home and agriculture, and eventually phase out its use. Flea collars containing Dursban will not have to be off the shelves until December 31, 2001. If this product has such detrimental effects on children who are exposed to it through lawn spraying or because it has been sprayed on some fruits and vegetables, what about the animals wearing this toxic substance around their neck every day for months? Avoid Dursban at all costs.

Many of the over-the-counter flea products contain pyrethrins, which are natural extracts from the flowers of the chrysanthemum plant and are usually considered safe for dogs and cats. However, some animals, especially cats, may experience a reaction, including salivating, tremors, vomiting, and possible seizures.

Some flea and tick products contain permethrin, a human-made form of the naturally occurring pyethrin. Jill Richardson, DVM, from the ASPCA National Animal Poison Control Center, suggests, "Never use flea control products that contain permethrin on your cats, unless they are specifically labeled for use on cats. There are some products that are labeled for use on cats that contain small concentrations of permethrin, usually less than 0.1%."[27] Some people feel that they can apply the same flea and tick products to cats as they do to dogs but this is not the case. Many flea and tick preparations, deemed safe for dogs, can be deadly to cats. Most products containing permethrin that are available over the counter, are for use on dogs only.

When using sprays, shampoos, or mousse for treatment and prevention of fleas and ticks on your feline, avoid the ears and eyes because some of the ingredients can cause irritation. Make sure that you use the product as directed, and be sure that your cats do not lick their coats until the solution is completely dry. If your cat experiences any unusual behavior, or becomes weak or lethargic, seek veterinary assistance. If left untreated, the cat's reaction could be fatal.

Some of the products purchased at veterinary clinics contain the active ingredients Imidacloprid (Advantage) and Fipronil (Frontline), which kill adult fleas but have no effect on ticks. Both Imidacloprid and Fipronil are topical preparations, and are a monthly insecticide. Holly Frisby, DVM, explains how these products work: "The drug collects in the hair follicles from which it is slowly released."[28] As with most products, animals can have reactions to these products.

Lufenuron is the ingredient in a product called Program to be administered orally once a month. This product is not for dogs who have flea-bite allergies. Dara Johns, DVM, who writes a column for the *Northwest Florida Daily News*, lives in an area where fleas can be a serious problem nearly all year. Her opinion of Program: "It does not kill adult fleas, but when the female fleas take blood meal from dogs that are taking Program, their eggs will not develop properly. It breaks the life cycle at the egg stage, so if you have a lot of fleas, you will need to use another product to kill adults."[29]

As of January 2001 Revolution is the latest in flea and tick prevention. This product incorporates ingredients that also act on ear mites and give a month of heartworm prevention. The chemical ingredient is selamectin, which is in the class of chemicals known as avertmectins, and a derivative of dormectin.[30] Revolution is also a topical product that is supposed to kill fleas and prevent eggs from hatching for one month. Ross Becker, who wrote the initial article on Revolution for *Good Dog! Magazine*, posted an update in April 2000: "We have received some initial reports of two or three dogs dying after use of Revolution. Sage, for example, had a history of bruising, and died of cardiovascular collapse resulting from hemorrhage. This occurred following the use of Revolution. No other anticoagulatory toxins showed up in her autopsy. We are following these stories and will report when there is more information available."[31]

Ticks are blood-sucking parasites that can attach themselves to both animals and humans. The United States and Canada have about two hundred tick species. Dixie Farley from the U.S. Food and Drug Administration (FDA) found that "adult females [ticks] of some species lay about 100 eggs at a time. Others lay 3,000 to 6,000 eggs each time."[32] Ticks feed on blood by biting into the skin of animals. This can result in transmitting numerous diseases that can be dangerous if not deadly.

Lyme disease is one such disease spread by ticks. Some of the signs of Lyme disease in humans include flu-like symptoms, dizziness, and arthritic-like symptoms. In dogs, Lyme disease symptoms include lethargy, joint pain, and sudden lameness. In addition to Lyme disease, ticks can cause Rocky Mountain spotted fever, tularema, babesiosis, and tickborne relapsing fever in both pets and humans.

Moist conditions can be a breeding ground for ticks. If possible, avoid thickly wooded areas when taking your dogs for a walk. When you come home from your walk, examine your dogs thoroughly for ticks. Long-haired dogs obviously are at a higher risk of contracting diseases from ticks.

If you find ticks, Jeff Feinman, DVM, suggests the following course of action: "If only a few ticks are present on an animal, they may be plucked off individually. Tweezers should be used to remove the ticks as ticks may carry organisms infectious to people. To remove a tick, grab the head firmly while gently depressing the skin around the tick. Pull straight out without twisting. After removing a tick swab the area well with peroxide or alcohol. A red raised area is normal if the tick was embedded, and does not mean that your pet will get Lyme disease."[33] If you are unable to remove the head along with the body of the tick, Dr. Feinman advises that your pet will eventually eliminate it as it would any other foreign material. If the area appears to be infected seek veterinary attention.

In June 1992, the United States Department of Agriculture (USDA) licensed a vaccine to prevent Lyme disease in dogs. In most cases, immunity lasts for at least five or six months. The vaccination recommendations are for dogs most likely to be exposed to ticks. For dogs in apartments, who seldom if ever get outside, or who reside in regions where Lyme disease isn't prevalent, this vaccination is not necessary. Your veterinarian or a local health official could advise if the incidents of Lyme disease are high in the area where you live.

Commercial flea and tick preparations are available but be sure and read the labels and use only as directed. Before using any of these products on your pets, acquire all the information available so you can make an informed decision. Also consider using one of the safer alternatives described in the following section.

Safe Alternatives for Flea and Tick Problems

Instead of the conventional chemical-laden flea and tick collars for cats and dogs, there are flea collars that contain only all-natural, non-toxic repellents. These natural flea and tick collars usually contain herbs such as flea bane, myrrh, eucalyptus, cedarwood, rosemary, lavender, geranium, red cedar, Asian mint, and bay. Some companies also produce flea and tick sprays. These contain virtually the same herbs mixed in an oil and can be applied to the dog's coat before and after visiting a tick-infested area. These collars and sprays do not kill the ticks and fleas but the scent repels them. Many of these collars can be purchased at pet stores or health-product stores.

Although my animal companions have not had fleas for many years, one solution that worked well for me was to slice about six lemons and pour boiling water over the lemons. Let the water stand overnight, then strain the liquid into a spray bottle. Start at the back of the dog and work toward the neck, making sure every inch of the dog or cat is covered with the lemon-water spray.

Cats are not as cooperative and don't take kindly to being sprayed. You might try dabbing the solution on your cat with a cotton ball. Spray the bedding with this solution as it will repel and kill fleas. Check the pet and bedding every few days to make sure that all fleas are killed and eggs have not hatched. Combing your cat or dog daily with a fine-tooth comb also works very well in eliminating fleas as well as being pleasurable for most cats. Be sure to invest in a quality steel flea comb to successfully rid your cat of fleas. Make sure you have a bucket of soapy water handy to drown the fleas as you comb them from your pet.

To remove fleas in the house the best advice is to vacuum thoroughly, including furniture and baseboards. Mothballs can be put in the vacuum cleaner bag and the camphor and naphthalene in the mothballs will kill fleas or flea eggs. (Be careful that your animals do not ingest the mothballs.) If you are bothered by the odor of mothballs discard the vacuum cleaner bags as soon as you are finished. Wash all pet bedding frequently. Another recommendation is to use cedar chips in and around the pet's bed because fleas cannot tolerate the cedar chip scent. Many years ago when my pets had fleas I sprinkled and rubbed plain table salt into the carpet, left it for a day or so, and then vacuumed. After using this treatment twice in the span of two weeks, I had no further flea problems.

A company called Flea Busters uses a borate powder, which is a salt and boric acid compound. Borate powder is purportedly harmless to pets and humans. The borate powder is put on the carpet and left for a few days then vacuumed. Basically, the product dehydrates and kills fleas and flea larvae. If your dog goes outside and picks up more fleas and brings them in the house, the borate powder will take care of that as well. People who have used this service find that it is very effective and lasts for a year or more. In addition, this product is safe for animals and children, and contains no harmful chemicals. Flea Busters has locations in the United States, Europe, and New Zealand and can be found in the Yellow Pages under "Pest Contro."

A laundry product which, according to some, works extremely well in killing fleas and eggs in carpets is 20 Mule Team Borax. Comprised of minerals this substance can be sprinkled on carpets and furniture and then vacuumed up in twenty-four hours.

In his book, *Natural Remedies for Dogs*, Martin Zucker mentions a safe alternative for flea control recommended by Roger DeHaan, DVM. Dr. DeHaan suggests using the following mixture, which is an antiseptic shampoo that kills fleas and soothes irritated skin:

> "Add 10 drops of tea tree oil and 1 tablespoon of aloe vera into an 8 ounce bottle of your regular pet shampoo. Then, separately, add 1 tablespoon of apple cider vinegar to 1 pint of water. Shampoo the animal as normal and let the shampoo stand for six to ten minutes. Rinse off well. Then rinse with the apple cider-spiked water."[34]

There are various methods that can be used to repel or kill these insects but before using any commercial product on your pet or to spray your home, be sure you are aware of all the hazards these products may pose. Although natural approaches may take longer to work, and take more of your time, in the long run they may well be worth it for the long-term health of your animal companions and yourself.

Household Cleaning Products

The dangers of cleaning products must also be considered by pet owners. If cats or dogs walk or roll in a cleaning substance and then lick themselves, they will ingest any toxic substances that may be in that cleaning product. For instance, if you use a cleaning product on your kitchen floor, and your cats or dogs walk across the floor, this product could make them sick.

One of the substances used in cleaning products is coal tar found in phenolic compounds. According to the Feline Advisory Bureau Information Sheet, "Many derivatives of the phenols are available, probably the best known being 'TCP' (2,4,6-Trichlorophenol)."[35] These coal tar substances can be found in such cleaning products as Lysol and Stericol, to name only two. In addition, be careful not to use a shampoo on your animal companions that is not specifically designed for them. Some shampoos that humans use contain tar derivatives.

Symptoms for pets, especially cats, who have ingested one of these substances can range from vomiting to burns in the mouth and esophagus, hyperactivity, panting, and apprehension. "Their toxicity can progress to include shock, cardiac arrhythmia and coma,"[36] note Nina Anderson and Howard Peiper in their book, *Are You Poisoning Your Pet?* In particular, Anderson and Peiper explain that pine oil can affect cats in a similar manner and if cats ingest much of this substance they can die within twelve hours. Pine oil products are very toxic to cats so avoid cleaning kitty litter trays, floors, or any surface that animals might lick that may contain this substance. Some products to steer clear of are Pine Sol and Lysol. Baking soda is a much safer alternative.

Toilet cleaning products contain corrosive materials that can severely burn the mouth and esophagus of dogs and cats if they drink out of the toilet. Keep the toilet lid closed as a precautionary measure. Take great care when using any cleaning products and make sure pets are kept out of any area that has been recently cleaned.

There are safer cleaning alternatives that can be used without the fear of harming pets or children. Baking soda with water makes an all-purpose cleaner. White vinegar in water is a great window cleaner as is basic soda water. Borax or diluted bleach have been suggested as a safe alternative to the caustic toilet cleaners. Remember that pets are inquisitive, so keep all cleaning products tightly closed to prevent accidental spills and ingestion.

If you suspect your dog or cat has had contact with any cleaning product or shows any of the symptoms listed above, do not hesitate to contact your veterinarian immediately.

Toxic Plants

Many years ago I learned that there are certain plants that you must keep out of the house and garden if you own pets, especially cats who enjoy nibbling on greens. Toxic house plants include, but are not limited to, English ivy, Boston ivy, azalea, mistletoe, saddleleaf, umbrella plant, amaryllis, Christmas cherry, poinsettias, sago palm, and dieffenbachia. Outdoor plants include Japanese yew, begonia, rhododendrons, lily-of-the-valley, laurel, castor bean, oleander, azalea, foxglove, Chinese lantern, ornamental pepper, honey-suckle, hydrangea, narcissus, hyacinth, narcissus, iris, daffodils, morning glory, and rhubarb leaves.

The American Veterinary Medical Association, (AVMA) advises: "It is worth noting here that dogs and cats often vomit after chewing on plants; this probably does not represent 'poisoning' or any dangerous exposure. Only severe or persistent vomiting is a danger sign in small animals."[37]

Some plants are not as toxic as others but according to the AVMA, the yew plants are extremely poisonous and an animal needs to eat only one-tenth of one percent of its body weight to get a toxic dose. "The toxin in the Yew is an alkaloid and works by depressing electrical activity in the heart. Signs may include sudden death from heart failure. If the animal shows clinical signs of toxicosis other than sudden death those could include: trembling, incoor-dination, diarrhea, and collapse."[38] The AVMA advises against having a yew as an ornamental plant for your home landscape. Before you bring any plants into your home or plant any shrubs or flowers around your home, check to be sure that they are pet safe.

I have plants in my home, all pet safe, but because my cats are indoor cats they like to nibble, therefore most of my plants are hanging plants. If you want to provide some greens for your animal companions, which are an excellent source of minerals, try growing various types of grasses for them. Wheat grass is just one of the many grasses that makes a wonderful treat and grows very quickly. Most cats are fond of catnip and this also can be grown in pots indoors and out.

The National Animal Poison Control Center (NAPCC) and the American Veterinary Medical Association provide a list of plants that can be toxic to pets. Obtain a copy of one of these lists and refer to it before purchasing plants for your home or outdoors.

Drugs

Do not give your animal companions any kind of drugs unless recommended by your veterinarian. Many of the drugs that humans use can be toxic, even deadly, when given to pets. The National Animal Poison Control Center (NAPCC) advises that toxic exposure to drugs accounts for a vast percentage of deaths as a result of accidental ingestion. Dogs rate higher then cats for ingesting these substances. Never give a cat a medicine that has been prescribed for a dog. Cats do not metabolize medications the same as a dog does.

The NAPCC advises, "Store medications for all family members and pets in high cabinets, out of reach. With their curiosity and strong teeth, dogs can crack open a pill bottle and swallow the entire contents in a very short time." In addition, the NAPCC recommends, "Medications that come in tubes may also pose a large risk. Most pets have sharp teeth and can chew into a tube within seconds. Creams and ointments that may be quite safe when applied to the skin can cause serious problems when eaten."[39] Never give your pet human pain killers, cold medicines, anti-depressants, or diet pills as they can be lethal to animals, even in small doses.

Tylenol is generally a safe painkiller in humans but cats have less of the enzyme required to detoxify the drug following ingestion. One regular strength (325 mg) tablet can poison a cat. Small dogs are also susceptible to the toxic effects of these tablets although in larger dogs the dose would have to be somewhat higher to cause a toxic reaction. Symptoms of toxicity can develop quickly and can include salivation, vomiting, weakness, and abdominal pain.

Aspirin, ibuprofen, phenylbutazone, naproxen, and nonsteroidal anti-inflammatory drugs (NSAIDs) are widely prescribed with caution by veterinarians to relieve pain from arthritis and other conditions. Animal doses, however, are much lower than human dosages. "These pain relievers cause signs of poisoning by decreasing the mucous production of the stomach," according to the "Common Small Animal Poisons" guide from the AVMA. "Mucous serves to protect the stomach from acids it secretes and reduction of mucous production decreases the protection the stomach has from acid secretion and increases the likelihood of ulcer formation."[40] These drugs can also indirectly decrease the blood flow to vital organs, particularly the kidneys, and can result in significant kidney damage. Cats are more sensitive to these types of drugs.

The best advice: don't leave medications where a dog or cat may have access. Never give a dog or cat any form of human medication unless prescribed by a veterinarian.

– Ten –

The Ultimate Health Risk: Cruelty

Writing this chapter has been difficult. Difficult because like anyone who loves animals, I try to pretend cruelty does not exist. My denial tries to convince me that people could not possibly treat animals with such blatant abuse. However, in working on this book, I have encountered numerous reminders that cruelty to animals continues to be a major problem worldwide. Even though my research leads me down "health-related" avenues for cats and dogs, cruelty looms as the ultimate health risk.

How do we extend our caring to those animals who need advocates? How do we work together to stop the cruel attitudes and treatment of animals? There are many places to begin and organizations to support that work on animal abuse issues daily. Educating people about the abuses and how they may be unknowingly participating is an important step. In this chapter I touch on a few subjects that involve animal companion abuse in order to heighten awareness around these issues.

Pet Shops and Puppy Mills

How many of us have walked past a pet shop and seen that cute puppy or kitten in the window, paused, and considered the possibility of taking one home? Or maybe we even considered purchasing a kitten or puppy to "rescue" him or her from the pet shop? In many instances, pet shop purchases are spur-of-the-moment decisions. Although many people have good intentions, this is not the way to bring an animal companion into your life. First and foremost, purchases from pet shops support the cruel practice of puppy and kitten mills. Pet mills are a loosely regulated industry fraught with inhumane conditions and practices.

Many of these pet stores acquire puppies and kittens from mills located throughout the United States and Canada. It has been estimated that more then four thousand puppy mills exist in the United States alone. The Humane Society of the United States (HSUS) published a report on puppy mills that describes deplorable conditions: "The documented problems of puppy mills include: over breeding dams, inbreeding, minimal veterinary care, poor quality food and shelter, lack of socialization with humans, over-crowded cages, and killing unwanted animals."[1] You can read this report on The Humane Society's website listed in the Resource section.

These animals spend their entire lives in these deplorable conditions. Kim Townsend has undertaken extensive research into puppy mills as well as the breeders, brokers, pet shops, and auctions. According to Townsend the minimum kennel space allowed by the United States Department of Agriculture, (USDA) for these animals is very small. Townsend calculated that the space required by the USDA for a Miniature Schnauzer, Linus, who she rescued from an auction, was unbelievably small. Based on the parameters established by the USDA, "Sec. 3.6 Primary enclosures" Townsend determined, "Linus must have 6.25 square feet of floor space to run, play, eat, sleep, urinate, defecate and live out his life. In other words, Linus must have a cage slightly bigger than 2 foot by 3 foot."[2] Townsend also noted that the USDA height requirement for Linus was that his head had to have six inches of clearance from the top of his cage when he was standing in an upright position.

Adult animals are kept at puppy mills for only one reason, to reproduce. Once a dog's reproductive capacity wanes, she or he is killed.

In a "Special Feature" report for *Reader's Digest* in February 1999, William Ecenbarger describes the conditions at a puppy mill near Bunnell, Florida that had been closed down six months previously. He writes, "When police and humane officials arrived they were greeted at the gate by dozens of dogs, many of them sick or injured. On the porch of the ramshackle farmhouse was a stack of filthy cages where the decomposing carcass of a terrier dripped fluids onto a live poodle below."[3] Officials seized 358 dogs from that facility, and some had to be euthanized because of their condition. This is just one case of blatant neglect and cruelty, but unfortunately, not an isolated one.

Who Inspects the Puppy and Kitten Mills?

According to HSUS, inspecting puppy and kitten mills is the responsibility of the USDA. "The agency uses a force of approximately 70 inspectors to enforce its code with an average of 57 facilities per agent per year that need inspection."[4] There are many times that these places are inspected by USDA representatives and still the deplorable conditions continue.

In 1999 an investigator from the People for the Ethical Treatment of Animals (PETA) worked at Nielsen Farms, a puppy mill in Kansas. His job was to clean up, feed, and water hundreds of dogs. "The animals had no comforts, no bedding on the hard wire, little to no protection from the searing hot summers or frigid winters and no regular veterinary care, even when they were ill," reported the PETA representative. The investigator found animals with "crusted oozing eyes, raging ear infections, mange that turned their skin into a mass of red scabs, abscessed feet from the unforgiving wire floors, all were ignored or inadequately treated."[5]

In an exposé precipitated by the PETA investigation, and with footage provide by PETA, the TV show "Dateline" visited the facility and reported on the neglect and abuse. This same facility had been inspected by a USDA inspector just one month prior to the "Dateline" visit. The USDA official report did not state that there were any problems. Since the program aired in April 2000, Nielsen Farms closed its doors, but thousands more of these puppy mills continue to operate. When I asked PETA Research Associate, Peter Wood, if the puppy mill situation had improved, he responded, "I am sorry to report that nothing has changed. The indifference on the part of local, state, and federal officials to the animal suffering in these facilities is unbelievable."[6]

Misguided pet store personnel often are advised by breeders that these puppies come from inspected USDA kennels and that the American Kennel Club (AKC) would not provide papers for a dog unless the breeders had passed rigorous standards. "Dateline" investigators found that this was not the case. As was previously mentioned, USDA inspections are inadequate in reporting mistreatment, not the least of which is taking puppies away from their mothers before they have been weaned.

As for the AKC, it appears this organization's main job is to shuffle papers. Chris Hansen, a reporter for "Dateline," stated, "In truth, obtaining papers from the AKC has been relatively easy. You send in your registration fee and they send you the papers. No questions asked."[7] "Dateline" revealed just how worthless AKC papers really are by successfully getting two domestic cats registered as purebred Golden Retrievers.

The horrific conditions of puppy mills was also cited by Karl Stark, a writer for the *Philadelphia Inquirer*. His December 1995 story revolved around the puppy mills in Lancaster County, Pennsylvania, which is called the "puppy mill capital of the East Coast." Lancaster County is the heart of Amish and Mennonite country. According to Stark, "Farmers and kennel owners in Lancaster County say they breed and sell dogs to make money. For many, dog breeding has become more profitable than pig breeding and other farming business. And, several kennel owners say, they treat dogs as farm animals, not pets."[8]

Most of these kennel owners do not allow visitors and prohibit photographs. In his newspaper article, Stark describes the inside of some of these facilities, "The floors of many kennels are covered with urine and feces, and the kennels are sometimes contaminated with viruses. At times, waste is allowed to collect for days. The dog's hair grows matted. The animals receive minimal human contact."[9] In January 2000, I contacted Stark to get an update on the puppy mill problems he first reported on in 1996. Stark responded, "Many of the problems we wrote about are still going on, not just here but across the country."[10]

The puppy mills of Pennsylvania were also reported on by the *New York Post* in a shocking article in 1996, "4.4M Puppy Mill Scandal." Tucked away amid the picturesque barns and rolling farmland of the Amish in Pennslyvania the puppy mills continue to operate. "They bring in $4 million a year for the 100 Amish and Mennonite farmers who supply boutique dog-shop markets, including at least two New York dealers."[11] The farmers sell twenty thousand puppies a year to wholesalers for an average $223 a pup according to government records. One of these farmers has had his license suspended for numerous animal welfare violations and fined $51,250. However, it appears that he continues to sell pups. At least three other farmers, operating in the same area, have also had their licenses suspended yet continue to sell pups according to the same *New York Post* article.

It is seldom that puppy mill breeders will actually sell the pups directly to a pet store. Brokers are agents who purchase puppies and kittens from the breeders and sell them to pet stores. Brokers are classified as "B" Dealers with the USDA. This means that they can obtain "random source" puppies and kittens from various puppy and kitten mills as well as from breeders, and then sell them to pet shops. Some brokers are also breeders.

Brokers usually ship animals to pet stores when the animals are only eight weeks old and barely weaned. These puppies and kittens can spend days in crowded cages in the back of a truck, and some arrive at pet shops sick, stressed, and even dead. Pet shop employees bathe the surviving animals, fluff them up, and place them in a cage, waiting for a buyer.

In addition to supporting puppy and kitten mills when you purchase an animal from a pet shop, the general health of the purchased animal is questionable. A spur-of-the-moment purchase invites numerous and potential health, genetic, and personality problems. Once bonded with your new animal companion, it is difficult to part with the new addition and the vet bills begin to mount. Also, if you do not know much about the particular breed purchased, you may find yourself unprepared, and this could quickly lead to one more animal relinquished at the local humane society.

Perhaps some of the most tragic impulse buys are those inspired by popular movies such as *101 Dalmatians* or *Beethoven*, or television's hit children's program, "Wishbone." Dalmatians and Jack Russell Terriers are two breeds that have very specific needs and personality considerations. Saint Bernards became a popular breed after the film *Beethoven* and led to inbreeding and vicious Saint Bernards.

A word of advice: *never* purchase a pup or kitten from a pet store. You may think you are saving an animal from a miserable life but in fact you are supporting puppy and kitten mills. Although kitten mills are not as prevalent as puppy mills, they do exist. If you are looking for an animal companion to offer you years of love and friendship, consider adopting from a humane society or animal rescue organization. You will not only have a loving companion but you will also be saving a life.

Sadly, only one out of every four dogs born in the United States ever finds a permanent home. And approximately every six seconds a dog is euthanized in the United States, the majority of them mutts. Genetically speaking, mixed-breed dogs are the healthiest, and each dog has a wonderful unique personality. As Karen Derrico so aptly states in her book, *Unforgettable Mutts: Pure of Heart Not of Breed*, "When you think of it, most of us are 'mutts.' The vast majority of the world's human population comes from a blended lineage, and the same applies to the world's canine population, including the dogs we refer to today as 'purebred.'"[12]

If you plan on buying a purebred dog, first, read all you can on the specific breed that interests you. Second, go to a reputable kennel that handles just one or two breeds, and if possible, see the mother and father of the pups. The breeder can provide a significant amount of information about a puppy, including temperament, the pup's diet, and the genetic background of the parents and grandparents. If you encounter a problem with your new animal companion, then you can go back to that breeder for assistance.

Drop Boxes

A shocking fact came to my attention during a typical day of research. Some shelters have what is called a "drop box," which is used to deposit unwanted dogs and cats at local shelters. One such facility is located in Tennessee's Rutherford County. The HSUS "Today's News" described what transpired at this particular drop box: "Animals were slipped through a flap into a chute, fell several feet, and landed on a concrete floor. There was no protection from heat or cold and no protection from other animals. Dogs were dropped next to cats, sick animals next to healthy ones."[13]

Some argue that a drop box is better then having animals dumped off along the side of the road, but others are opposed to drop boxes as just another inhumane form of abandonment. Drop boxes do not hold pet owners accountable.

If for some reason you cannot keep your pet, never forget that your animal companion is a living creature and deserves to be treated with respect and compassion. If you learn that a local shelter uses a drop box, encourage it to seek more humane ways of relinquishing animal companions. We must continue to educate ourselves and one another that animals, domesticated or wild, are not products or conveniences. In my opinion, drop boxes are not a part of the solution, but rather one more way to treat animals inhumanely.

Cat and Dog Fur for Consumers

On December 13, 1999, "Dateline" aired an investigation sponsored by The Humane Society of the United States in which undercover investigators revealed the use of dog and cat fur for human clothing. This eighteen-month investigation sponsored by the HSUS spanned China, Thailand, and the Philippines. "The investigation concluded that more than 2 million dogs and cats were slaughtered each year for their fur, mainly in Asia,"[14] stated the HSUS chief investigator, Rick Swain, in the "Dateline" interview.

As a part of that same investigation, the undercover agents toured two toy factories in the People's Republic of China in 1998. While there they surreptitiously filmed lifelike replicas of pets made out of molded plastic and covered with fur. The fur on these figurines looked realistic because it actually came from dogs and cats. *Reuters News* reported, "HSUS investigators estimate twenty percent of fur-covered figurines are made from the pelts of brutally slaughtered dogs and cats. Hundreds of thousands of figurines covered in domestic cat or dog fur are sold each year. This amounts to hundreds of thousands of dogs and cats who are killed for trinkets. Each of those figurines represents one dead animal."[15] These figurines are being sold in flea markets and stores across the United States, costing from $20 to $40 a piece.

Asked if he could be sure that these toys definitely include cat and dog fur, Swain responded, "We know because of forensic testing. A total of 47 figurines were tested, 22 tested positive for dog and cat."[16] Many of these figurines are coming into the United States deceptively labeled as containing rabbit fur rather than dog and cat fur, as if this is more acceptable. Personally, I am very much opposed to the use of any animal being used for fur, whether dogs, cats, rabbits, mink, seal, beaver, or any other kind of animal.

In 1999 a large coat retailer, Burlington Coat Factory Warehouse Corporation, recalled hundreds of men's parkas because this same HSUS investigation revealed that the fur trim on the coats imported from China was dog fur. The coats retailed for about $90, and about 140 coats had been sold in the United States when the problem was discovered. Burlington Coat Factory executives denied any knowledge about the fur being cat and dog fur, and stated that they had inadvertently bought these coats from an undisclosed supplier. People who had purchased coats were offered a store credit for returned items.

The HSUS also issued a report by animal organizations investigating further the use of dog and cat fur on products imported from overseas. "In California, the San Diego Humane Society and SPCA, Los Angeles SPCA, and the Humane Society of San Bernadino Valley have all investigated vendors to see if they were selling figurines made with dog and/or cat fur. Because the sale of items containing dog or cat fur is illegal in California, when samples from these stores tested positive for dog and/or cat fur, charges were brought against these stores."[17] There is also a concern about the health risks of these figurines. When U.S. Customs Service labs examined these skins, they where shocked to find vermin and bug life. Most of these products were imported by the United States, Germany, and France. To the best of my knowledge, none of these cat and dog fur products found their way into Canada.

In November 2000, President Clinton signed a ban on dog and cat fur products being imported, exported, or sold in the United States. Up until now any products with fur valued at less than $150 did not need to be labeled. The new law states: "(1) Sets penalties of up to $10,000 for each item containing dog or cat fur. (2) Makes it possible to prohibit repeat offenders from selling any fur product. (3) Calls on the U.S. Customs Service to publish a list of businesses and individuals known to trade in dog and cat fur. (4) Directs the U.S. Custom Service to certify laboratories that are qualified to determine whether an item contains dog or cat fur. (5) Establishes a $500 reward for information leading to the successful imposition of a civil penalty, forfeiture, or debarment."[18]

As a consumer, if you suspect any item such as the trim on coats, hats, gloves, or figurines, is made from dog or cat fur, notify the HSUS or U.S. Customs officials. Most of these products are made in China or other parts of Asia. This is a practice that must be stopped. Although there is a ban on the selling, importing, or exporting these products there is no doubt that some products still remain on the shelves. The labels do not need to state that it is dog or cat skin used in these items.

Breeding and killing any kind of animal for fur is simply unnecessary because of all the alternatives available, but most important, it is cruel. Consider how the animals suffer so humans can derive pleasure from wearing fur coats, fur hats, fur-lined gloves, fur-lined or fur-trimmed shoes and boots. Michael W. Fox, a veterinarian who has worked in animal welfare with the HSUS for more then twenty-five years, describes the horrendous treatment of animals raised for fur in his book, *Eating with Conscience: The Bioethics of Food*: "Foxes, mink, chinchillas, and other wild creatures are raised in small cages on factory ranches until they are killed to make fur coats. I have been sickened by the sight of mink and foxes spinning and pacing neurotically in the tiny cages they are confined to on fur farms. So as not to damage their pelts, they are often killed with an electrified rod shoved into their rectums."[19]

Greyhound Racing

In my estimation one of the most blatant forms of cruelty that is legal and popular among many people is dog racing. While this sport looks harmless on the surface, this industry is fraught with abuse and cruelty to Greyhounds bred for racing. Since dog racing first began in the United States in Emeryville,

California around 1919, the Greyhound Protection League estimates that over one million Greyhounds have been killed. The dog racing industry admits to the deaths of seven thousand dogs a year; however, those working to protect Greyhounds believe this figure is much higher.

Greyhounds, docile, loving dogs, are often subjected to deplorable living conditions, spending most of their lives in pens, crates, or fenced enclosures with limited human contact. Greyhounds are often muzzled for long periods of time in their pens because too many dogs kept in close proximity will fight. In addition, they are over-bred by breeders looking for the fastest dogs. The racing industry exists for entertainment and profit at the expense of animals who suffer and die needlessly.

In Canada, there is no longer Greyhound racing because Canadian law only allows betting on horse racing. However, as of 1999 in the United States, there are forty-nine tracks open for dog racing in fifteen states. Currently, U.S. Greyhound racing is legal in sixteen states including Alabama with three tracks; Arkansas with one track; Arizona with three tracks; Colorado with five tracks; Connecticut with two tracks; Florida with seventeen tracks; Iowa with two tracks; Kansas with two tracks; Massachusetts with two tracks; New Hampshire with three tracks; Oregon with one track; Rhode Island with one track; South Dakota allows dog racing but there are no formal race tracks as of 2000; Texas with two tracks; West Virginia with two tracks; and Wisconsin with three tracks.[20] According to Connie Thiel, Director of Oregon Defenders of Greyhounds, "It is estimated that between 1,000 and 1,200 dogs are needed at any given time to operate a dog track."[21]

In recent years, several states have banned dog racing, including Washington, Idaho, and Nevada. "Idaho did so after dog trainers were discovered electrocuting losing Greyhounds during midnight cocaine parties," reported Theil in her article, "You Bet They Die: A look at the Dark Side of the Greyhound Racing Industry." "Upon passing the legislation, Idaho Governor Phil Batt stated, 'It hardly seems worth it to breed and breed to get a winner, and kill the ones that can't compete, just to have the sport.'"[22]

The HSUS vociferously opposes the practice of Greyhound racing. On HSUS's website is a scathing report, "Greyhound Racing Facts," that reports: "Every year, the industry breeds tens of thousands of Greyhounds, more than it can place at race tracks. This over breeding is motivated by the incentive to produce 'winning' dogs. (Hundreds of Greyhounds raced at each track are disposed of yearly in order to bring in a 'fresh' group of dogs.) A dog's racing career is usually over at 3.5 to 4 years of age."[23] The average life span for a Greyhound raised as a companion animal is thirteen years.

Unproductive Greyhounds are considered "losers" and are disposed of often by owners and racetrack personnel using the least expensive methods available. The Greyhound Protection League lists some of the "documented disposal methods" as "euthanasia, mass euthanasia, gunshot, starvation, bludgeoning, sale/donation to medical research, abandonment (often muzzled), sale to racing interests in Third World countries, and electrocution."[24] The suffering and pain many of these dogs are put through prior to their deaths is incomprehensible.

Many examples of cruelty related to Greyhound racing have been reported in the press. The *Connecticut Hartford Courant* published an article on January 12, 1997 on nine emaciated Greyhounds who were apparently deprived of bedding and food and were brought to a veterinary clinic by rescue workers. These animals had been in the care of a trainer. One of the animals was unconscious and near death due to kidney failure. "The Greyhounds were covered with sores, fleas, and ticks: several were 20-25 pounds underweight."[25] The veterinarian in charge stated that they were basically starving to death.

For those Greyhounds who do not get discarded and are used for racing or breeding, the conditions are often inhumane. In particular, the diet of racing Greyhounds is usually raw meat because many owners assume that this diet will make them run faster. Unfortunately, many animals become ill due to the substandard meat, which comes in large part from 4-D (dead, diseased, dying, and disabled) animals. According to an article on the Greyhound Protection website, "4-D meat is produced by animal rendering plants. Many of the larger companies such as Qual-Pet, a subsidiary of National By-Products (parent company: Holly Farms Corp.), provide perks to racetracks, including freezers and jackets displaying the company name free of charge to kennels that continue to purchase their products."[26]

This food is sold to Greyhound tracks frozen, and the tracks often leave the food out to thaw, exposed to flies and filth. The major consequence for this kind of feeding for racing Greyhounds is called Alabama Rot, because it was first recognized at a Greyhound track in that state. In humans, this same illness is called E. coli poisoning, and both can cause acute renal failure. The E. coli bacteria are common to the environment and can be found in undercooked or raw meat.

The Greyhound Protection League is an excellent source for learning more about what you can do to stop the abuse of Greyhounds. Education is the number-one step to protect Greyhounds from abuse at the track. If people know what is going on behind the scenes at these dog races, perhaps their lives would change more quickly.

Janet Skinner from the Greyhound Protection League in Florida suggests, "If you have one of these tracks in the city where you live, write 'Letters to the Editor,' protest, inform people how the animals are suffering, volunteer or become an adoptive parent to one of these dogs."

Most of these Greyhound organizations, including the Greyhound Protective League, and the Greyhound Network News are nonprofits and staffed entirely by volunteers. If you don't have the time, but you have the means, consider a donation since expenses can be high. (See Resources.) As for Canada, most of the adoptable Greyhounds originate from the various adoption agencies in the United States.

Animals cannot speak for themselves. They rely on us to take the necessary steps to stop human cruelty to animals.

Eleven

Healthy Recipes

For over twelve years I have fed my animal companions a home-made diet and they all have done exceptionally well. It is not complicated to feed your cats and dogs a balanced, nutritious homemade diet. Yes, homemade diets are more time-consuming then opening a can or bag but at least I know what I am feeding them. In the years I have fed a home-made diet my veterinary bills have declined to almost nothing. The time you spend preparing food for your animal companion will save time and money in veterinary visits.

Despite what the pet food industry advises, despite what your veteri-narian tells you, pets do extremely well on either healthy table scraps or a homemade diet. In these past twelve years I have had no more then five veterinary bills for all five pets. When I was feeding them commercial food I was a regular visitor to our vet clinic. There are two things to which I attribute to my animal companions' longevity: a homemade diet and no vaccinations other then the initial puppy and kitten vaccines. (I monitor their immunity levels with titer tests.)

Cooking for Your Cats and Dogs

More and more books are published on the topic of homemade diets and there are two I recommend if you plan to feed your animal companions an alternative to commercial foods. If you are looking for a diet for a specific dog breed pick up William Cusick's *Canine Nutrition*. This book provides a brief history of the breed and also recommends food for that particular breed. If your animal companion is experiencing health problems, heart disease, skin disease, allergies, gastrointestinal disease, renal disease, etcetera, I highly recommend a book by Donald R. Strombeck, DVM, *Home Prepared Dog and Cat Diets*. With the permission of Dr. Strombeck and his publisher, Iowa State University Press, I have included a couple of the book's recipes. This book provides numerous home-cooked diets for dogs and cats who are healthy as well as for those suffering from various health-related problems.

When I began feeding my pets a homemade diet, I was very apprehensive. For years, many veterinarians advised against feeding a homemade diet or table scraps believing that this type of diet is neither nutritious nor balanced. It was not until I began my research on commercial pet foods that I realized that with a meal made with food fit for human consumption that I was providing a far more nutritious diet. Not only could it improve their health but it could add years to their lives.

Older veterinarians reminded me that prior to the advent of commercial pet foods our cats and dogs were fed basically table scraps. Nina Anderson and Howard Peiper, DVM, in their book *Super Nutrition for Dogs n' Cats*, also note this fact: "Household pets die younger now than ever before. Statistics show that the normal life span for the average pet dog or cat in the United States has decreased by approximately eighteen percent in the last forty years. The problem is that our pets are becoming nutritionally deficient, due to the fact that most commercial pet foods lack sufficient minerals, enzymes and proper nutrients."[1]

Veterinarians who practiced thirty or forty years ago claim they did not see the diseases in cats and dogs that they see today. Now, companion animals face high rates of cancer, heart disease, allergies, skin problems, and autoimmune diseases. I believe this is due in part to over-processed commercial foods as well as from over-vaccination.

The animal companions I have now are not fed table scraps although my dog will eat any meat, vegetable, pasta, grain, or even salad that is left over from our dinner. This never amounts to much and I always feed him his own meals. Because Sarge is a large dog he is fed two meals per day: morning and evening. The cats are fed three times a day: morning, noon, and night, and they often have a bedtime snack. I never leave food sitting out. If the animals do not eat a meal within twenty minutes to half an hour, I either refrigerate the food or throw it out. Usually I cook twice a week, and unless my animal companions eat their food that day, I freeze it.

With one or two small dogs or cats, you can prepare their food once a week and refrigerate or freeze it until you are ready to use the food. The easiest method I have found is to take the food out of the freezer the night before, and place it in the refrigerator to thaw. Slightly heat the food when you are ready to feed it to your pets. Be careful if you use a microwave because foods heat quickly. When we take trips with the dog we put the frozen meals in a thermal container packed with ice. This keeps the meals frozen until we reach our destination.

If you decide to cook meals for your animal companions, there are a few things you should consider. The food for dogs and cats, although basically the same ingredients, are a little different.

Cats are carnivores and require meat because they need the amino acid, taurine, which is found only in meat or by adding taurine as a supplement to the food. However, do not feed your cat an all-meat diet because this would be too low in minerals. Although cats do not require as high a level of minerals in their diet as dogs, minerals are necessary so an animal can absorb vitamins. Pat Lazarus notes in her book, *Keep Your Pet Healthy the Natural Way*, "Another problem with an all-meat diet is that carbohydrates, which are present in grains, fruits and vegetables but not in meat, are needed to help your cat's body use proteins. Without carbohydrates, your cat can't efficiently use the proteins in the meat that his body needs so much."[2] Small amounts of grains and mashed raw vegetables or fruit should always be added to a cat's diet.

The diet I feed my cats is comprised of two-thirds meat and the other one-third grains and vegetables. I use primarily chicken, turkey, beef or lamb, in that order. Fish, especially sardines, are a good source of B12. About once a week I substitute salmon or tuna for meat. Avoid pork because pork can cause diarrhea in some pets. Although liver is a good source of vitamin B12, liver can also contain levels of vitamins A and D, which in excess amounts can be toxic. I also add about a tablespoon of cottage cheese or yogurt as a source of calcium.

For my dog, I use the same ingredients I use for the cats, only in different amounts. One-third of the dog diet is comprised of protein. One-third is comprised of grains, potatoes, pasta, or whole-grain cereals, and the other one-third is comprised of vegetables or fruit. As with the cats, I add cottage cheese or yogurt plus a small amount of vegetable oil. Flax seed oil is also an excellent source of Omega-3 fatty acids. (Note that dogs are not strictly carnivores, however, I feed my dog meat. There are a growing number of books on vegetarian meals for dogs that provide healthy, balanced recipes.)

Usually I use brown rice but potatoes, mashed or boiled, are good, too. Sometimes I will use millet, or a whole-grain cereal. Some people also mix in barley as another source of grain. My Newfoundland, Charlie, loved to have oatmeal for breakfast and now Sarge also enjoys the occasional bowl of oatmeal. Being owned by a number of breeds of dogs over the years, I have found that some breeds cannot tolerate eggs. My Old English Sheepdog loved eggs but within minutes of eating them I would get them back. My sister's dog, a Dachshund, could not tolerate eggs.

Vegetables, for both dogs and cats, should be finely chopped or run through the food processor for better digestion. Both my dog and cats enjoy a wide variety of vegetables and fruits. If you are starting to cook for your animal companion, you might start off by adding carrots or zucchini, both of which are well tolerated. Celery, squash, mushrooms, and green and yellow beans are also well tolerated.

Dogs enjoy apples, pears, peaches, mashed bananas, but remember each dog has likes and dislikes. Alfalfa sprouts and bean sprouts are healthy ingredients, and alfalfa sprouts provide high levels of both vitamins and minerals. Do not feed large amounts of the gas-producing vegetables such as cabbage, broccoli, or brussel sprouts. If you mix in table scraps with your homemade food, avoid highly spiced foods, processed lunch meats, or anything containing chocolate. Avoid fried foods as well.

Although I have never done it, some cooks add a multi-vitamin and mineral supplement to their animal companions diets after cooking the meal. As for treats, dog snacks can be anything from carrot and celery sticks kept in a container in the refrigerator to little bits of cheese. For your cats, try growing cat grass that is comprised of various grass seeds, or wheat grass. Both provide an abundance of vitamins and minerals and cats love them.

A little advice that you may find helpful when you begin feeding a homemade diet to your pet: After eating commercial foods for a number of years pets, especially cats, are not thrilled with being offered a new diet. Try adding a small amount of the new food to the commercial food they have been eating. Gradually reduce the amount of the commercial food. This may take days or even a couple of weeks. Be sure that your animal companion has free access to fresh water at all times.

Beware of Commercial Pet Treats

All of us like to give our pets treats once in awhile and there is a wide variety on the market. Beware of rawhide bones and pigs' ears for dogs. Rawhide bones can cause a very serious problem if a piece of this material becomes lodged in the animal's throat. When a piece becomes wet from saliva it tends to swell either in the throat or in the stomach. The dog can either choke to death or has to undergo an expensive operation to have the material removed.

In October 1999 the FDA issued an advisory on contaminated pet treats. These included pigs' ears, beef jerky treats, smoked hooves, pig skins, etc. The warning was issued to pet owners who might be handling the treats. The FDA was not necessarily concerned that pets were ingesting them! The advisory warned: "The Food and Drug Administration today issued a nationwide public health warning alerting consumers about a number of recent cases in Canada of human illnesses apparently related to contact with dog chew products made from pork or beef derived materials."[3] The FDA advised consumers to handle the treats carefully and if they come in contact with them to wash their hands with hot soap and water. Another concern was that these pet treats were often left in the pet's bowl where a human infant might have access to them.

One company manufacturing such a product is Farm Meats Canada Ltd. of High River, Alberta. This is the company from which many of the contaminated products originated. In a letter put out by the Alberta Crops and Beef of Agriculture Canada, Mike Lamb wrote, "Farm Meats processes packing plant wastes such as beef hooves, gristle, leg bones and even bull penises, along with pigs' ears and inedible lamb and turkey parts. The company markets a full selection of dog food and chews under the Rollover brand name."[4] Prior to writing *Food Pets Die For* I had been in contact with this company and they advised that they used 3-D meats in their pet foods. When I asked them which of the 4-D meats they did not use—dead, dying, downed or disabled—I did not receive a reply.

As with commercial pet food, be sure to read the labels on any special pet treats you may buy. They may contain highly toxic ingredients that can legally be used in pet foods. One final word on treats, avoid sweets—a dog (or an owner) does not require excess sugar. The following are some easy and healthy recipes for cats and dogs, both treats and main meals.

✦ ✦ *RECIPES FOR CATS* ✦ ✦

— FOWL DINNER —

2 cups of ground chicken or turkey, cooked
1 cup of cooked brown rice
1/4 cup grated carrots
4 teaspoons cottage cheese or plain yogurt
4 teaspoons vegetable oil

Combine all ingredients and serve at room temperature. This should feed two cats for one to one and a half days. Refrigerate leftovers.

— SOMETHING FISHY —

1 15-ounce can of salmon
1 cup of cooked brown rice
1/4 cup chopped parsley or celery
4 teaspoons yogurt or cottage cheese
4 teaspoons vegetable oil. If salmon is packed in oil omit adding
   vegetable oil.

Combine all ingredients and serve at room temperature. Refrigerate leftovers.

— KITTY STEW —

2 cups cooked stewing beef, finely chopped.
1 cup cooked brown rice
1/4 cup peas
1/4 cup raw carrot, shredded
1/4 cup zucchini, shredded
1 tablespoon vegetable oil
1 tablespoon cottage cheese

Combine all ingredients and serve warm, not hot. Refrigerate leftovers.

— ALLERGY DIET —

2 cups of cooked ground lamb
1/2 cup grated carrots or zucchini
1/2 cup cooked brown rice
1/4 cup yogurt
1/4 teaspoon garlic powder

Combine all ingredients and either mix in a blender or serve as is at room temperature.

— CHICKEN AND RICE DIET —

Dr. Donald R. Strombeck recommends this recipe for cats with renal disease. This is low-protein, low phosphorus, normal potassium, normal sodium diet providing 46.4 grams protein/1000 kilograms.

1/4 cup cooked chicken breast
1/2 ounce clams, canned, chopped in juice
1/2 cup rice, long-grain, cooked
1 tablespoon chicken fat
1/8 teaspoon salt substitute, potassium chloride
1 calcium carbonate tablet (400 milligrams calcium)
1/4 multiple vitamin-mineral tablet
1/10 B complex - trace mineral tablet

— TOFU AND SARDINES DIET —

Dr. Strombeck recommends this diet for cats with urinary tract stone disease.

3 1/3 ounces tofu, raw firm
1 1/4 ounces sardines, canned, tomato sauce
1/2 yolk of egg, large, hard-boiled
1/2 ounce clams, canned, chopped in juice
1/3 cup brown rice, long-grain, cooked
2 teaspoon vegetable (canola) oil
1/2 ounce brewer's yeast
1 bone meal tablet (10 grain or equivalent)
1/2 multiple vitamin-mineral tablet.[5]

— CATS PAJAMAS –

Joe Bodewes, DVM, a veterinarian with Drs. Foster and Smith, Rhinelander, Wisconsin, suggests this recipe.

1 pound cooked ground beef
1/4 cup liver
1 cup cooked rice
1 teaspoon vegetable oil
1 teaspoon calcium carbonate
Multi-vitamin/mineral tablet.[6]

✦ *Kitten Formulas* ✦

From the "Cats and Diets" website, here are two kitten formula recipes. These can be used short term until you can obtain a commercial milk substitute from your veterinarian.

— FORMULA ONE —

1 cup of whole milk
2 egg yokes
2 teaspoons of Karo syrup

— FORMULA TWO —

1 egg yolk
1 teaspoon Karo or maple syrup per pint mixture
1 teaspoon brewer's year or bee pollen per pint mixture
A vitamin-mineral supplement like Fauve or Vital Nutrition.[7]

✦ *Dry Treats Especially for Cats* ✦

— GO FISH —

1 envelope (2 1/4 teaspoons) dry active yeast
1/4 cup warm water (110°F to 115°F)
1 cup warm chicken or fish stock

2 tablespoons molasses
2 cups all-purpose flour (approximate)
1 1/2 cups whole-wheat flour
1 cup cracked wheat
1/2 cup cornmeal
1/2 cup dry milk powder
1/3 cup fish food flakes
1 teaspoon salt (I'd use less then that)
2 teaspoons garlic powder
1 large egg
1 tablespoon milk

Combine yeast and warm water. Let stand 5 minutes. Stir in broth and molasses. Add 1 cup of all-purpose flour and all the rest except the egg and milk. Turn dough out onto a floured surface. Knead in enough of remaining flour to make a very stiff dough (5 minutes), divide in half. Cover and let rest 10 to 15 minutes. Roll out each portion to 1/4-inch thickness. Cut into shapes, preferably 1-inch fish shapes. Place on ungreased cookie sheet. Combine beaten egg with milk and brush over biscuits. Bake 300°F for 35 minutes. Turn off oven and let biscuits cool in oven overnight.

— TUNA COOKIES —

1 8-ounce can tuna in oil
2 cups cornmeal
2 cups flour
3/4 cup water
2/3 cup vegetable oil
1/2 teaspoon salt

Mix all ingredients well, kneading just to combine. On floured surface, roll out and cut into little squares or other shapes. Place on greased baking sheet. Bake at 350°F for 25 to 30 minutes. Cool on wire rack. Store in air-tight container in refrigerator.

✦ ✦ *Recipes for Dogs* ✦ ✦

— High-Fiber Breakfast —

2 cups of bran cereal
2 tablespoons of vegetable oil
1 cup cooked chicken

Top with alfalfa sprouts. Mix together and serve.

— Pasta, Liver, and Veggie Dinner —

2 cups pasta, cooked
2 pieces beef liver cooked in butter or vegetable oil
1 can of mixed vegetables. (Thawed frozen vegetables may also be used).

Chop liver slices in pieces. Add pasta and vegetables. Sprinkle with 1/4 teaspoon garlic powder (not garlic salt). Serve.

— Chicken Feast —

2 cups cooked cubed chicken or 2 cups cooked ground chicken
3/4 cup chopped celery
3/4 cup chopped apples
1 cup cooked brown rice
1/2 cup plain yogurt
2 tablespoons vegetable oil

Mix all ingredients together and serve at room temperature. Refrigerate leftovers.

— Pot Roast —

1 3- or 4-pound cheap cut of beef, cut into pieces
2 large potatoes, skin on, cut into pieces
2 carrots cut into pieces
1 cup of green beans
1/2 teaspoon garlic powder
1 cup of tomato or V-8 Juice.

Place all ingredients in slow cooker for approximately 5 or 6 hours or until vegetables are tender. Cool and serve. Store any leftovers in refrigerator.

— UNDER THE WEATHER —

2 cups of cooked cream of wheat (use oatmeal if your dog has a wheat allergy)
1 cup plain yogurt
3 tablespoons liquid honey
1 cup of cooked, chopped chicken livers

Mix together and serve warm.

— FOX'S NATURAL CANINE STEW —

Dr. Michael Fox, veterinarian and author, suggests this homemade natural diet for dogs.

6 cups rice or barley, rolled oats, or pasta noodles (cooked)
3 cloves of garlic
pinch of salt
1 tablespoon vegetable oil (flax seed or safflower oil)
1 tablespoon wheat germ
1 tablespoon white vinegar
1 teaspoon brewer's yeast
1 teaspoon bone meal
1 teaspoon dried kelp
2 deboned chicken backs (remove excess fat) or pieces of meat from soup bones
1 pound lean hamburger, ground lamb, or turkey

Combine all above ingredients. Add water to cover ingredients, simmer, stir, and add more water as need until cooked. Should be thick enough to be molded into patties. (Add bran or soya protein to thicken).

You can add well-cooked lentils, chick peas, lima beans as a meat substitute. Add sprinkling of raw, grated carrots, raw yams or alfalfa sprouts.[8]

— Beef and Potato Diet —

From Dr. Strombeck's *Home Prepared Dog and Cat Diets*, this recipe is for dogs with heart disease. This meal contains normal protein, high potassium, minimum sodium, moderate fat.

8 ounces lean ground beef (raw weight) cooked
3 cups potato, boiled with skin
5 bone meal tablets (10-grain or equivalent)
1 multi-vitamin mineral tablet[9]

✦ *For Active Dogs* ✦

Joe Bodewes, DVM, recommends this recipe for those "get up and go" canines!

— Healthy and Hearty —

1 pound of meat with fat included
2 cups of cooked cream of wheat
1 1/2 cups cottage cheese
1 hard-boiled egg
2 tablespoons brewer's yeast
3 tablespoons sugar
1 tablespoon vegetable oil
1 teaspoon potassium chloride
1 teaspoon dicalcium phosphate
1 teaspoon calcium carbonate
Multi-vitamin/mineral tablet.

— Raring to Go! —

Another recipe recommended by Joe Bodewes, DVM, for active canines.

1 pound ground meat with fat included
4 hard-boiled eggs
1 cup cooked oatmeal
1 cooked potato
1/4 cup wheat germ

1/2 cup raw carrots
1/2 cup raw green vegetables
3 tablespoons olive oil
2 tablespoons minced garlic
Multi-vitamin/mineral tablet.[10]

— DIET FOR DOGS WITH CANCER —

4 ounce pork back fat (boiled, baked, or fried in olive oil)
4 ounce tofu (firm soybean curd)
2 teaspoon extra virgin oil
2 whole carrots (boiled and then cut up)
1 cup spinach (cooked)
4 tablespoons green bell pepper (chopped and steamed)
4 broccoli spears (boiled and then cut up)
2 sardines (in olive oil, drained)
2 cloves raw garlic (crushed and added before serving)
1/2 teaspoon dry, ground ginger (add before serving)
1/2 teaspoon dry, yellow mustard (add before serving)[11]

— NO-MEAT TATER TOT SPECIAL —

This is a tasty vegetarian dish for dogs.

1 1/2 cups Green Giant vegetable protein crumbles (available at most grocery
   stores in the frozen food section or the organic foods section).
1 package frozen tater tots
1 can cream of potato condensed soup
1 can cream of celery condensed soup
1/2 cup of milk.

Preheat oven to 375°F. Mix all ingredients except tater tots in 1 quart
casserole dish. Top evenly with tater tots. Bake uncovered for 45 minutes.
Let stand 5 minutes, or until cool and serve.

— VEGAN DOG BISCUITS —

From People for the Ethical Treatment of Animals (PETA), a vegan dog biscuit recipe.

9 cups whole-wheat flour
1 cup nutritional yeast
1 tablespoon salt
1 tablespoon garlic powder

Mix dry ingredients. Add approximately 3 cups of water. Knead into a pliable dough. Roll out to 1/8-inch thickness. Cut into desired shapes. Bake for 10 to 15 minutes at 350°F. Important: After turning off the oven, leave biscuits in the oven overnight or for an 8-hour period so they become hard and crunchy.[12]

— TURKEY JERKY: A DOG'S FAVORITE TREAT —

From Bethany Bain-Chamberlain, The Pet Cottage Pet Sitter, a couple of dog treat recipes.

1 pound ground turkey, or substitute ground chicken or beef
3 teaspoons teriyaki sauce (use a low-sodium teriyaki sauce, especially for older dogs)
1 to 2 cloves of garlic
1/2 teaspoon ginger

Preheat oven to the lowest setting, 150°F to 170°F. Mix all ingredients and spread thinly onto a cookie sheet. Place in the oven and bake for two hours. During baking, keep the oven door propped open. After two hours, remove the jerky from the oven and blot any grease with paper towels. Slice the jerky into one or two-inch strips. Turn the slices over and return to the oven and bake two more hours. Allow them to cool, then store in the freezer. Makes about 2 dozen treats.

— PEANUT BUTTER DOG BISCUITS —

1 1/2 cup water
1/2 cup vegetable oil
2 medium eggs

1/4 cup natural crunchy peanut butter
1 tablespoons vanilla
2 1/2 cups whole-wheat flour
3/4 unbleached flour
1 cup cornmeal
3/4 cup rolled oats

Preheat oven to 400°F. In a medium bowl, mix together the water, oil, eggs, peanut butter, and vanilla. In the bowl of an electric mixer, combine the dry ingredients. Pour the wet mixture into the dry ingredients and beat with an electric mixer until smooth. Roll the dough into a ball and place it on a sheet of floured wax paper. Roll or pat the dough to a thickness of 1/4 inch to 1/2 inch. Cut the dough with a cookie cutter (preferably one shaped like a dog biscuit) and place the biscuits on an ungreased cookie sheet. Bake for 20 minutes. Turn off the heat and leave the biscuits in the oven for one hour. Makes 1 to 2 dozen biscuits, depending on the size of your cookie cutter.[13]

✦ ✦ DRY FOOD FOR DOGS AND CATS ✦ ✦

These recipes should not be fed as the main diet for animals, they are more of a snack.

— HEALTHY COOKIES —

1 1/2 cups whole-wheat flour
1 1/2 cups rye flour
1 1/2 cups brown rice flour
1 cup wheat germ
1 teaspoon dried kelp or alfalfa
4 tablespoons vegetable oil
1 teaspoon garlic powder
1 1/4 cups beef or chicken broth or stock
Dried catnip or brewer's yeast.

Mix dry ingredients. Slowly add broth and vegetable oil. Roll out into a thin sheet. Place on cookie sheet and bake at 350°F until golden brown. Cool and break into bite-size pieces. Toss lightly in brewer's yeast. Store in air-tight container in refrigerator.

— HIGH PROTEIN DRY FOOD —

This dry food diet could be fed more often to dogs and cats then the one above. This diet provides a higher level of protein and seems to be a better balanced diet.

1 1/2 pounds chicken wings, necks, backs, and liver, cooked and ground
1 15-ounce can of salmon, mackerel, or tuna
1 1/2 cups rye flour
2 1/2 cups whole-wheat flour
1 1/2 cups brown rice flour
1 1/2 cups wheat germ
2 teaspoons garlic powder
4 tablespoons powdered kelp
1 1/2 cups powdered milk
3/4 cups brewer's yeast
3 1/2 cups of beef or chicken stock or broth
5 tablespoons of vegetable oil
1 whole egg

Mix dry ingredients together. Mix ground chicken and fish together. Mix vegetable oil, egg, and broth together. Blend ground chicken and fish with vegetable oil, egg and broth and mix into dry ingredients. Roll to 1/4-inch thickness and place on cookie sheet. Bake at 350°F until golden brown. Break into pieces and store in air-tight container in refrigerator.

— CAT AND DOG COOKIES —

These are a couple of recipes for dog and kitty treats from the Newf Friends website.

1 1/2 cups plain flour
1 teaspoon toasted wheat germ
1/2 cup brown sugar
1/4 cup sesame seeds
rind of 1 lemon
1/2 teaspoon butter or margarine
1/2 cup ground walnuts
1/2 teaspoon vanilla extract

Combine all ingredients. Knead until thoroughly blended. Divide into six parts. Roll each into a log. Wrap loosely in wax paper. Freeze. When needed, thaw and slice into 1/2-thick slices (across roll). Preheat oven to 375°F. Place cookies on an ungreased cookie pan. Bake about 12 minutes.

— NEWF BREAKFAST BARS —

This recipe was contributed by Martha Taylor-Young, from the Newfoundland dog website. (See Resources.)

12 cups oatmeal
4 cups whole wheat flour
8 eggs
3/4 cups oil
2/3 cup honey
1/2 cup molasses
2 cups milk
1 large can solid pack pumpkin (optional)
3 to 4 mashed bananas (optional)

Preheat oven to 325°F. Grease 2 cookie sheets. Dump everything into a very large bowl. Mix everything together. Pat onto greased cookie sheets and bake at 325°F for 1 hour. After 1 hour turn oven off, crack oven door, and allow cookies to cool down in oven. Break into whatever size you want.[14]

Helpful Hints If an Animal Won't Eat

If you have a cat recovering from surgery or is as old as one of mine (twenty-four) and refusing to eat, try an all-meat baby food. Over the last twenty years I have used this numerous times when a cat has been ill or recovering from surgery. It has worked every time. Do not make this a steady diet but feed them this until they are ready to accept their usual diet. If you are using a syringe to feed them, the baby food may have to be watered down a little. I've tried feeding the combination meat and vegetable diets but have not had much luck. The all-meat baby food may also be used for small dogs who will not eat their normal diet. It could be cost prohibitive to feed a large dog baby food!

Alternative Pet Food Companies

Be assured that not all pet foods contain the deleterious substances described in this book. These are usually smaller companies that are truly concerned about the health of our pets. They have seen the ills that many of the commercial foods cause and have gone further to devise a product that is as safe for humans to consume as it is for pets.

The owners of these companies are very open and more than willing to answer, forthright, any questions you may have about their products. Yes, their foods are more expensive than the ones you purchase at the supermarket, but the price is well worth it because of the quality ingredients used. Finally, consider the money you will save on veterinary bills by feeding your animal companions whole, healthy foods.

RESOURCES

SUGGESTED READING MATERIAL

Anderson, N., Peiper, H., DVM, *Are You Poisoning Your Pet?* East Canaan, Connecticut: Safe Goods Publishing, 1995.

Anderson, N., Peiper, H., DVM, *Super-Nutrition for Dogs n' Cats*, East Canaan, Connecticut: Safe Goods Publishing, 2000.

Belfield, W., DVM, Zucker, M., *How to Have a Healthier Dog*, New York, New York: Doubleday & Co., Inc., 1981.

Cusick, W.D., *Canine Nutrition*, Wilsonville, Oregon: Doral Publishing Inc., 1997.

Derrico, Karen, *Unforgettable Mutts: Pure of Heart Not of Breed*, Troutdale, Oregon: NewSage Press, 1999.

Downing, R., DVM, *Pets Living with Cancer*, Lakewood, Colorado: American Animal Hospital Association Press, 2000.

Eisnitz, G.A., *Slaughterhouse*, Amherst, New York: Prometheus Books, 1997.

Fox, M.W., DVM, *Eating with Conscience: The Bioethics of Food*, Troutdale, Oregon: NewSage Press, 1997.

Goldstein, M., DVM, *The Nature of Animal Healing*, New York, New York: Alfred A. Knopf, 1999.

Merwick, Katie, *People Food For Dogs*, Seattle, Washington: Elfin Cove Press, 1997.

O'Driscoll, C., *What Vets Don't Tell About Vaccines*, Longnor, U.K.: Abbeywood Publishing, 1998. (This book is available through NewSage Press.)

Schlosser, Eric, *Fast Food Nation: The Dark Side of the American Meal*, New York, New York: Houghton Mifflin, 2001.

Straw, D., *Why Is Cancer Killing Our Pets?* Rochester, Vermont: Healing Arts Press, 2000.

Strombeck, D.R., DVM, *Home Prepared Dog and Cat Diets*, Ames, Iowa: Iowa State University Press, 1999.

Zucker, M., *Natural Remedies for Cats*, New York, New York: Three Rivers Press, 1999.

Zucker, M., *Natural Remedies for Dogs*, New York, New York: Three Rivers Press, 1999.

INFORMATIVE WEBSITES

American Board of Veterinary Toxicology. Provides addresses and various links to toxicology sites. www.abvt.org/

Animal Protection Institute. An organization that informs, educates, and advocates the humane treatment of all animals. www.api4animals/org/

Canine Health Census. Take part in the worldwide survey on what role vaccines are causing in the various illnesses in our pets. www.members@aol.com/k9health/wwwk9h/vac_intr.htm

Foster and Smith, DVM. A site devoted to many ailments in puppies, kittens, dogs, and cats. www.peteducation.com

Greyhound Protection League. Devoted to preventing abuse in these animals: www. greyhound.org. Also, the Greyhound Network News: www.greyhound.org/gnn (These are national organizations and have contact with the many other Greyhound organizations located in the U.S. and Canada.)

Humane Society of the United States. Provides an interesting website that describes the work it does for animals, wild and domestic: www.hsus.org/

Katie Marwick. The Second Chance Ranch, provides insight into adopting, training, and nutrition of animals: www.mybluedog.com

Laurelhurst Veterinary Hospital Library. This site provides information on various illnesses in pets: www.lvhvet.com/library.html

Omaha Vaccine Company. Lists the various vaccines that are available and provides price lists: www.omahavaccine.com

Pet Vaccination Education. Covers many aspects of pet vaccinations: www.mobilepetcare.com/diseasedog.htm

Robert Wayne, Ph.D. This site discusses the difference in dogs and wolves: www.kc.net/~wolf2dog/way2.htm

Senior Dog Project. If you have a pet on Rimadyl be sure and check this site: www.srdogs.com/Pages/rimadyl.html

USDA Nutrient Data Laboratory. Provides extensive date on the various vitamins, minerals, amino acids in foods: www.nal.usda.gov/fnic/foodcomp/

Wendell Belfield, DVM. Site provides information on the treatment of various pet illnesses: www.belfield.com

ORGANIZATIONS

Academy for Veterinary Homeopathy
1283 Lincoln Street
Eugene, OR 97401
541-342-7665

American Holistic Veterinary
Medical Association
2214 Old Emmorton Road
Bel Air, MD 21015
410-569-0795

American Veterinary
Chiropractic Association
623 Main Street
Hillsdale, IL 61257
309-658-2920

Food and Drug Administration,
Center for Veterinary Medicine
(FDA/CVM)
George Graber, Ph.D, Director
Division of Animal Feeds
Office of Surveillance and Compliance
Center for Veterinary Medicine
HFV-220
7500 Standish Place
Rockville, MD 20855
Telephone: 301-827-6651
Fax: 301-594-1812
E-mail: ggraber@bangate.fda.gov

Food and Drug Administration,
Center for Veterinary Medicine
(FDA/CVM)
Sharon Benz, DVM
Office of Surveillance and Compliance
Leader, Nutrition and Labeling Team
Division of Animal Feeds
Center for Veterinary Medicine HFV-228
7500 Standish Place
Rockville, MD 20855
Telephone: 301-594-1731

International Veterinary
Acupuncture Society
PO Box 1478
Longmont, CO 80502-1478
303-682-1167

National Association of Pet Funeral Directors
210 Andersontown Road
Mechanicsburg, PA 17055
888-422-1745

National Renderers Association, Inc.
801 Fairfax St., Suite 207
Alexandria, VA 22314
703-683-0155

Pet Food Institute
2025 M Street, N.W. Suite 800
Washington, DC 20036
202-367-1120

AGENCIES TO CONTACT IF YOU SUSPECT THE PET FOOD YOU ARE USING IS CONTAMINATED.

UNITED STATES

ALABAMA

Lance Hester, Director
Agricultural Commodities Inspection Division
Department of Agriculture and Industries
Richard Beard Building
PO Box 3336
Montgomery, AL 36109-0336
Telephone: 334-240-7202
Fax: 334-240-7177

ALASKA

Douglas R. Warner, Chief
Alaska Department of Natural Resources,
Division of Agriculture

1800 Glenn Highway, Suite 12
Palmer, AK 99645
Telephone: 907-745-7200
Fax: 907-745-7112
E-mail: Douglas_Warner@dnr.state.ak.us

ARIZONA

Jack Peterson, Associate Director
Arizona Department of Agriculture
Environmental Services Division
1688 West Adams
Phoenix, AZ 85007
Telephone: 602-542-3579
Fax: 602-542-0466
E-mail: jpeter@getnet.com

ARKANSAS

Jamey Johnson, Director
Division of Feed and Fertilizer
State Plant Board
1 Natural Resources Drive
Little Rock, AR 72205
Telephone: 501-225-1598
Fax: 501-225-3590
E-mail: JohnsonJ@aspb.state.ar.us

CALIFORNIA

Steve Wong, Branch Chief
California Department of Food and Agriculture
Ag Commodities and Regulatory Services Branch
1220 N Street - Room A 472
Sacramento, CA 95814-5621
Telephone: 916-654-0574
Fax: 916-653-2407
E-mail: Swong@cdfa.ca.gov

COLORADO

Julie Zimmerman, Program Administrator
Colorado Department of Agriculture Feed Control
2331 W. 31st Avenue
Denver, CO 80211
Telephone: 303-477-0081
Fax: 303-480-9236
E-mail: Julie.Zimmerman@ag.state.co.us

CONNECTICUT

Alton A. VanDyke, Ag. Commodities Division
Bureau of Regulation and Inspection
Connecticut Department of Agriculture
765 Asylum Avenue, Room 337
Hartford, CT 06105
Telephone: 860-713-2513
Fax: 860-713-2515

DELAWARE

Teresa A. Crenshaw
Agriculture Compliance Officer
Division of Consumer Protection
Delaware Department of Agriculture
2320 South DuPont Highway
Dover, DE 19901
Telephone: 302-739-4811
Fax: 302-697-6287
E-mail: teresa@smtp.dda.state.de.us

FLORIDA

No regulations.
Arthur B. Frassrand, Administrator
Feed Section
Florida Department of

Agriculture and Consumer Services
3125 Conner Boulevard, ME-2
Tallahassee, FL 32399-1650
Telephone: 850-488-7626
Fax: 850-488-8498

GEORGIA

Director
Plant Food, Feed and Grain Division
Georgia Department of Agriculture
Capitol Square
Atlanta, GA 30334
Telephone: 404-656-3637
Fax: 404-463-6670
E-mail: cfrank@agr.state.ga.us

HAWAII

Jeri Kahana, Program Specialist
Eggs and Feeds Unit
Hawaii Department of Agriculture
PO Box 22159
Honolulu, HI 96823-2159
Telephone: 808-973-9566
Fax: 808-973-9565

IDAHO

Michael E. Cooper, Chief
Bureau of Feeds and Plant Services
Idaho Department of Agriculture
PO Box 790
Boise, ID 83701
Telephone: 208-332-8620
Fax: 208-334-2283
E-mail: mcooper@agri.state.id.us

ILLINOIS

Mark Ringler, Bureau Manager
Bureau of Agricultural Products Inspection
Fairgrounds, PO Box 19281
Springfield, IL 62794
Telephone: 217-785-1082
Fax: 217-524-7801
E-mail: mringler@agr084r1.state.il.us

INDIANA

Dr. Alan R. Hanks, State Chemist
Office of Indiana State Chemist
Purdue University
1154 Biochemistry
West Lafayette, IN 47907-1154
Telephone: 765-494-1492
Fax: 765-494-4331
E-mail: hanksa@isco.purdue.edu

IOWA

Larry Blunt
Feed Bureau Administrator
State Chemical Laboratory Division
Iowa Department of Agriculture
Wallace State Office Building
Des Moines, IA 50319
Telephone: 515-281-8597
Fax: 515-281-4185
E-mail: larry.blunt@idals.state.ia.us

KANSAS

Fred Gatlin, Program Manager
Kansas Department of Agriculture
Agriculture Commodities Assurance Program
901 S. Kansas Avenue - 7th Floor
Topeka, KS 66612-1272
Telephone: 785-296-3558
Fax: 785-296-0673

KENTUCKY

Wilbur Frye, Director
Division of Regulatory Services
Room 103, Regulatory Services Building
University of Kentucky
Lexington, KY 40546-0275
Telephone: 606-257-2827
Fax: 606-323-9931
E-mail: wfrye@ca.uky.edu

LOUISINANA

Hershel F. Morris, Jr., Director
Louisiana Department of Agriculture and Forestry
Division of Agricultural Chemistry
PO Box 25060, University Station
Baton Rouge, LA 70894-5060
Telephone: 202-342-5812
Fax: 202-342-0027

MAINE

David Gagnon, Director
Division of Quality Assurance and Regulations
Department of Agriculture,
Food and Rural Resources
State House Station No. 28
Augusta, ME 04333
Telephone: 207-287-2161
Fax: 207-287-5576
E-mail: David.Gagnon@state.me.us

MARYLAND

Warren R. Bontoyan, State Chemist
Maryland Department of Agriculture
50 Harry S. Truman Parkway
Annapolis, MD 21401

Telephone: 410-841-2721
Fax: 410-841-2765

MASSACHUSETTS

George M. Porter, Chief
Bureau of Farm Products
Massachusetts Department
of Food and Agriculture
Leverett Saltonstall Building
100 Cambridge Street
Boston, MA 02202
Telephone: 617-727-3020, extension 141
Fax: 617-727-7235

MICHIGAN

Steven M. Martin, Feed and Drug Coordinator
Michigan Department of Agriculture
Pesticide and Plant Pest Management Division
PO Box 30017
Lansing, MI 48909
Telephone: 517-373-9749
Fax: 517-335-4540
E-mail: martinsm@state.mi.us

MINNESOTA

Paul M. Bachman, Supervisor
Agronomy Regulatory Unit
Agronomy and Plant Protection Division
Minnesota Department of Agriculture
90 West Plato Boulevard
St. Paul, MN 55107
Telephone: 651-297-7176
Fax: 651-297-2271
E-mail: paul.bachman@state.mn.us

MISSISSIPPI

Harry Ballard
Feed, Fertilizer, Seed and Lime Division
Mississippi Department of Agriculture
PO Box 5207
Mississippi State,
Starkville, MS 39762
Telephone: 662-325-3390
Fax: 662-325-8397
E-mail: harryb@mdacstate.ms.us

MISSOURI

Kent R. Jones, Program Administrator
Bureau of Feed and Seed
Plant Industries Division
Missouri Department of Agriculture
PO Box 630
Jefferson City, MO 65102-0630
Telephone: 573-751-4310
Fax: 573-751-0005

MONTANA
David Taylor
Montana Department of Agriculture
Agricultural Sciences Division
PO Box 200201
Helena, MT 59620-0201
Telephone: 406-444-3730
Fax: 406-444-5409
E-mail: dtaylor@state.mt.us

NEBRASKA
Ken Jackson, Program Manager
Bureau of Plant Industry
Nebraska Department of Agriculture
PO Box 94756
Lincoln, NB 68509
Telephone: 402-471-2394
Fax: 402-471-6892
E-mail: kencj@agr.state.ne.us

NEVADA
Robert Gronowski, Chief
Bureau of Plant Industry
Nevada Division of Agriculture
350 Capitol Hill Avenue
Reno, NV 89502
Telephone: 702-688-1180
Fax: 702-688-1178
E-mail: rgronow@govemail.state.nv.us

NEW HAMPSHIRE
Richard Uncles, Supervisor
New Hampshire Department of Agriculture,
Markets and Food
25 Capitol Street
PO Box 2042
Concord, NH 03302-2042
Telephone: 603-271-3685
Fax: 603-271-1109
E-mail: runcles@compuserve.com

NEW JERSEY
David T. Shang
Bureau of Agricultural Chemistry
Division of Regulatory Services
New Jersey Department of Agriculture
CN 330
Trenton, NJ 08625
Telephone: 609-984-2222
Fax: 609-984-2508
E-mail: agrshan@ag.state.nj.us

NEW MEXICO
Larry J. Dominguez, Division Director
Agriculture and Environmental Specialist

PO Box 30005, Dept. 3150
Las Cruces, NM 88003-0005
Telephone: 505-646-3208
Fax: 505-646-5977

NEW YORK
Robert Whiting
Division of Food Safety and Inspection
Department of Agriculture and Markets
Capital Plaza - I - Winners Circle
Albany, NY 12235
Telephone: 518-457-5457
Fax: 518-485-8986

NORTH CAROLINA
Dr. Jack Van Stavern, Feed Administrator
Food and Drug Protection Division
North Carolina Department of Agriculture
4000 Reedy Creek Road
Raleigh, NC 27606
Telephone: 919-733-7366
Fax: 919-733-6801

NORTH DAKOTA
Garry W. Wagner, Registration Specialist
Plant Industries
North Dakota Department of Agriculture
600 E. Boulevard, 6th Floor
Bismarck, ND 58505-0020
Telephone: 701-328-1501
Fax: 701-328-4567
E-mail: gwagner@state.nd.us

OHIO
Bill Goodman, Specialist in Charge
Feed and Fertilizer Section
Ohio Department of Agriculture
8995 E. Main Street
Reynoldsburg, OH 43068-3399
Telephone: 614-728-6397
Fax: 614-728-4221
E-mail: goodman@odant.agri.state.oh.us

OKLAHOMA
Sancho Dickinson, Acting Director
Oklahoma Department of Agriculture
Plant Industry and Consumer Services
2800 N. Lincoln Boulevard
Oklahoma City, OK 73105-4298
Telephone: 405-521-3864
Fax: 405-521-4912

OREGON
Richard Tan Eyck, Feed Specialist
Oregon Department of Agriculture

635 Capitol Street, NE
Salem, OR 97310-0110
Telephone: 503-986-4691
Fax: 503-986-4734
E-mail: rteneyck@oda.state.or.us

PENNSYLVANIA

John Breitsman
Feed Program Specialist
Pennsylvania Department of Agriculture
Bureau of Plant Industry
2301 N. Cameron Street
Harrisburg, PA 17110-9408
Telephone: 717-772-5213
Fax: 717-783-3275
E-mail: jbreitsman@pda005.pda.state.pa.us

PUERTO RICO

Arline D. de Gonzalez, Chief
Puerto Rico Department of Agriculture
Apartado 10163
Santurce, PR 00908-1163
Telephone: 787-796-1710
Fax: 787-796-4426

RHODE ISLAND

Stephen M. Volpe, Deputy Chief
Rhode Island Division of Agriculture
Rhode Island Department
of Environmental Management
235 Promenade Street, Room 370
Providence, RI 02908-5767
Telephone: 401-222-2781
Fax: 401-222-6047

SOUTH CAROLINA

Peggy C. Knox, Registration Officer
South Carolina Department of Agriculture
Laboratory Division
PO Box 11280
Columbia, SC 29211-1280
Telephone: 803-737-9700
Fax: 803-737-9703
E-mail: pknox@scda.state.sc.us

SOUTH DAKOTA

Brad Berven, Administrator
South Dakota Department of Agriculture
Division of Regulatory Services
523 East Capitol - Foss Building
Pierre, SD 57501-3182
Telephone: 605-773-4432
Fax: 605-773-3481
E-mail: bradb@doa.state.sd.us

TENNESSEE

Jimmy Hopper, Director
Division of Quality and Standards
Tennessee Department of Agriculture
PO Box 40627, Melrose Station
Nashville, TN 37204
Telephone: 615-837-5152
Fax: 615-837-5335
E-mail: jhopper2@mail.state.tn.us

TEXAS

Roger Hoestenbach, Head
Office of the Texas State Chemist
PO Box 3160
College Station, TX 77841-3160
Telephone: 409-845-1121
Fax: 409-845-1389
E-mail: r-hoestenbach@tamu.edu

UTAH

Stephen T. Burningham
Utah Department of Agriculture
350 North Redwood Road
Box 146500
Salt Lake City, UT 84114-6500
Telephone: 801-538-7183
Fax: 801-538-7189
E-mail: agmain.sburning@email.state.ut.us

VERMONT

Philip R. Benedict, Director
Plant Industry, Laboratory and
Consumer Assurance Division
116 State Street, Drawer 20
Montpelier, VT 05620-2901
Telephone: 802-828-2431
Fax: 802-828-2361
E-mail: phil@agr.state.vt.us

VIRGINIA

J.R. (Jay) Crane, Program Supervisor
Office of Product and Industry Standards
Virginia Department of Agriculture
and Consumer Services
PO Box 1163
Richmond, VA 23218
Telephone: 804-786-3542
Fax: 804-786-1571
E-mail: jcrane@vdacs.state.va.us

WASHINGTON

Ali Kashani
Feed and Fertilizer Program Administrator

Washington Department of Agriculture
PO Box 42589
Olympia, WA 98504-2589
Telephone: 360-902-2028
Fax: 360-902-2093
E-mail: akashani@agr.wa.gov

WEST VIRGINIA

Herma Johnson, Assistant Director
Regulatory Protection Division
West Virginia Department of Agriculture
1900 Kanawha Boulevard, East
Charleston, WV 25305
Telephone: 304-558-2227
Fax: 360-558-3594

WISCONSIN

Nicholas J. Neher, Administrator
Agricultural Resource Management Division
Wisconsin Department of Agriculture
PO Box 8911
Madison, WI 53708
Telephone: 608-224-4567
Fax: 608-224-4656
E-mail: nehernj@wheel.datcp.state.wi.us

WYOMING

Henry R. Uhden,
Consumer Protection Supervisor
Wyoming Department of Agriculture
2219 Carey Avenue
Cheyenne, WY 82002-0100
Telephone: 307-777-6574
Fax: 307-777-6593
E-mail: huhden@state.wy.us

CANADA

Canadian Food Inspection Agency
Linda Morrison, Associate Director
Feed Section
Plant Products Division
59 Camelot Drive
Nepean, ON
Canada K1A 0Y9
Telephone: 613-225-2342
Fax: 613-228-6614

ENDNOTES

CHAPTER TWO: RENDERING PLANTS AND PET FOOD

1. Paula Rausch, "Country Seeks Pet Disposal Alternative," *Gainsville Sun*, January 5, 2000.

2. Stan Gudenkauf, American Proteins, personal correspondence, March 7, 2000.

3. Kevin Kuhni, John Kuhni and Sons, March 7, 2000. Humphry Koch, West Coast Reduction Ltd., March 10, 2000. Dean Carlson, National By-Products Inc., March 7, 2000, personal correspondence.

4. Michele Sullivan, "Shelter Has Nowhere to Dispose of Animals," *The Warren Sentinel*, March 8, 2000.

5. Charlie Powell, Public Information Officer, College of Veterinary Medicine, Washington State University, personal correspondence, August 2, 2000.

6. Kathy Connell, DVM, Assistant State Veterinarian, Washington State Department of Agriculture Food Safety and Animal Health Division. Olympia, Washington, personal correspondence, August 3, 2000.

7. Department of Health and Human Services, FDA, Rockville Maryland, personal correspondence, July 12, 1994.

8. Association of American Feed Control Officials (AAFCO), Ingredient Definitions, 1994.

9. Ibid.

10. Delmer Jones, Chairman, National Joint Council, USDA Meat Inspectors, personal correspondence, March 16, 2000.

11. Op. cit., AAFCO.

12. Elizabeth Cohen, Medical Correspondent, CNN Interactive, "USDA denies company request to recondition recalled meat," April 14, 1999.

13. J.W. Schroeder, "By-Products and Regionally Available Alternative Feedstuffs for Dairy Cattle," North Dakota State University, September 1999.

14. Op. cit., AAFCO.

15. Animal Protection Institute. Veterinary Survey, 1998.

16. Tara Parker-Pope, "For You, My Pet, *Wall Street Journal*," November 3, 1997.

17. The American Veterinary Medical Association. "Bayer, Hill's Make a Commitment.... Not Seen Before," press release, September 15, 1997.

18. University of Colorado College of Veterinary Medicine, "Guidelines for Use of the Teaching Hospital by Veterinary Students," student handbook, December 20, 1999.

19. The American Veterinary Medical Association. AVMA Sponsor Spotlight. "Hill's Pet Nutrition, Inc.," newsletter, 1997.

20. Jill McPhillips, "Ralston Purina Gift Begins Student Leadership Award," University of Minnesota, press release, November 1998.

21. Ibid.

22. Ralston Purina Public Relations, "Ralston Purina Funds New Veterinary Residency at Tufts University," News from Checker-board Square, St. Louis, Missouri, September 1, 1999.

23. *Nexus Magazine,* "News Snippets from Australia," "Vet Threatened Over Pet Food Danger Claims," June-July 1997.

24. Tom Lonsdale, DVM, "A Modern Veterinary Snafu," Faculty of Veterinary Science, lecture, Massey University, Palmerston North, New Zealand, September 9, 1993.

CHAPTER THREE: A TOXIC FEAST

1. Rana Aron Silver, "Consumer Reports Find 71 Percent of Store-Bought Chicken Contains Harmful Bacteria" Consumer Union, Yonkers Office, press release, February 23, 1998.

2. John J. O'Connor, DVM, MPH, Clarence M. Stowe, VMD, Ph.D, Robert R. Robinson, BVSc, MPH, Ph.D, "Fate of Sodium Pentobarbital in Rendered Products," *American Journal of Veterinary Medicine*, Vol. 46, No 8, August 1985, p. 1721.

3. Ashley Robinson, BVSc, MPH, Ph.D,

University of Minnesota, personal correspondence, August 26, 1994.

4. Michael Fox, DVM, *Eating with Conscience: The Bioethics of Food*, Troutdale, Oregon: NewSage Press, 1997, p. 34.

5. The Humane Farming Association, "The Truth About Factory Farming," paper, 1996.

6. Ibid.

7. The Humane Society of the United States, letter to Jane Henney, MD, March 9, 1999.

8. University of Wisconsin, "Antimicrobial Use Guidelines," "Chloramphenicol" Eighth Edition, July 1995 to June 1996.

9. Duane Miksch, Warrie Means, Hohn Johns, Food Safety Department, "Residues in Animal-Derived Foods," pamphlet, August 1990.

10. Mark Papich, DVM, MS, North Carolina State University, personal correspondence, March 1, 1995.

11. K.O. Honikel, U. Schmidt, W. Woltersdorf, L. Leistner, "Effects of Storage and Processing on Tetracycline Residues in Meat and Bones," *Journal of the Association of Official Analytical Chemists*, September 1978, 61 (5) pp. 1222-7.

12. The American Board of Veterinary Toxicology, "Ionophore Toxicosis," website: www.abvt.org/ionop.html.

13. N. Safran, I. Aizenberg, H. Bark, "Paralytic Syndrome Attributed to Lasalocid Residues in a Commercial Ration Fed to Dogs," Koret School of Veterinary Medicine, Hebrew University of Jerusalem, Rehovot, Isreal, *Journal of the Veterinary Medical Association*, April 15, 1993, 202(8) pp. 1273-5.

14. J.J. Vanes and others, "Epidemic of Nutritional Polyneuropathy in Cats," Final Report of the Investigative Team, Tijdschr Diergeneesky, The Netherlands, research paper, 122 (21), November 1, 1997, pp. 604-7.

15. "FDA Approved Animal Drug Products", Drug Product Abstract 128-409 (Rx/OTC), January 4, 1999, website: dil.vetmed.vt.edu/FDA/Advanced/NedaPrint.cfm?NadaString=128-409

16. D.M. Houston, J. Parent, K.J. Matushek, "Ivermetic Toxicosis in a Dog," *Journal of the*

American Veterinary Medical Association, 191 (1) July 1, 1987, pp. 78-80.

17. K.D. Hopkins, K.L. Marcella, A.E. Strecker, "Ivermectin Toxicosis in a Dog," *Journal of the American Veterinary Medical Association*, 197 (1) July 1, 1990 pp. 93-94.

18. "Remember the Beef," "Dairy Initiatives Newsletter," University of Minnesota, Vol. 7, Issue 2, Fall 1998.

19. Food and Drug Administration, "The Use of Hormones for Growth Promotion in Food-Producing Animals," information sheet, May 1996.

20. *The Globe and Mail* (Canada) "Cover-Up Alleged at Health Canada, Were Pushed to Approve Drug, Scientists Say," September 17, 1998.

21. Lee Townsend, BS, MS, Ph.D, Extension Entomologist, "Insecticide-Impregnated Cattle Ear Tags," University of Kentucky College of Agriculture, website:www.uky.edu/Agriculture/Entomology/entfacts/livestc/cf505.html.

22. Gordon L. Coppoc, DVM, Ph.D, "Pharmacology of Pesticides," Professor of Veterinary Pharmacology, School of Veterinary Medicine, Purdue University, paper, February 20, 1996.

23. Mark Redman, "Organophosphates: The Pyramid of Exposure." *The Food Magazine*, Issue 23, 1993.

24. Tom Kenworthy, "EPA Pesticide Limits Irk Farmers, Environmentalists," *The Washington Post*, August 3, 1999.

25. United States Information Services, "EPA Bans Pesticide Methyl Parathion," fact sheet, April 8, 1999.

26. CVM MEMO, CVMM-19 "Monitoring for Residues in Food Animals," Food and Drug Administration, Center for Veterinary Medicine, Communications and Education Branch HFV-121, 301/594-1755 D.H.H.S. Pub. No. (FDA) 94-6001, Revised March 1994.

27. R.M. Corwin, Jule Nahm, DVM, "Insecticides" University of Missouri, College of Veterinary Medicine, 1999, website:missouri.edu/~vmicrorc/Drugs/Insecticides.html.

28. CNN Health, "EPA Bans Pesticides

Dursban, Says Alternatives Available," report, June 8, 2000.

29. Cecil F. Brownie, DVM, Ph.D, DABVT, DABT, Toxicologist, North Carolina State University, College of Veterinary Medicine, personal correspondence, October 25, 1991.

30. Lester Hankin, G.H. Heichel, and Richard Botsford, "Lead Content of Pet Foods," Connecticut Agriculture Experimental Station, publication, 1975, pp. 630-632.

31. Ibid.

32. Timothy A. Gbodi, National Veterinary Research Institute, Toxicology Section, Vom Nigeria, Nwako Nwude, Faculty of Veterinary Medicine, Department of Physiology and Pharmacology, Ahmadu Bello University, Ziaria, Nigeria, "Mycotoxicoses in Domestic Animals: A Review," *Veterinary and Human Toxicology*, 30 (3), June 1988.

33. J. Michael Parkert, "Aflatoxin Poisoning, Dogs, Texas," *San Antonio Express*, November 3, 1998.

34. C.E. Wolf-Hall, M.A. Hanna, L.B. Bullerman, "Stability of Deoxynivalenol in Heat-Treated Foods," Food and Nutrition Department, South Dakota State University, *Journal of Food Protection*, August 1999, 62 (8); pp. 962-4.

35. FDA "Enforcement Report," Recalls and Field Corrections: Veterinary Products - Class 11, October 11, 1995.

36. Food Safety and Inspection Service, U.S. Department of Agriculture, "Clenbuterol," information sheet, July 1995.

37. Julia Prodis, "Cheating with Clenbuterol in Livestock Shows," Animal People Online News Service, August 20, 1995.

38. Gail A. Eisnitz, *Slaughterhouse*, Amherst, New York: Prometheus Books, 1997, p. 278.

39. Jay Richards, "Clenbuterol Should be OK'd to Help Racehorses," *Las Vegas Review Journal*, August 2, 1998.

40. Center for Veterinary Medicine, "Veterinarian Sentenced in Animal Drug Smuggling Case," bulletin, January 6, 1999, p. 37.

41. Wendell Belfield, DVM and Martin Zucker,

How to Have a Healthier Dog, Garden City, New York: Doubleday & Co., Ltd., 1981, p. 38.

42. Jeff Bender and Ashley Robinson, "Health Concerns Relating to the Feeding of Raw Meat to Companion Performance Animals," paper, University of Minnesota: Department of Clinical and Population Sciences, 1994.

43. Donald R. Strombeck, DVM, Ph.D, *Home Prepared Dog and Cat Diets*, Ames, Iowa: Iowa State University Press, 1999, p. 47.

44. Russell Research Center, "The Presence of Listeria Monocytogenses in the Integrated Poultry Industry," paper, Athens, GA, August 16, 1996.

45. H. Schroeder, I.B. Reusburg, "Generalised Listeria Monocytogenes Infection in a Dog," Department of Medicine, Faculty of Veterinary Medicine, University of Pretoria, Onderstepoort, Republic of South Africa, *Journal of South Africa Veterinary Association*, September 1993, 64(3): pp. 133-6.

46. Institute of Food Science and Technology. "Foodborne Campylobacteriosis - and How to Safeguard Against It," paper, 1999.

47. Op. cit., Meat Industry Insights News Service, citing *New York Times*, October 23, 1997.

48. Linda March, Information Specialist, "Have Dogs Tested for Canine Brucellosis Before Breeding," University of Illinois, College of Veterinary Medicine, Pet Column of the Week, August 8, 1994.

49. Ibid.

50. Donald B. Hudson, DVM, District Extension Specialist, Veterinary Science, University of Nebraska, paper, File G417: Animal Diseases, September 1978.

51. E.J. Richey, E.L. Bliss, DVMs, "Clostridial (Blackleg) Disease of Cattle," Cooperative Extension Service, Institute of Food and Agriculture Sciences, University of Florida, Gainesville, website:edis.ifas.utl.edu/BODY_VM039

52. The American-International Charolais Association and American-International Junior Charolais Association, "Focus on Herd Health," paper, September 2000.

53. Charles H. Courtney, DVM, Ph.D, "Strategic Parasite Control -Practices That Pay,"

44th Annual Florida Beef Cattle Short Course Proceedings: University of Florida (Gainsville): Animal Science Department, Gainsville, Florida, May 3-5 1995, p. 166.

54. Texas A&M University, "Viral Diseases (Exclusive of Respiratory Disease)" Section 4, website: www.gallus.tamu.edu/Diseases/PDSec4.html#LEUKOSIS

55. Physicians Committee for Responsible Medicine, "Mad Cow Disease: The Risk to the U.S.," paper, Washington DC, Summer 1996, p. 5.

56. Op. cit., Texas A&M University.

CHAPTER FOUR: PET FOOD REGULATIONS

1. "Nutrition: Government Regulations," Ralston Purina, 1999, website: www.ivillage.com/pets/features/purinadogcaretips/nutrition/articles/0,4437,16808,00.html

2. Linda Grassie, Center for Veterinary Medicine, personal correspondence, February 17, 2000.

3. Douglas Hepper, DVM, Staff Veterinarian, Meat and Poultry Inspection Branch, personal correspondence, February 21, 2000.

4. FDA Consumer, "Understanding Pet Food Labels," Vol. 28, No. 8, report, October 1994, p. 12.

5. "Ethoxyquin Study Results," Petfood Industry, May/June 1996.

6. CVM Update Bulletin "FDA Requests That Ethoxyquin Levels Be Reduced in Dog Foods," August 14, 1997.

7. Op. cit., FDA Consumer, p. 12.

8. "Selected Portions of the Food, Drug, and Cosmetic Act As Amended," U.S. Food and Drug Administration (FDA) April 22, 1996.

9. David A. Dzanis, DVM, Ph.D, DACVN, Information for Consumers, "Interpreting Pet Food Labels," 1995, website: www.fda.gov/cvm/fda/infores/consumer/petlabel.html.

10. Association of American Feed Control Officials, "Ingredient Definitions," 1994.

11. Mississippi State Chemist, February 25, 2000. New Hampshire Department of Agriculture, personal correspondence, February 11, 2000.

12. Tony Claxton, Missouri Department of Agriculture, Bureau of Feed and Seed, Jefferson City, Missouri, personal correspondence, February 10, 2000.

13. Ken Jackson, Nebraska Department of Agriculture, Bureau of Plant Industry, Lincoln Nebraska, personal correspondence, February 17, 2000.

14. Donna DiCesare, Agency Program Aide, New York Department of Agriculture, personal correspondence, February 16, 2000.

15. Ann Brueck, Program Specialist, Department of Agriculture, Indiana, personal correspondence, February 9, 2000.

16. Richard Ten Eyck, Feed Specialist, Oregon Department of Agriculture, personal correspondence, February 9, 2000.

17. Steve Wong, Branch Chief, California Department of Food and Agriculture, Commodities and Regulatory Services, personal correspondence, February 16, 2000.

18. Federal Trade Commission. 16 CFR Part 241 "Request for Comment Concerning Guides for the Dog and Cat Food Industry," March 18, 1999, website: www.ftc.gov/os/1999/9903/dogandcatfoodguidesfrn.html.

19. Federal Meat Inspection. Title 21-Food and Drugs. Chapter 12 - Meat Inspection Section 606. 1999.

20. "Meat Inspection" Meat Science at Texas A&M University, 1998, website: savell-j-tamu.edu/meat.insp.html.

21. Ibid.

22. Douglas Hepper, DVM, Staff Veterinarian, Meat and Poultry Inspection Branch, personal correspondence, February 21, 2000.

23. "USDA Denies Petition and Allows Diseased Animals into Human Food Supply," March 25, 1999, website: www/nodowners.org/usdadeniespetition.html.

24. Ibid.

25. Nancy Cook, Director, Technical and Regulatory Affairs, Pet Food Institute, personal correspondence, April 28, 2000.

26. Ibid.

27. Duane Ekedahl, Executive Director, Pet Food Institute, personal correspondence, August 23, 2000.

28. Ibid, September 6, 2000.

29. Sonia Mertens-Scott, Information Center, Industry Canada, personal correspondence, February 14, 2000.

30. Canadian Veterinary Medical Association, Ottawa, Ontario, personal correspondence, August 5, 1994.

31. Pet Food Association of Canada, "Nutritional Assurance Program," brochure, Mississauga, Ontario, March 1990.

32. Alison Walker, Pet Food Manufacturers Association, England, personal correspondence, February 24, 2000.

33. Jill Carey, "Negotiating the Cat Food Jungle," *Cats Magazine*, November 1996, p. 38.

34. "Putting the Pieces Together," *The Pet Dealer*, July 1992, p. 48.

35. Dr. Rodney Noel, Secretary-Treasurer of the AAFCO, Indiana, personal correspondence, February 22, 2000.

36. Ibid.

37. Ali Kashani, Department of Agriculture, Washington, personal correspondence, February 28, 2000.

CHAPTER 5: THE LATEST ON MAD COW DISEASE AND PET FOOD

1. USDA, "Bovine Spongiform Encephalopathy," Veterinary Services, paper, September 1999.

2. Martin Groschup, DVM, Federal Research Center for Virus Diseases of Animals, "Bovine Spongiform Encephalopathy (BSE)," Info Memo - Hearing No. 17, June 24, 25, 1996.

3. Stanley B. Prusiner, MD, " The Prion Diseases," *Scientific American*, January 1995, p. 50.

4. M.M. Leggett, J. Dukes, H.M. Pirie, "A Spongiform Encephalopathy in a Cat," *Veterinary Record*, U.K., 1990, 127 24, pp. 586-588.

5. Alison Walker, Pet Food Manufacturers' Association Ltd., U.K., personal correspondence,

February 24, 2000.

6. Ministry of Agriculture, Food and Fisheries, "Your Feed Ban Questions Answered BSE," information sheet, U.K., 2000.

7. Anthony Bevins, Political Editor, "BSE Fear for Millions of British Pets," *The Independent*, October 16, 1996.

8. Ibid.

9. Ministry of Agriculture, Food and Fisheries, "Other TSEs," MAFF BSE Information Bulletin, July 31, 2000.

10. Richard Savill, "Injured Lion Destroyed by Zoo Had Feline BSE," *The Telegraph*, U.K., November 15, 2000.

11. *The Reuters European Business Report*, "Mad Dogs Nip at Heels of British Beef," April 28, 1997.

12. Paul Brown citing Dr. Stephen Dealler, MD, Environmental Correspondent, *The Guardian*, U.K., April 29, 1997.

13. Iain McGill, DVM, BSE Inquiry, Statement No. 67, June 8, 1998, cites Robert Higgins, DVM, letter, 1990.

14. Ibid.

15. Ibid.

16. *The Associated Press*, "Dog's Death Linked to Brit Dog Food," April 22, 1997.

17. Stephen Dealler, MD, Ph.D, Microbiologist, personal correspondence, March 22, 2000.

18. Richard Pitcairn, DVM, Eugene, Oregon, personal correspondence, August 5, 1996.

19. Rick LeCouteur, DVM, University of California at Davis, personal correspondence, March 15, 2000.

20. Andrew Mackin, DVM, Royal School of Veterinary Medicine, Edinburgh, Scotland, personal correspondence, October 28, 1996.

21. United States Department of Agriculture, Veterinary Services, "Transmissible Mink Encephalopathy," paper, September 1999.

22. "Pet Food Labeling Alarm," *Petfood Industry*

magazine, March/April 1997, p. 68.

23. Duane Ekedahl, Executive Director of the Pet Food Institute, Food and Drug Administration, Public Forum, statement, St. Louis, Missouri, February 4, 1997.

24. Kevin Custer, American Protein, Food and Drug Administration, Public Forum, statement, St. Louis, Missouri, February 4, 1997.

25. Jim Corbin, DVM, "Pet Foods and Feeding," *Foodstuffs*, July 17, 1996, p. 84.

CHAPTER SIX: THE CONTROVERSY OF THE RAW MEAT DIET

1. Ian Billinghurst, DVM, personal correspondence, November 4, 2000.

2. Wendell Belfield, DVM, "Raw Meat Diets for Companion Animals," Your Animal's Health, Jan/Feb 1999, website: www.belfield.com.

3. Ibid.

4. Martin Goldstein, DVM, *The Nature of Animal Healing*, New York, New York: Alfred A. Knopf, 1999, p. 62.

5. Sharon Gwaltney Brant, DVM, Ph.D, National Animal Poison Control Center, personal correspondence. June 12, 1997.

6. L. Beutin, DVM, "Escherichia coli as a Pathogen in Dogs and Cats," *Journal of Veterinary Research*, (2-3), March-June 30, 1999, pp. 285-98.

7. Y. Sato, R. Kuwamoto, DVM, "A Case of Canine Salmonellosis Due to Salmonella Infantis," *Journal of Veterinary Medical Science*, 61: (1), January, 1999, pp. 71-72.

8. Carla Haddix DVM, Haddix Animal Hospital, Florida, personal correspondence, September 26, 1999.

9. Joe Bartges, DVM, Department of Small Animal Clinical Sciences, College of Veterinary Medicine, The University of Tennessee, personal correspondence, September 14, 1999.

10. Ibid.

11. Dan Hendrix, DVM, Heights Veterinary Clinic, Houston, Texas, personal correspondence, September 1999.

12. Elizabeth Poole, Foodborne and Diarrheal Diseases. Division of Bacterial and Mycotic Diseases, National Center for Infectious Diseases, Centers for Disease Control and Prevention, personal correspondence, October 6, 1999.

13. Dennis J. Blodgett, Toxicologist, College of Veterinary Medicine. Virginia Tech., personal correspondence, September 18, 1999.

14. Donald R. Strombeck, DVM, Ph.D., *Home Prepared Dog and Cat Diets: The Healthful Alternative*, Ames, Iowa: Iowa State University Press, 1999, p. 49.

15. Gerry Henningsen, DVM, Ph.D, DABVT, personal correspondence, September 25, 1999.

16. Ian Billinghurst, DVM, "A Response to My Blue Dog," August 4, 2000, website: www. geocities.com/Heatland/Flats/7244/bluedog.html.

17. Ian Billinghurst, DVM, *Give Your Dog a Bone*, published by Ian Billinghurst, NSW Australia, 1993, p. 164.

18. Ibid, p. 156.

19. Noah's Ark Wildlife Coalition, "Parasites in Kangaroo Meat," paper, citing Dr. David Obendore, Wildlife Veterinary Pathologist, Tasmania, 1999.

20. Carol Pickett, MD, "Campylobacter on Chicken Carcasses Surveyed for a Potential Virulence Factor," presentation, 98th General Meeting of the American Society of Microbiology, Atlanta Georgia, May 17-21, 1998.

21. Ibid.

22. Op cit., Ian Billinghurst, *Give Your Dog a Bone,* p.120.

23. Ibid, p. 135.

24. Wendy Powell, DVM, Ontario Veterinary College University of Guelph, personal correspondence, October 5, 1999.

25. Allan Sachs DC, CCN, "The Alternative Guide to Grapefruit Seed Extract," website: www.patmckay.com/Product_11.html.

26. Diane Gerken, DVM, Ph.D, Department of Veterinary Biosciences, College of Veterinary Medicine, Ohio State University, personal correspondence, November, 8, 2000.

27. GSE Report, "FDA Testing Shows Grape-fruit Seed Extract Effective Against Protozoan Infection." Vol.1, Issue 1, citing Dr. Louis Parish, MD.

28. NutriTeam, "Pets and Grapefruit Extract," 2000, website: www.nutriteam.com/pets.html.

29. Pat McKay, *Reigning Cats and Dogs*, Pasadena, California: Oscar Publications, 1997, p. 116.

30. Op cit., Ian Billinghurst, *Give Your Dog a Bone,* p. 121.

31. Judy Rochette, DVM, FAVD, Dipl. AVDC, Burnaby, BC, personal correspondence, October 10, 2000.

32. Fraser Hale, DVM, FAVD, Dip. AVDC, Guelph, Ontario, personal correspondence, October 10, 2000.

33. Gregg Dupont, DVM, Seattle, Washington, personal correspondence, October 10, 2000.

34. David Clark, DVM, NSW, personal corre-spondence, October 11, 2000.

35. Op cit., Fraser Hale, DVM.

36. G. Steenkamp, C. Gorrel, DVM, "Oral and Dental Conditions in Adult African Wild Dogs: A Preliminary Report," *Journal of Veterinary Dentistry*, June 1999, 16(2), pp. 65-8.

37. Linda Dugger, DVM, personal correspon-dence, September 20,1999.

38. Douglas Macintire, DVM, personal corre-spondence, August 30 1999.

39. Richard Hill, MA, VetMB, Ph.D, Dip. ACVIM, MRCVS, personal correspondence, October 10, 2000.

40. William Duke, DVM, Martin-Clark Animal Hospital, Dothan, Alabama, personal correspon-dence, September 22, 1999.

41. Mark W. Jackson, Clinical Assistant Professor, Intern Medicine, Department of Clinical Sciences, North Carolina State University, personal corre-spondence, September 20, 1999.

42. Geoff Stein, DVM, Studio City Animal Hospital. Studio City, California, personal corre-spondence, September 24, 1999.

43. Michael Fox, DVM, *Eating with Conscience: The Bioethics of Food*, Troutdale, Oregon: NewSage Press, 1997, p. 26.

44. Marian Burros, *New York Times*, "USDA to Allow Meat to be Labeled Organic," January 15, 1999, website: www.organic-mlt.com/usda-mlabel-srpt990121.html#nyt

45. Elliott Japin, Scott Montgomery, "US Non-Organic Meat Is Filthy," *Cox News Service*, Washington, DC, January 21, 1998.

46. George Anthan, "USDA Reports Filth in Meat," *Register Washington Bureau*, April 12, 1999.

47. Francis M. Pottenger, MD, "Pottenger's Cats - A Study in Nutrition," Price-Pottenger Foundation, 1997.

48. Ibid.

49. John Coupland, Ph.D, Food Chemistry, Assistant Professor of FoodScience, Pennsylvania State University, personal correspondence, October 21, 2000.

50. Ibid.

51. Hosni Hassan, Ph.D, Microbiology, Head, Department of Microbiology and Interim Head, Department of Toxicology, North Carolina State University, Raleigh, personal correspondence, October 23, 2000.

52. Robert C. Backus, DVM, Ph.d, Assistant Research Physiologist, Department of Molecular Biosciences, University of California, Davis, personal correspondence, October 23, 2000.

53. Nick Costa, Associate, Ph.D Nutrition and Biochemistry, Professor of Biochemistry and Nutrition, School of Veterinary Biology and Biomedical Science, Division of Veterinary and Biomedical Sciences, Murdoch University, Australia, personal correspondence, October 22, 2000.

54. Ibid.

55. Christopher Cowell, MS., Nutritionist, VETMED List. July 9, 1998.

56. David Klurfeld, MD, "Live Enzymes from Your Food," Chairman and Professor of the Department of Nutrition and Food Science, Wayne State University, paper, April 1, 1999.

57. William J. Burkholder, DVM, Ph.D, Dip ACVM, College of Veterinary Medicine, Texas A&M University, personal correspondence, September 20, 1999.

58. Enzymes "Go Ask Alice, "Columbia University's Health Education Program, February 9, 1996, website: www.goaskalice.columbia.edu/0785.html.

59. Thomas Cowan, MD, "Raw Milk Is Good For You," 1999, website: www.//lilipoh.com/issues/articles/rawmilk.html.

60. Robert K. Wayne, Ph.D, "Molecular Evolution of the Dog Family," 1993, website: www.kc.net/--wolf2dog/wayne2.html.

61. Ibid.

62. Ibid.

63. Robert Lee Hotz, "Man Found Dog 100,000 year ago," *Seattle Times*, June13, 1997.

64. Norma Bennett Woolf, "The Wolf: Father and Brother to the Dog," *Dog Owner's Guide Profile: The Wolf*, "Canis Major Publications," Cincinnati, Ohio, 2000.

65. Lioncrusher's Domain, "Wolf-Dog Hybrids," September 22, 2000, website:www.geocities.com/~lioncrusher/wolves/wolf_11_wolfdogs.html.

66. USGS-Northern Prairie Wildlife Research Center, "Wolf Depredation on Livestock in Minnesota: The Problem in Perspective," website: www.npwrc.usgs.gov/resource/1998/minnwolf/persoec.html.

67. Rosalind Dalefield, BVSc, Ph.D, Diplomate American Board of Veterinary Toxicology, Royal Veterinary College, UK, personal correspondence, September 21, 1999.

68. Ibid.

CHAPTER SEVEN: OVER-VACCINATION
AND ANIMALS

1. Rabies Prevention in Washington State: A Guide for Practitioners. "The Epidemiology of Rabies," bulletin, 1997.

2. Pet Vaccination Education. "Diseases Your Pet Should Be Protected Against," Vet Care Vaccination Services, Inc. Huntington Beach, California, website: www.mobilepetcare.com/diseasedog.html.

3. Ibid.

4. Michael Paul, DVM, "AAHA releases Opinion Paper on Vaccine Issues," *DVM* magazine, November 1999.

5. Jean Dodds, DVM, Lisa Twark, DVM, "Clinical Use of Serum Parvovirus and Distemper Virus Antibody Titers for Determining Revaccination Strategies in Healthy Dogs" *Journal of the American Veterinary Medical Association*, 217: 2000, pp. 1021-1024.

6. Ibid.

7. Charles Loops, DVM, "The Dangers of Vaccinations, and the Advantages of Nosodes in Disease Prevention," July 3, 2000, website: www.geocities.com/HotSprings/1158/NOSODES.HTML.

8. Pat Lazarus, *Keep Your Pet Healthy the Natural Way*, New Canaan, Connecticut: Keats Publishing, Inc., 1983 citing Dr. Michael Lemmon, DVM, p. 120.

9. Health World On Line. "'Vaccination in Animals," excerpted from *Wolf Clan Magazine*, April/May 1995, web-site:www.healthy.net/library/articles/ivn/animals.html.

10. Ibid. Christina Chambreau, *Wolf Clan Magazine*.

11. Lynne Brakeman, Senior Editor, DVM Breaking News. "Extra: Vaccine Associated Feline Sarcomas. Coalition Organizes Research into Feline Sarcomas," *DVM Newsmagazine*, August 1997.

12. American Veterinary Medical Association, "Feline Sarcoma Task Force Meets," 1997, web-site: www.avma.org/onlnews/javma/feb97/s020197f.html.

13. American Veterinary Medical Assocation, "Vaccine-Associated Feline Sarcoma Task Force," 1998, website: www.avma.org/vafstf/sitercmnd.asp.

14.Theresa A. Fuess, Ph.D, Information Specialist, University of Illinois, College of Veterinary Medicine. "Study Will Pinpoint Cancer Risk in Cat Vaccines," Pet Column for the Week of August 18, 1997.

15. C. Guillermo Couto, DVM, Dennis W. Macy, DVM, MS, "Vaccine Associated Feline Sarcoma Task Force," American Veterinary Medical Association, presentation, 1998.

16. Wendy C. Brooks, DVM, DABVP, "Vaccine FAQs and General Information," The Pet Care Forum, paper, 2000.

17. Katherine James, DVM, Veterinary Medical Info: Dogs and Cats, "Vaccines Can Cause Cancer in Cats: Feline Vaccine-Associated Sarcomas, " July 11, 1997, website: www.suite101.com/article. cfm/veterinary info/2217.

18. Martin Goldstein, DVM, *The Nature of Animal Healing*, New York, New York: Alfred A. Knopf, 1999, p. 94.

19. Ibid.

20. Susan Little, DVM, Diplomate ABVP (Feline) "Feline Leukemia Virus," Cat Fanciers Association Health Committee, report, 2000.

21. Ibid.

22. Ibid.

23. Catherine O'Driscoll, "Pet Vaccine Myths," 1997, website: www.members.aol.com/ abywood/www/vac_myth.html.

24. Catherine O'Driscoll, personal correspondence, December 7, 2000.

25. Canine Health Census, "Vaccination Survey," Derbyshire, U.K., 1996.

26. Omaha Vaccine Company, "Dog Vaccines," 2000, website: www.omahavaccine.com/ets/show-page.cgi?producttable=/_private.../vaccine-canine. html.

27. Catherine O'Driscoll, "The Vaccine Debate," 1997, website: www.members.aol.com/abywood/ www/vaccine.html.

28. Colorado State College of Veterinary Medicine and Biomedical Sciences, "Colorado State University's Small Animal Vaccination Protocol," January 1998, website: www. Cvmbs. colostate.edu/vth/savp2.html.

29. Ibid.

30. Ibid.

31. Stephen Kruth, DVM, DACVM (Internal Medicine) Professor and Chair, Department of Clinical Studies, University of Guelph, personal correspondence, April 15, 2000.

32. Susan Goldstein and Robert Goldstein, DVMs, "To Vaccinate or Not To Vaccinate: Solve the Dilemma With Titer Testing," *Earth Animal*, 1997, website: www.earthanimal.com

33. Bill Fortney, DVM, Assistant Professor of Clinical Sciences, "Leptospirosis Vaccination Not Recommended for Puppies," Kansas State University News Service, paper, November 9, 1999.

34. Donna Starita Mehan, "The Dangers of Vaccinations, and the Advantages of Nosodes for Disease Prevention," paper, July 3, 2000.

35. Ibid.

36. Dee Blanco, DVM, "Vaccines — Are They Safe for Your Dog?" seminar, March 26, 2000.

37. Ibid.

38. Christopher Day, MRCVS, "Isopathic Prevention of Kennel Cough, Is Vaccination Justified?" *International Journal for Homeopathy*, Vol. 2, No. 1, April 1987, pp. 45-50.

39. Op. cit., Donna Starita Mehan.

40. Susan G. Wynn, DVM, "Vaccination Decision," *Alternative Veterinary Medicine*, 2000.

41. Ibid.

42. Debra Tibbitts, DVM, "What is Vaccination?" paper, 1999, website: www.teddyfreezer.com/ proforum/vet_july00.html.

43. T.R. Phillips, DVM; R. Schultz, Ph.D, Diplomate ACVM (Hon.), "Canine and Feline Vaccines," *Current Veterinary Therapy*, 1992, p. 205.

44. Don Hamilton, DVM, "Vaccinations in Veterinary Medicine: Dogs and Cats," paper, 1999, website: www.members.aol.com/ifta2/ vaccine1.html.

45. John Fudens, DVM, "The Big-Scam-Rabies Vaccination," *Tiger Tribe Magazine*, September/ October 1992.

46. Ibid.

47. Catherine O'Driscoll, "For Love's Sake, Let Us Protect the Animals," *Caduceus*, Issue 37, Autumn 1997, p. 12.

CHAPTER 8: CANCER IN PETS

1. Ralph A. Henderson, DVM, MS, Professor of Surgery and Oncology, Department of Veterinary Clinical Sciences, College of Veterinary Medicine, College of Veterinary Medicine, Auburn University, personal correspondence, February 1, 2001.

2. Martin Goldstein, DVM, "A Vet's Pet Peeves," *People Magazine*, September 13, 1999.

3. Martin Goldstein, DVM, *The Nature of Animal Healing*, New York, New York: Alfred A. Knopf, 1999, p. 5.

4. Ihor Basko, DVM, Kauai, Hawaii, personal correspondence, December 14, 2000.

5. Lori Tapp, DVM, Ashville, North Carolina, personal correspondence, December 16, 2000.

6. American Veterinary Medical Association. "Animal Cancer, Common Signs of Cancer in Small Animals," paper, 1999.

7. Michael H. Goldschmidt, DVM, Professor of Pathology and head of the Surgical Pathology Services, "Breed Related Cancers," Cancer in Dogs: The 28th Annual Canine Symposium, January 31, 1998.

8. Theresa A. Fuess, Ph.D, Information Specialist, "Cancer Risks in Cats and Dogs," University of Illinois, College of Veterinary Medicine, January 19, 1998, website: www.cvm.uiuc.edu/ceps/petcolumns/cancercb.html.

9. Ibid.

10. Kim Cronin, DVM, "Cancer in Dogs," The 28th Annual Canine Symposuim, University of Pennsylvania, January 31, 1998.

11. "No More Sneak Cancer Treatments - Pets Get Their Own Care Center," April 22, 1999, website: www.animals.co.za/services/news/domestic/pet_cancer_centre.html.

12. Karin Sorenmo, DVM, "Cancer Treatment Options, " The 28th Annual Canine Symposium, University of Pennsylvania, January 31, 1998.

13. Vet Network, Condensed from the KSU Press, "Progressive Approach to Reducing Tumors in Cats and Dogs, " bulletin, March 27, 2000.

14. *DVM News Magazine*, "Canine Cancer Treatment Under Review," Small Animal Treatment, November 2000.

15. "Nutritional Requirements of Dogs and Cats with Cancer," Clinical Oncology Service, Veterinary Hospital of Pennsylvania, September 20, 1998, paper, revised August 26, 1999.

16. Ibid.

17. Op. cit., Igor Basko.

18. Ibid.

19. "The Dog Owner's Guide," "The Tellington Touch: The Touch that Heals," Canis Major Publishing, Cincinnati, Ohio, 2001.

20. Barbara Janelle, MA (Medical Geography), "TTeam for Cats - Communication Through Touch" Human Innovations and Alternatives, pp. 354-368, 1993.

21. Ibid.

22. Barbara Janelle, MA, personal correspondence, December 18, 2000.

23. Nurse Healers-Professional Associates International, "Therapeutic Touch," paper, 2000, website: www.therapeutic-touch.org/ttouch.html.

24. Robin Downing, DVM, *Pets Living With Cancer*, Lakewood, Colorado: AAHA Press, 2000, p. 67.

25. Dr. Gary Tram, DVM, Louisville, KY, personal correspondence, December 16, 2000.

26. Jordan Kocen, DVM, "Holistic Approaches to Cancer Therapy," newsletter, Spring 1997.

27. R.M. Clemmons, DVM, Ph.D, Associated Professor of Neurology and Neurosurgery, Department of Small Animal Clinical Sciences, University of Florida, "Integrative Treatment of Cancer in Dogs," paper, 1997.

28. Deborah Straw, *Why Is Cancer Killing Our Pets?* Rochester, Vermont: Healing Arts Press, 2000, p. 157.

29. Elissa Leibowitz, "Owners Can Save Pets' Lives with Costly Cancer Treatment," *Washington Post*, January 20, 1999.

CHAPTER NINE: OTHER HEALTH CONCERNS

1. Chris Adams, "Most Arthritic Dogs Do Well On This Pill, Except Ones That Die," *Wall Street Journal*, March 13, 2000.

2. Michael Meyer "When Pets Pop Pills," *Newsweek*, October 11, 1999, pp. 60-61.

3. Op. cit., Chris Adams.

4. Center For Veterinary Medicine, "Update on Rimadyl," bulletin, December 1, 1999.

5. Ibid.

6. Russell Swift, DVM, "Rimadyl: Wolf in Sheep's Clothing," *The Pet Tribune*, May 1, 2000.

7. Ibid.

8. The Senior Dog Project, "The History of Rimadyl," 2000, website:www.srdogs.com/Pages/rimadyl.html.

9. Ibid.

10. Jean Townsend, personal correspondence, December 28, 2000.

11. Katharine Delahaye Paine, "Lessons Learned in the Branding Corral. How to Rope 'em In and Make Your Mark Stick," *The Gauge*, Vol. 11, No 4, article, July- August 1998.

12. Joe Bodewes, Holly Frisby, DVM, "Non-surgical Management of Arthritis in Dogs," 2000, website: www.peteducation.com/dogs/treatmentdjd.html.

13. Ibid.

14. Wendell Belfield, DVM, "Arthritis and Related Joint Disease of the Canine," Summer 2000, website: www.belfield.com

15. Martin Goldstein, DVM, *The Nature of Animal Healing*, New York, New York: Ballantine Books, p. 188.

16. Jocelynn Jacobs-Knoll, DVM. "Bloat In Review," American Canine Association, news-letter, Volume 45, No. 1, January 1997.

17. School of Veterinary Medicine. Purdue University, "Bloat Notes," January 1998, website: www.vet.purdue.edu/depts/vad/cae/bnjan98.html.

18. L.T. Glickman, DVM, N.W. Glickman MPH, D.B. Schellenberg, MS, G.C. Lantz, DVM, "Multiple Risk Factors for the Gastric Dilatation-Volvulus Syndrome in Dogs; a Practitioner/Owner Case-Control Study," *Journal of the American Animal Hospital Association,* 33(3), May-June 1999, pp. 197-204.

19. L.T. Glickman, DVM, D.B. Schellenberg, MS, Gary Lantz, DVM, William Widmer, SVM,MS, Nita Glickman, MS, MPH, "Clues to Bloat Prevention Emerging from Case-Control Study," "Bloat Notes," April 1996, website: www.vet.purdue.edu/depts/vad/cae/bnaprwb.html.

20. W.P. Bredal, DVM, Department of Small Animal Clinical Sciences, Norwegian College of Veterinary Medicine, Oslo, Norway. "Pneumonyssoides Caninum Infection - A Risk Factor for Gastric Dilatation-Volvulus in Dogs," *Veterinary Research Communications*, June 22, 1998. (4) pp. 225-231.

21. Op. cit., Martin Goldstein, p. 218.

22. Kathy Hutton, DVM, Introduction: The Physiology of Bloat Treatment and Prevention, Deep-Chested Dogs are Susceptible to Gastric Torsion: The Dreaded Bloat," website: www.geocities.com/Heartland/Plains/8870/bloat.html.

23. Morbidity & Mortality Weekly Report. "Illnesses Associated with Occupational Use of Flea- Control Products — California, Texas, and Washington, 1989-1997," paper, June 4, 1999.

24. Ibid.

25. Sylvie Farrell of Mothers & Others, with reporting by Aisha Ikramuddin, "Healthy Pets, No Fleas, How to Control Fleas without Resorting to Chemical Warfare." *San Diego Earth Times*, June 1996.

26. Natural Resources Defense Council, Paper "A Summary of the Hazards of Dursban (Chlorpyrifos)," report, May 9, 2000.

27. Jill Richardson, DVM, "Miscellaneous Pet Care: How Can I Safely Use Flea Control Products On My Pets?" paper, ASPCA National Animal Poison Control Center, 1999.

28. Holly Frisby, DVM, "Ingredients in Tick and Flea Control Products," Drs. Foster &

Smith, Inc. Veterinary Services Department, website: www.peteduction.com.

29. Dara Johns, DVM, "Pet Peeves: Fipronil-based Products Prove Superior in Fight Against Fleas," *Northwest Florida Daily News*, February 20, 2000.

30. Ross Becker, "Revolution: Just a Few Drops Kills Fleas, Ticks and Ear mites, Plus Gives a Month of Heart-worm Prevention," *Good Dog Magazine*, September/October 1999.

31. Ross Becker, Update, *Good Dog Magazine*, April 24, 2000.

32. Dixie Farley, "Fighting Fleas and Ticks," U.S. Food and Drug Administration, paper, July-August 1996.

33. Jeff Feinman, DVM, "Fleas and Ticks," 1996-1997, website:www.homevet.com/index.html.

34. Martin Zucker, *The Veterinarians' Guide to Natural Remedies for Dogs*, New York: Three Rivers Press, 1999, citing Roger DeHaan, DVM, p. 239.

35. The Feline Advisory Bureau, "Disinfectants," information sheet, 2000.

36. Nina Anderson, Howard Peiper, *Are You Poisoning Your Pet?*, East Canaan, Connecticut: Safe Goods, 1995, p. 20.

37. The American Veterinary Medical Association, "A Pet Owner's Guide to Common Small Animal Poisons," information sheet, 2000.

38. Ibid.

39. National Animal Poison Control Center, "Medications," information sheet, 2000.

40. Op. cit., AVMA.

CHAPTER TEN: THE ULTIMATE HEALTH RISK: CRUELTY

1. The Human Society of the United States. "Dateline Joins Battle Against Puppy Mills," April 27, 2000.

2. Kim Townsend, "Housing of Dogs in Commercial Kennels," 2001, website: www.nopuppymills.com/housing.html.

3. William Ecenbarger, "Scandal of America's Puppy Mills," *Reader's Digest*, February 1999.

4. Op. cit., The Humane Society of the United States.

5. People for The Ethical Treatment of Animals (PETA), "Puppy Mill Prison," 2000, website: www.helppuppies.com/nc/index.html.

6. Peter Wood, Research Associate, People for the Ethical Treatment of Animals, (PETA), personal correspondence, January 4, 2001.

7. Chris Hansen, "Puppies for Sale," "Dateline," April 26, 2000.

8. Karl Stark, "Breeding Dogs," *The Philadelphia Inquirer*, December 10, 1995.

9. Ibid.

10. Karl Stark, *The Philadelphia Inquirer*, personal correspondence, January 3, 2001.

11. Laura Italiano, "4.4M Puppy Mill Scandal," *New York Post*, Sunday, September 22, 1996.

12. Karen Derrico, *Unforgettable Mutts: Pure of Heart Not of Breed*, Troutdale, Oregon: NewSage Press, 1999.

13. The Humane Society of the United States. "The Rutherford County Animal Drop Boxes," Today's News," 1999.

14. MSNBC "Dateline," Interview with Rick Swain, HSUS, December 13, 1999, website: www.msnbc.com/news/346373.asp?cp1=1

15. Animal Alert News, "Millions of Dogs and Cats Tortured and Killed Annually for their Fur," *Reuters, Philadelphia*, December 16, 1999.

16. The Humane Society of the United States. "Fatal Figurines," bulletin, 1999.

17. Ibid.

18. The Humane Society of the United States, "Clinton Signs Dog and Cat Fur Ban," news release, November 14, 2000.

19. Michael Fox, DVM, *Eating with Conscience: The Bioethics of Food*, Troutdale, Oregon: NewSage Press, 1997, p. 165.

20. Greyhound Protection League, "The Status

of Greyhound Racing in the United States," paper, 1999.

21. Connie Thiel, "You Bet They Die," *Dog Gone News*, December 2000.

22. Ibid.

23. The Humane Society of the United States, "Greyhound Racing Facts," 1999, website: www. hsus.org/programs/companion/pet_cruelty/ greyhound_racing.html.

24. Greyhound Protection League, "The Darkside of Dog Racing," paper, 1999.

25. Lynn Bixby, "Greyhound Abuse," *The Hartford Courant*, January 12, 1997.

26. The Greyhound Protection League, "You Wouldn't Feed It to a Dog....," 1999, website: www.Greyhounds.org/gpl/contents/meat.html.

CHAPTER ELEVEN: HEALTHY RECIPES

1. Nina Anderson, Howard Peiper, DVM, *Super Nutrition for Dogs n' Cats*, East Canaan, Connecticut: Safe Goods Publishing, 2000, p. 17.

2. Pat Lazarus, *Keep Your Pet Healthy the Natural Way*, New Canaan, Connecticut: Keats Publishing Inc, 1983, p. 36.

3. United States Department of Health and Human Services, "FDA Issues Nationwide Public Health Advisory about Contaminated Chews," press release, October 1, 1999.

4. Mike Lamb, Agriculture Canada, "Alberta Turns Sows' Ears Into Silk Purses," "Alberta Crops and Beef," newsletter, Spring 1999.

5. Donald R. Strombeck, DVM, Ph.D, *Home Prepared Dog and Cat Diets*, Ames Iowa: Iowa State University Press, 1999, Chicken and Rice Diet, p. 269, Tofu and Sardines Diet, p. 285.

6. Joe Bodewes, DVM, "Homemade Diets," Drs. Foster & Smith, Inc. Veterinary Services Department, website:www.pededucation.com/nutrition/ homemadediets.html.

7. Cats and Diets, "Homemade Recipe for Short-term Use," website: www.cats-and-diets. com/html/formulas.html.

8. Michael Fox, DVM, "Dog Diet," Health and Nutrition, website:www.petcity.com/directory/ health_nutrition_recipe.asp.

9. Ibid, Beef and Potato Diet, p. 313.

10. Op. cit., Joe Bodewes.

11. R.M. Clemmons, DVM, Ph.D, Associated Professor of Neurology and Neurosurgery, Department of Small Animal Clinical Sciences, University of Florida, "Integrative Treatment of Cancer in Dogs," paper, 1997.

12. People for the Ethical Treatment of Animals, (PETA), Vegan Dog Biscuit Recipe, "Companion Animals: Meatless Meals for Dogs and Cats," newsletter, 1999.

13. Bethany Bain-Chamberlain, "Dog-Gone Delicious and Nutritious Treats," February 2000, website: www.petcottage.com.

14. Treat Recipes Newf Friends "Goodies Dog Treats," website:www.geocities.com/Heartland/ Ranch/1011/.

INDEX

A

Acupuncture, 121, 130
Advantage (imidacloprid), 137
Aflatoxins, 45
Alachuca County Shelter, 8
American International
  Charolais Association, 37
American Veterinary Medical
  Association (AVMA), 15,
  114, 142
Amino acids, 83, 87
Animal Protection Institute, 5,
  14
Antibiotics, 20, 22-23, 26
  Ampicillin, 25
  Chloramphenicol, 24-25
  Oxytetracycline, 24-25
  Penicillin, 23
  Streptomycin, 25
  Sulphadimidine, 23, 25
  Tetracycline, 23
Antibodies, 105
Antibody titers, 93, *see also*
  Titers
Aspirin, 143
Association of American Feed
  Control Officials, (AAFCO)
  14, 22, 33, 39, 43-47, 50,
  54-55
Australian Veterinary
  Association (AVA), 16-17

B

Backus, Robert, 84
Bacteria, 8, 35-36, 38, 72,
  75-76
Baker Commodities, 8, 10
Bartges, Joe, 72
Basko, Ihor, 113, 118
Beet pulp, 14
Belfield, Wendell, 33, 69-70,
  130
Bender, Jeff, 33
Benz, Sharon, 2
Billinghurst, Ian, 67-69, 73-74,
  77, 90
Blanco, Dee, 107
Bloat, 131-133
Bloat study, Purdue University,
  131-133
Blodgett, Dennis, 72
Bodewes, Joe, 129, 164, 168
Bones, 67, 76-78, 81, 90

Bones and Raw Food (BARF)
  74, 78, 80, 82, 88, 90
Botulism, 74
Bovine growth hormone, 27
Bovine spongiform encephalop-
  athy (BSE), 3, 37-38, 53,
  59, 61-62, 65
Bowel perforations, 79
Brownie, Cecil, 29
Brucellosis, 35-36
Burkholder, William, 86
Burlington Coat Factory, 151

C

Campylobacter, 20, 34-35,
  69-72, 74
Canadian Veterinary Medical
  Association, (CVMA), 1, 22,
  39, 43, 51, 55
Cancer, 113-114
  Bone, 114-115
  Fibrosarcoma, 114
  Intestinal carcinomas, 115
  Leukemia, 99-100
  Lymphosarcoma, 116
  Melanoma, 115
  Neoplasma, 117
  Sarcomas, 117
  Salivary carcinomas, 115
  Skin, 115
Canine Health Census, 100-101
Center for Disease Control,
  (CDC), 70
Center for Veterinary Medicine,
  28, 32, 40-41, 49, 54-55,
  64, 126
Chan, L., 16
Chambreau, Christine, 94
Charolais cattle, 37
Chemotherapy, 116, 118, 121
Chondroitin, 130
Clark, David, 78
Clemmons, R.M., 122
Clenbuterol, 32
Condemned materials, 12, 21,
  40, 47
Contaminated meat, 80
Cook, Nancy, 3, 49-50
Cook, Tom, 9
Corbin, Jim, 64
Corn gluten meal, 13
Costa, Nick, 84-85
Coupland, John, 84

Couto, Guillermo, 96
Creutzfeldt-Jakob disease (CJD)
  37, 58-59

D

4-D animals, 4, 12, 33, 50, 63,
  154, 161
D&D Disposal, 7-8
"Dateline" tv show, 147, 150
Day, Christopher, 99-100, 108
Dealler, Steve, 62
DeHaan, Roger, 140
Dehydrated garbage, 12
Detwiler, Linda, 4
Diarrhea, 71,75, 79, 81, 90-91
Dodds, Jean, 93, 97-99, 100,
  105-106
Downer livestock, 48-49
Downing, Robin, 121
Drugs, 40, 52
Dugger, Linda, 78
Duke, William, 79
DuPont, Gregg, 77
Dursban, 29, 136

E

E. coli, 20, 33-34, 69-71, 75,
  154-155
Eisnitz, Gail, 32, 69, 74
Ekedahl, Duane, 4, 50-51, 64
Encephalopathy, *see* Bovine
  Spongiform Encephalopathy
  (BSE)
Endotoxin, 72-73
Enzymes, 85-86
Esophageal, 79
Estradiol, 26
Ethoxyquin, 41-42

F

Factory farming, 23
Farm Sanctuary, 48-49
Federal Trade Commission,
  46-47
Feinman, Jeff, 138
Feline leukemia, 95-98, 114
Feline Urological Syndrome
  (FUS), 40
Feline sarcomas, 96
Fibrosarcomas, 95
Fleas and flea control, 134-140
Flea Busters, 140
Food and Drug Administration

(FDA), 1-2, 28, 39, 43, 47, 49-50, 64, 126, 161
Fox, Michael, 23, 80, 69, 152, 167
Frisby, Holly, 129
Frontline (fipronil), 137
Fudens, John, 110
Fur trade, 150-151

G
Gerken, Diane, 75
Glickman, Larry, 132-133
Glucosamine, 130
Goldschmidt, Michael, 114-115
Goldstein, Martin, 70, 97, 113, 130, 133
Goldstein, Susan and Robert, 106
Graber, George, 2-3
Grapefruit seed extract (GSE), 75
Greyhound Network News, 155
Greyhound Protection League, 153, 155
Greyhounds, 152
Griffin Industries, 9
Groschup, Martin, 57-58
Gwaltney Brant, Sharon, 71

H
Haddix, Carla, 71
Hale, Fraser, 77-78
Hamilton, Don, 110
Hazard Analysis and Critical Control Points (HACCP), 9
Heavy Metals, 38, 40, 52
Hendrick, Mattie, 94
Hendrix, Dan, 72
Henney, Jane, 3, 23
Herbs for cancer
    Cat's claw, 121
    Essiac, 121-122
    Garlic, 121
    Ginsing, 121
    Green tea, 121
    Milkthistle, 122
    Mistletoe, 121
    Pau d'arco, 121
    Shark cartilage, 122
Hill, Richard, 79
Hill's, 14-15
Homecooked pet food, 157-160
Hormones, 20, 25, 27, 38, 40
Humane Society of the United States (HSUS), 23,146,

150-151, 153
Humane Farming Association, 23
Hutton, Kathy, 134
Hydrolzyed hair, 12

I
Industry Canada, 51
Immune response, 93-94 106, 118
Insecticides, 27
Ivermectin, 25-26

J
Jacobs-Knoll, Jocelynn, 132
James, Katherine, 96
Janelle, Barbara, 120-121
John Kuhini and Sons, 9
Jones, Dara, 137

K
Kennel cough, 108
Kessler, David, 2
Klurfled, David, 85
Kocen, Jordan, 121
Koefran Services, 7-8
Kruth, Stephen, 104

L
Labeling pet food, 40-41, 51
Lazarus, Pat, 159
Lead, 29-30
LeCouteur, Rick, 62
Lemmon, Michael, 94
Listeria, 33-34. 71, 75
Little, Susan, 97
Liver flukes, 35, 37
Lonsdale, Tom, 16-17, 100
Loops, Charles, 94
Lyme disease, 138

M
Macintire, Douglas, 79
Mackin, Andrew, 62
Macy, Dennis, 96
Mad cow disease see Bovine spongiform encephalopathy
Manure, 12
McGill, Iain, 61
McKay, Pat, 76
Meat in pet foods, 11
Meat by-products, 8, 11-13, 54
Meat meal, 11-13, 35, 54
Mehan, Donna Starita, 107-108
Miller, Janice, 4
Minerals, 29

Ministry of Agriculture, Food and Fisheries (MAFF), 59
Monsanto, 41
Mycotoxin, 30-31, 38
    Aflotoxin B1, 30
    Deoxynivalenol, (Vomitoxin), 31
    Fumonisin, 45

N
National Research Council, 44
National Animal Poison Control Center, (NAPCC), 70, 142-143
National Research Council, 43
National By-Products, 9
National Renderers Association, 5, 43
Nosodes, 99, 108-109
Nutrition, teaching vets, 14-15

O
Obendore, David, 73
O'Driscoll, Catherine, 99, 101, 103
Omega 3 fatty acids. 68, 159
Organophosphates, 28, 136
Osteoarthritis, 125

P
Pancreatitis, 81
Papich, Mark, 24
Parasites, 76
Parish, Louis, 75
Pathogens, 40, 52
Peiper, Howard, 158
People for the Ethical Treatment of Animals (PETA), 147
Permethrin, 136-137
Pesticides, 20, 27-28, 35, 40, 52
Pet Food Institute, (PFI), 3, 49-50
Pet Food Manufacturer's Association (U.K.), 59
Pet Food Manufacturers Association, (PFMA), 51, 60
Pet Food Association of Canada (PFAC), 53
Pfizer, 103, 126-127, 128
Phillips, T.R., 109
Pickett, Carol, 74
Pitcairn, Richard, 62
Plants, toxic, 142
Pottenger, Francis, 81-82, 87-88
Pottenger study, 68-69

Poultry by-products, 14
Prednisone, 20
Prions, 58
Program (lufenuron), 137
Propylene glycol, 42
Prusiner, Stanley, 58
Puppy mills, 146-148
Pyrethrins, 136

R
Rabies, 110
Radiation, 116, 118
Radioactive beads, 116
Ralston Purina, 16, 39, 54
Raw material in pet foods, 6
Raw meat, 67, 72, 74-75 79-80,
  82-83, 85, 87, 90
Rendering, 1, 7, 35, 38, 49,
  59-60, 65
Rendered material, 63
Rendering plants, 8-11, 21,
  47-48, 65
Reno Rendering, 8
Revolution, 137
Rimadyl, 125-130
Robinson, Ashley, 21, 33
Rochette, Judy, 77

S
Sachs, Allan, 75
Salmonella, 20, 33, 69-72,
  74-75,
Scapie, 57, 61, 64-65
Scheibner, Viera, 100
Schultz, Ronald, 109
Slaughterhouse, 12, 47
Sodium pentobarbital 2-3,
  21-22
Sorenmo, Karin, 116
Splitting, 13
Stein, Geoff, 80
Strombeck, Donald, 34, 72,
  129, 157, 163
Sutton, Diane, 4
Swift, Russell, 127

T
Tapeworm, 73
Tapp, Lori, 114
Taurine, 51, 82-85
Tellington Touch Every Animal
  Method, (TTEAM), 119
Tellington-Jones, Linda, 119
Therapeutic Touch, 120
Tibbitts, Debra, 109
Ticks, 138

Titers, 102, 105, 109
Townsend, Jean, 128
Toxoplasmosis, 72
Tran, Gary, 121
Tryptophan, 83
Tylenol, 143

U
United Animal Owners
  Association, 41
United States Animal Health
  Association, 2
United States Department of
  Agriculture (USDA), 4, 34,
  39, 48, 57, 64, 83, 146-148

V
Vaccinations, 91-93, 100-102
  Adenovirus, 91, 103
  Bordetella, 91, 106, 107
  Calicivirus, 103, 107
  Cat typhoid, 92
  Coronavirus, 91, 106
  Distemper, 91, 103, 107
  Feline distemper, 92
  Feline leukemia, 103
  Feline rhinotrachetis, 107
  Feline panleukopenia, 107
  FeLV, 92
  Hepatitis, 107
  Infectious enteritis, 92
  Leptospirosis, 91, 106, 107
  Lyme disease, 106
  Parainfluenza, 91, 103, 107
  Parvovirus, 91, 107
  Rabies, 106
  Rhinotracheitis, 107
Valley Protein, 10

W
Washington State Department
  of Agriculture, 10
Wayne, Robert, 88
West Coast Rendering, 8-9
Wild dogs, 67, 78
Williams, Beth, 4
Wineland, Nora, 4
Wolves, 67, 70, 80, 88-89
Wynn, Susan, 109

Y
Yellow corn, 13

ABOUT THE AUTHOR

Ann N. Martin is internationally recognized as an authority on the commercial pet food controversy. For the past fourteen years, Ms. Martin has investigated and questioned exactly what goes into commercial pet foods. Her book, *Food Pets Die For: Shocking Facts About Pet Food,* was the first in-depth book to expose the hazards of commercial pet food. Ms. Martin's investigative reporting on this topic was selected for special recognition as "one of the most censored news stories of 1997" by Sonoma State University's *Project Censored,* which focuses on important news events that are largely ignored by mainstream media.

Ann Martin with Jake

Photo: Mary Chambers

In her second book, Ms. Martin continues her investigation of pet-related issues as well as other controversial topics, revealing more shocking facts. Ms. Martin also is a pet columnist on health issues for *Better Nutrition* magazine. Ms. Martin graduated with a B.A. in business from the University of Western Ontario, and worked in a tax office for several years. She lives in Ontario, Canada, with her animal companions, where she continues to question, research, and write about pet-related issues. She can be reached by email at: annmartin@execulink.com.

OTHER TITLES BY NEWSAGE PRESS

NewSage Press has published several titles related to animals. We hope these books will inspire humanity towards a more compassionate and respectful treatment of all living beings.

Food Pets Die For: Shocking Facts About Pet Food
by Ann N. Martin

Pets at Risk: From Allergies to Cancer, Remedies for an Unsuspected Epidemic
by Alfred J. Plechner, D.V.M.

When Your Pet Outlives You: Protecting Animal Companions After You Die
by David Congalton & Charlotte Alexander
Award Winner, CWA Muse Medallion 2002

Blessing the Bridge: What Animals Teach Us About Death, Dying, and Beyond
by Rita M. Reynolds

Three Cats, Two Dogs, One Journey Through Multiple Pet Loss
by David Congalton
Award Winner, Merial Human-Animal Bond, Best Book

*Conversations with Animals: Cherished Messages and Memories
as Told by an Animal Communicator*
by Lydia Hiby with Bonnie Weintraub

*Polar Dream: The First Solo Expedition by a Woman and
Her Dog to the Magnetic North Pole*
by Helen Thayer, Foreword by Sir Edmund Hillary

The Wolf, the Woman, the Wilderness: A True Story of Returning Home
by Teresa Tsimmu Martino

Singing to the Sound: Visions of Nature, Animals & Spirit
by Brenda Peterson

Unforgettable Mutts: Pure of Heart Not of Breed
by Karen Derrico

NEWSAGE

NewSage Press
PO Box 607, Troutdale, OR 97060-0607

Phone Toll Free 877-695-2211, Fax 503-695-5406
Email: info@newsagepress.com, or www.newsagepress.com

Distributed to bookstores by Publishers Group West
800-788-3123, PGW Canada 800-463-3981

PRESS